About Pearson

Pearson is the world's learning company, with presence across 70 countries worldwide. Our unique insights and world-class expertise comes from a long history of working closely with renowned teachers, authors and thought leaders, as a result of which, we have emerged as the preferred choice for millions of teachers and learners across the world.

We believe learning opens up opportunities, creates fulfilling careers and hence better lives. We hence collaborate with the best of minds to deliver you class-leading products, spread across the Higher Education and K12 spectrum.

Superior learning experience and improved outcomes are at the heart of everything we do. This product is the result of one such effort.

Your feedback plays a critical role in the evolution of our products and you can contact us - reachus@pearson.com. *We look forward to it.*

CLASS

8

Pearson IIT Foundation Series

Chemistry

Seventh Edition

CLASS

8

Pearson IIT Foundation Series

Chemistry

Seventh Edition

Trishna Knowledge Systems

Pearson

Photo Credits

Chapter 1 Opener: blueringmedia.123rf.com
Chapter 2 Opener: Tsz-shan Kwok. Pearson Education
Chapter 3 Opener: mikeledray. Shutterstock
Chapter 4 Opener: LSkywalker. Shutterstock
Chapter 5 Opener: Trevor Clifford. Pearson Education
Chapter 6 Opener: Blueringmedia. 123rf.com
Chapter 7 Opener: Rtimages. 123rf.com
Icons of Practice Questions: graphixmania. Shutterstock
Icons of Answer Keys: Viktor88. Shutterstock
Icons of Hints and Explanation: graphixmania. Shutterstock

Senior Editor—Acquisitions: Nandini Basu
Editor—Production: Sakshi Kansal

ISBN 978-93-528-6674-8

First Impression

Published by Pearson India Education Services Pvt. Ltd, CIN: U72200TN2005PTC057128

Head Office: 15th Floor, Tower-B, World Trade Tower, Plot No. 1, Block-C, Sector-16, Noida 201 301, Uttar Pradesh, India.
Registered Office: 4th Floor, Software Block, Elnet Software City, TS-140, Block 2 & 9, Rajiv Gandhi Salai, Taramani, Chennai 600 113, Tamil Nadu, India.
Fax: 080-30461003, Phone: 080-30461060
www.pearson.co.in, Email: companysecretary.india@pearson.com

Compositor: D Book Media
Printer in India at Saurabh Printers Pvt. Ltd.

Brief Contents

Contents

Preface

Pearson IIT Foundation Series has evolved into a trusted resource for students who aspire to be a part of the elite undergraduate institutions of India. As a result, it has become one of the best-selling series, providing authentic and class-tested content for effective preparation—strong foundation, and better scoring.

The structure of the content is not only student-friendly but also designed in such a manner that it motivates students to go beyond the usual school curriculum, and acts as a source of higher learning to strengthen the fundamental concepts of Physics, Chemistry, and Mathematics.

The core objective of the series is to be a one-stop solution for students preparing for various competitive examinations. Irrespective of the field of study that the student may choose to take up later, it is important to understand that Mathematics and Science form the basis for most modern-day activities. Hence, utmost effort has been made to develop student interest in these basic blocks through real-life examples and application-based problems. Ultimately, the aim is to ingrain the art of problem-solving in the mind of the reader.

To ensure high level of accuracy and practicality, this series has been authored by a team of highly qualified teachers with a rich experience, and are actively involved in grooming young minds. That said, we believe that there is always scope for doing things better and hence invite you to provide us with your feedback and suggestions on how this series can be improved further.

Chapter Insights

Remember

Before beginning this chapter, you should be able to:

- define substance, mixture, mass, weight, etc.
- know the states of matter solid, liquid and gas
- basic properties of matter

Remember section will help them to memories and review the previous learning on a particular topics

Key points will help the students to identify the essential points in a chapter

Key Ideas

After completing this chapter, you should be able to:

- define matter, molecule, atom etc.
- know the arrangement of molecules in three different states of matter.

INTRODUCTION

The planet earth has endowed us with the basic necessities of life like air, water, food etc. Among these, air is the most vital for life and hence indispensable.

Layers of Atmosphere

Our atmosphere is divided into five layers on the basis of variations in chemical composition, density, temperature at different heights from the surface of the earth.

(i) Troposphere

(a) The layer of atmosphere which begins at the earth's surface and extends up to 20 km height is called **troposphere**.

Text: concepts are explained in a well structured and lucid manner

Note boxes are some add-on information of related topics

Note: Diluted H_2SO_4 is not used for the preparation of CO_2 because the calcium sulphate formed being insoluble in water forms a layer over marble chips and thus marble chips do not come in contact with dil H_2SO_4 further.

EXAMPLE

Give the electronic configuration and geometrical representation of the following elements.

(a) Flourine **(b)** Sodium **(c)** Chlorine **(d)** Carbon

SOLUTION

(a) Florine Z = 9

Electronic configuration = 2, 7

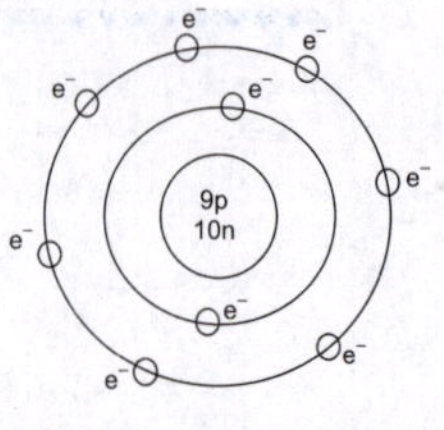

(b) Sodium Z = 11

Electronic configuration = 2, 8, 1

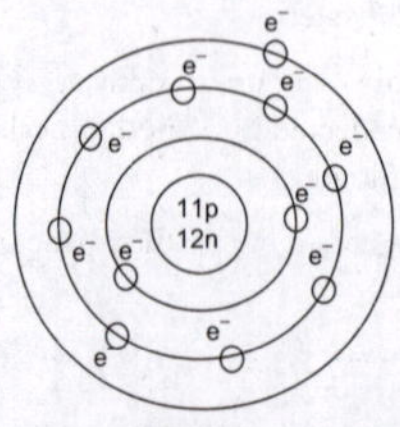

Examples given topic-wise to apply the concepts learned in a particular chapter

Illustrative examples solved in a logical and step-wise manner

TEST YOUR CONCEPTS

Very Short Answer Type Questions

Directions for questions 1 to 10: **Fill in the blanks.**

1. In a ______ properties of the constituents are retained.
2. A mixture of alcohol and water is an example of ______ mixture.
3. A substance which is formed by the chemical combination of two or more elements is called a ______.
4. Boiling point is the temperature at which ______ is converted to ______ at one atmospheric pressure.
5. Nonmetals usually exist in ______ state.
6. ______ show the properties of metals and nonmetals.
7. With an increase in the surface area of a liquid, the rate of evaporation______

16. Which among the following is an element?
    (a) Calcium oxide
    (b) Common salt
    (c) Ozone
    (d) Water
17. Evaporation is the process of conversion of
    (a) a liquid to its gaseous state below the boiling point of the substance
    (b) a liquid to its gaseous state at the boiling point of the substance
    (c) a solid to its liquid state at the melting point of the substance
    (d) a solid to its liquid state below the melting point of the substance

Different levels of questions have been included in the *Test Your Concept* as well as on *Concept Application* which will help students to develop the problem-solving skills

'Test Your Concepts' at the end of the chapter for classroom preparations

CONCEPT APPLICATION

Level 1

True or false

1. Gases have maximum intermolecular spaces.
2. Metals are highly ductile and malleable.
3. Evaporation takes place from the surface of a liquid and hence it is a surface phenomenon.
4. Pure substances are made up of identical molecules and hence are homogeneous in nature.
5. Tellurium is a metalloid and hence it shows properties of both metals and nonmetals.
6. Iodine is a lustrous nonmetal.
7. As the density of sodium is less than that of water it floats on water.
8. Ammonium chloride undergoes sublimation and hence it is a sublimable substance.
9. The constituents of a compound do not retain their properties and hence these cannot be separated by physical methods.
10. Sublimation is the process of the conversion of a solid to its gaseous state.

'Concept Application' section with problems divided as per complexity: Level 1; Level 2; and Level 3

38. Carbon fibre, a recently developed allotrope of carbon is ductile and has high tensile strength.
39. Sand is insoluble in water; hence, it can be separated by filtration. Glucone-D is soluble in water; hence, it can be separated by distillation and water is collected separately.
40. Rate of evaporation is directly proportional to surface area of the liquid. This is because more number of surface molecules are exposed to atmosphere which gain kinetic energy and escape into atmosphere.
41. (i) A mixture of sawdust and water is taken in a beaker
    (ii) A filter paper is folded in the form of a cone and fitted into a funnel by moistening it with a few drops of water
    (iii) The mixture is poured gently into the filter cone and collected into another beaker which is called a filtrate.
    (iv) The solid retained on the filter paper is called a residue.

Hints and Explanation for key questions along with highlights on the common mistakes that students usually make in the examinations

Series Chapter Flow

Class 7

1. Classification of Matter
2. Atomic Structure and Transformation of Matter
3. Acids, Bases and Salts
4. Air and Oxygen
5. Water
6. Chemistry in Daily Life

Class 9

1. Nature of Matter
2. Atomic Structure
3. Periodic Classification of Elements
4. Chemical Bonding
5. Mole Concept, Stoichiometry and Behaviour of Gases
6. Chemical Kinetics and Chemical Equilibrium
7. Water, Solution, Solubility and Hydrogen
8. Metals and Non-Metals
9. Organic Chemistry

Class 8

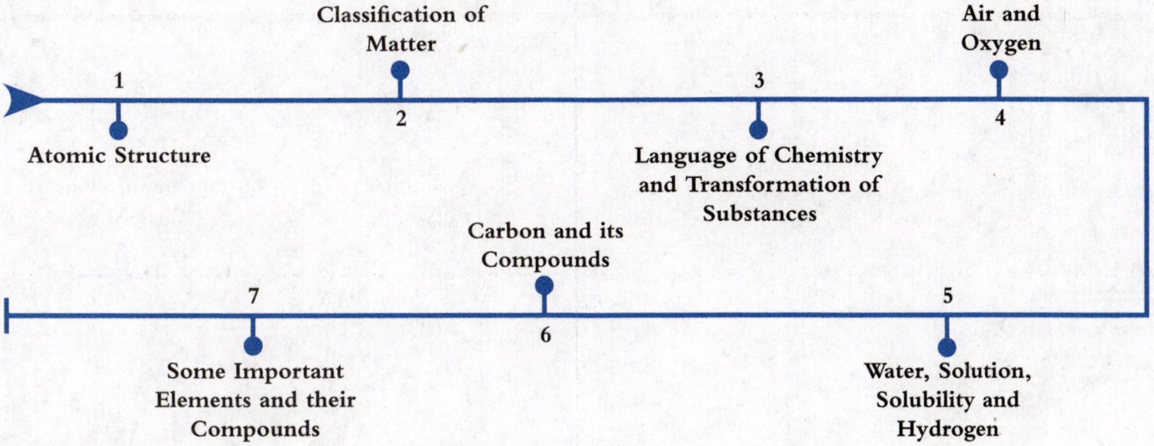

Class 10

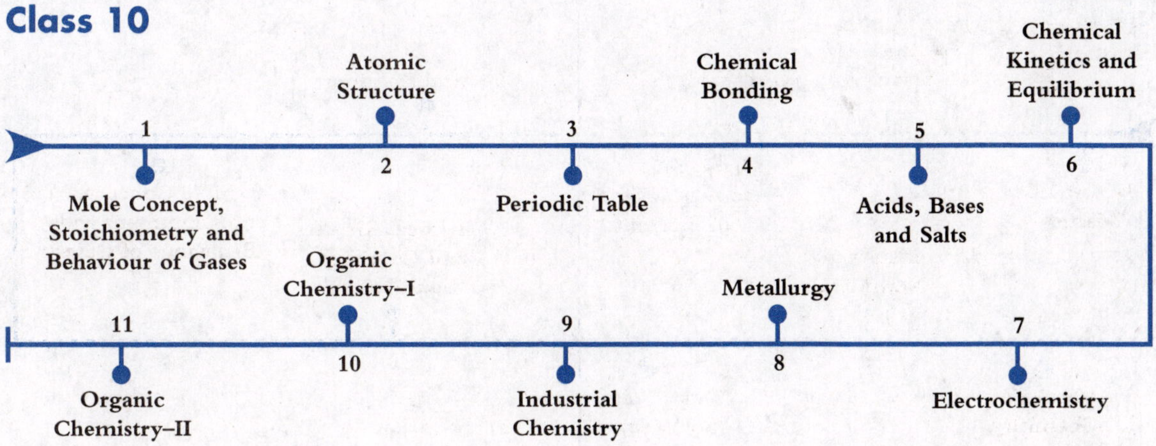

Chapter 1

Atomic Structure

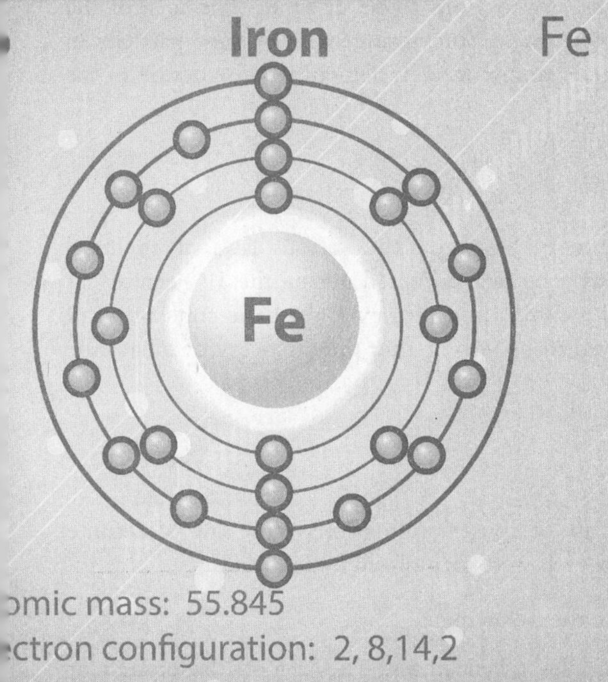

Remember

Before beginning this chapter, you should be able to:

- define matter and properties of matter.
- state atoms and molecules.

Key Ideas

After completing this chapter, you should be able to:

- understand the concept of atom as an indivisible particle.
- exaplin the models of an atom based on the concept of subatomic particles and the concept of nucleus.
- study concept of atomic number, mass number, isotopes and isobars.
- know about arrangement of electrons around the nucleus and form a structure of atom.

INTRODUCTION

The sun, the moon, the stars, etc., are some of the constituents of the universe by convention. In reality, there is matter and space. The study of matter dates back to as early as 600 BC where both ancient Indians and Greeks were important pioneers in the study of matter. In ancient India, Maharishi Kannada propounded that matter is made up of small indestructible particles called **Paramanu**. Ancient Greek philosophers, such as, Democritius, Epicurus and Leucippus theorised that matter is made up of small particles called **atoms**. The word atom is coined because these small particles of matter are assumed to be indestructible. In Greek language, atom means the 'incapability of being cut.' These achievements about atom were merely based on speculation. Later, based on experimentation, John Dalton postulated the theory of atoms. In due course, the discovery of electrons, protons and neutrons proved atom to be divisible. The idea of the subatomic particles paved the way for further researches on the arrangement of these particles in the atom, which led to the development of various atomic models depicting the structure of the atom.

Historical Aspects

In 1808, John Dalton proposed the atomic theory based on the various laws of chemical combination known at that time. The theory has been well accepted during the 19th century as it could help in explaining the laws of chemical combination. However, the basic conception of Dalton that an atom is indivisible has been proved to be wrong after the discovery of subatomic particles.

DALTON'S ATOMIC THEORY

Dalton's atomic theory is mainly based on the law of conservation of mass, the law of definite proportions and the law of multiple proportions which were formulated by Lavoisier.

The main postulates of Dalton's atomic theory are the following:

1. Matter is composed of tiny indivisible particles called atoms. They cannot be created or destroyed or transformed into atoms of another element.
2. Atoms of a given element are identical in all respects.
3. Atoms of different elements are different from each other.
4. Atoms of different elements take part in the chemical reaction and combine in a simple integral ratio to form compounds.
5. When elements react, the atoms may combine in more than one simple whole number ratio.

Dalton's atomic theory has been contradicted with the advancement of science, and hence, modified on the basis of further research and discoveries as listed here under:

1. With the discovery of subatomic particles, i.e., the electron, proton and neutron, it was concluded that atoms can be further divided.
2. Discovery of isotopes proved that atoms of the same element may possess different atomic weights, i.e., atoms of same elements may not be identical in all respects.

3. In some cases, atoms of different elements are found to have same mass number. For example, calcium and argon are found to have same mass number.

Though Dalton's atomic theory could not give convincing explanation to any of the above facts, it laid the foundation for the development of modern atomic theory.

The basic postulate of Dalton's atomic theory which says that 'atoms are the tiniest particles of matter which take part in the chemical reaction' is, however, accepted in modern atomic theory with experimental evidence.

The discovery of radioactivity led to the discovery of the fundamental particles in the atom.

DISCOVERY OF FUNDAMENTAL PARTICLES

An experiment to investigate the phenomenon that takes place when a high voltage is applied through a tube containing gas at low pressure laid the foundation to the discovery of fundamental particles.

In 1878, Sir William Crooke, while conducting an experiment using a special glass tube called discharge tube, found certain visible rays travelling between two metal electrodes. These rays are known as Crooke's rays or cathode rays. The discharge tube used in the experiment is now referred to as Crookes tube or more popularly as cathode ray tube (CRT).

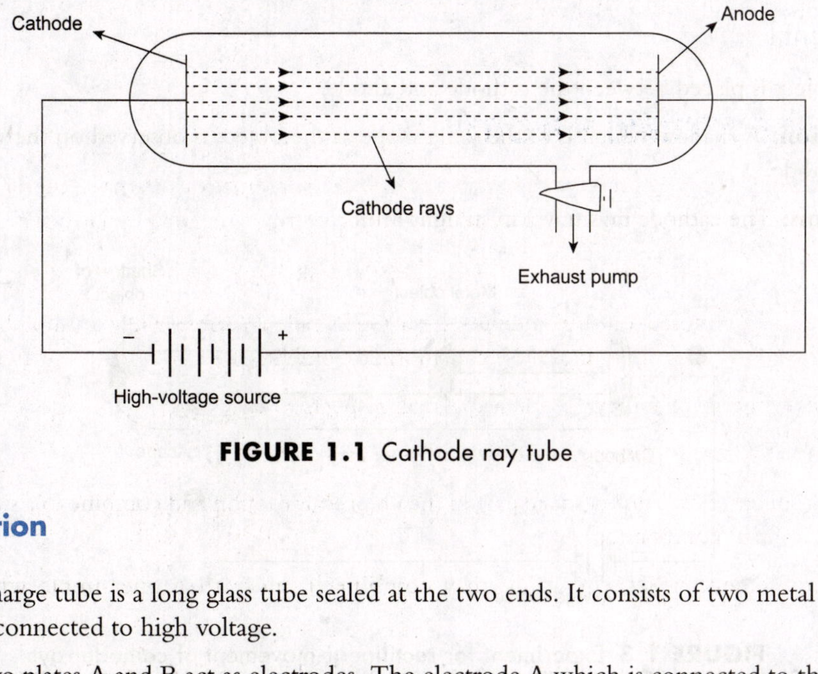

FIGURE 1.1 Cathode ray tube

Observation

1. A discharge tube is a long glass tube sealed at the two ends. It consists of two metal plates—A and B connected to high voltage.
2. The two plates A and B act as electrodes. The electrode A which is connected to the negative terminal of the battery is called **cathode** (negative electrode).
3. The electrode B which is connected to the positive terminal is called an **anode** (positive electrode).
4. There is a side tube which is connected to an exhaust pump. The exhaust pump is used for lowering the pressure inside the discharge tube.

Discovery of Electron

Later, J. J. Thomson also found that when a high voltage of 10,000 V was applied between the electrodes present in a partially evacuated CRT, a bright spot of light was formed on the screen coated with a fluorescent material, placed at the other end of the tube.

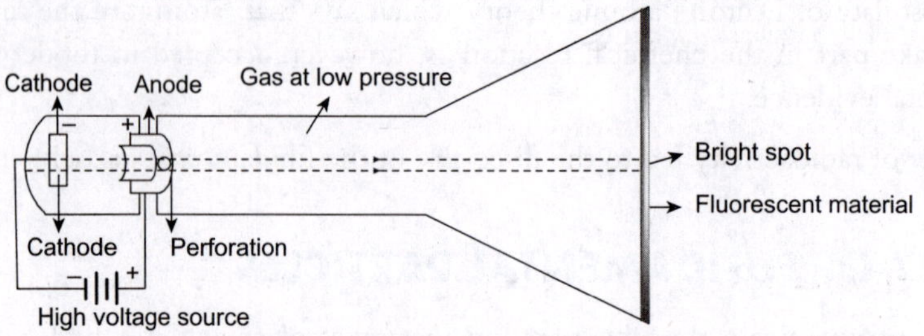

FIGURE 1.2 J. J. Thomson's cathode ray tube

The fluorescent material coated on the screen started to glow because it was struck by the rays which originated from the cathode. Since these rays were emitted by the cathode, he named these rays as cathode rays.

J. J. Thomson and others studied the properties of these cathode rays by conducting the following experiments:

Experiment I

A small object is placed between the cathode and anode.

Observation: A shadow which is of the same shape as the object is observed on the wall opposite to the cathode.

Conclusion: The cathode rays travel in straight lines.

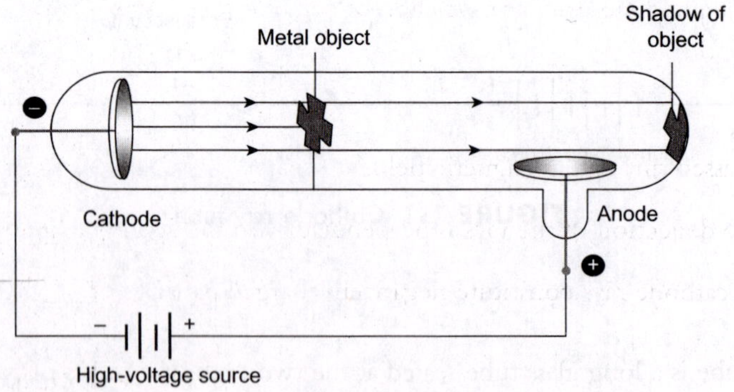

FIGURE 1.3 Experiment for rectilinear movement of cathode rays

Experiment II

A light paddle wheel is placed between the cathode and anode.

Observation: The wheel starts rotating.

Conclusion: Cathode rays are made up of small particles having mass and kinetic energy.

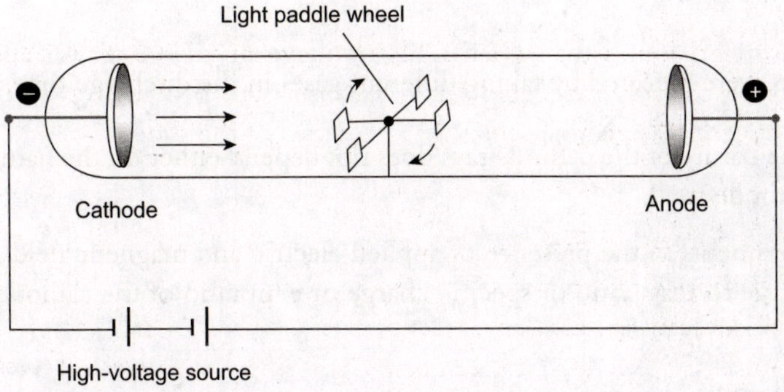

FIGURE 1.4 Experiment for proving cathode rays possess mass

Experiment III

Cathode rays are passed through an electric field.

Observation: The rays move on a curved path towards the positive plate of the electric field.

Conclusion: The cathode rays are negatively charged particles.

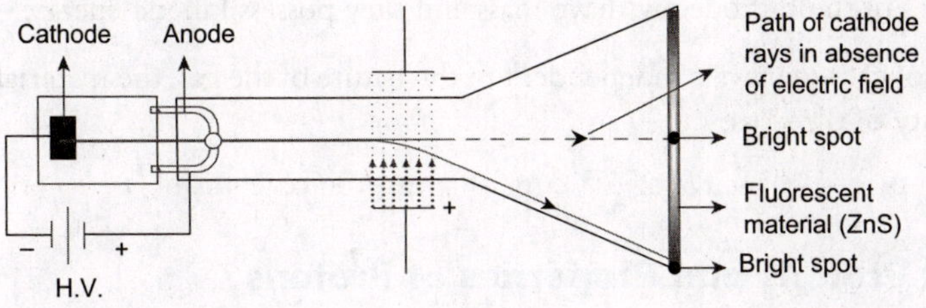

FIGURE 1.5 Schematic diagram of defelction of cathode rays in the presence of electrical field

Experiment IV

Cathode rays are passed through a magnetic field.

Observation: The deflection of the rays is perpendicular to the applied magnetic field.

Conclusion: The cathode rays constitute negatively charged particles.

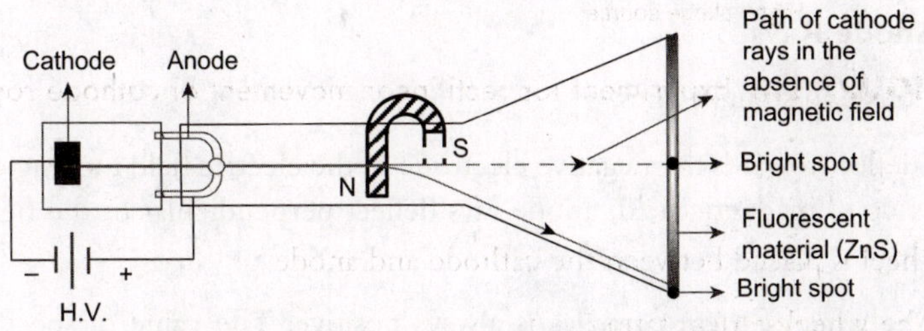

FIGURE 1.6 Schematic diagram of defelction of cathode rays in the presence of magnetic field

Experiment V

These experiments were repeated by taking different gases in the discharge tube.

Observation: The nature of the cathode rays does not depend either on the nature of the gas inside the tube or the cathode used.

During his experiments in the presence of applied electric and magnetic fields, he found out the concept called charge to mass ratio or specific charge or e/m ratio of the cathode rays.

Properties of the Cathode Rays

1. Cathode rays originate from cathode and travel towards anode.
2. Cathode rays travel in straight lines.
3. Cathode rays consist of a stream of particles.
4. The particles of the cathode rays are negatively charged. These negatively charged particles are called **electrons**.
5. Cathode rays deviate from their path in the presence of an electric field or a magnetic field.
6. The particles of the cathode rays have mass and they possess kinetic energy.
7. The nature of cathode rays is independent of the nature of the gas, the material of the electrodes and the quality of the glass.

Discovery of Protons and Properties of Protons

The presence of protons in the atom has been predicted by Goldstein based on the conception that atom being electrically neutral in nature should necessarily possess positively charged particles to balance the negatively charged electrons.

Goldstein's Experiment

Goldstein repeated the cathode ray experiment by using a perforated cathode.

Conclusion: In addition to the cathode rays originating from cathode some rays travelled from the anode towards the cathode. These rays were called anode rays or canal rays.

Properties of Anode Rays

1. Anode rays travel in straight lines.
2. Anode rays deflect towards the negative electrode of the electric field moving on a curved path. In the presence of magnetic field, anode rays deflect perpendicular to the field moving on an arc of a circle.
3. The electric charge of these particles is always positive. The value of specific charge of the particles varies with the nature of the gas taken in the discharge tube.
4. The mass of the particles was same as the atomic mass of the gas in the discharge tube.

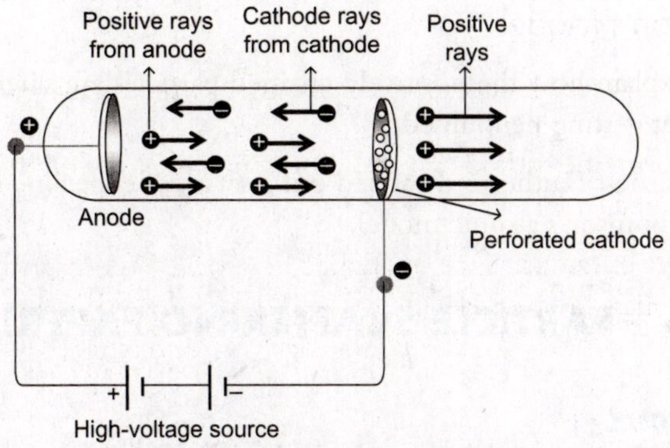

FIGURE 1.7 Discovery of protons

Goldstein assumed the rays (i.e., positive ions) travelling from anode to cathode as protons. Later discoveries proved that the lightest positively charged particle is that of hydrogen and is named proton.

The study of the properties of the fundamental particles, like, electrons and protons led to the conception of various atomic models.

Atomic model is the description of depicting the arrangement of various fundamental particles inside the atom.

Different atomic models have been proposed by John Dalton, J. J. Thomson, Rutherford and Bohr.

The systematic study of various basic atomic models gives an insight into the understanding of the primary structure of the atom.

Thomson's Atomic Model

J. J. Thomson proposed his atomic model in 1903 prior to the discovery of protons itself.

According to J. J. Thomson, an atom contains negatively charged-particles called **electrons** uniformly spread inside a sphere of thinly spread mass of positive charge. This model has been called by different names, such as, watermelon model, plum pudding model or an apple pie model. The total positive charge of the sphere is equal to the total negative charge of electrons and for this reason atom remains electrically neutral.

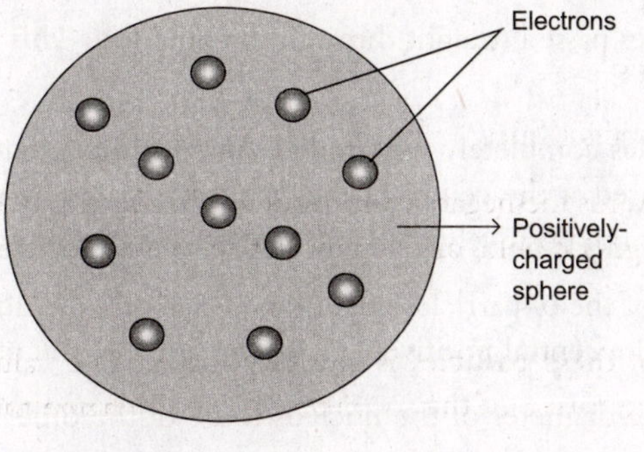

FIGURE 1.8 Thomson's atomic model

Drawback of Thomson's Model

The model could not explain how the positively charged particles are shielded from the negatively charged particles without getting neutralised.

After J. J. Thomson, Ernest Rutherford carried out a series of experiments from 1905 to 1911 to test the correctness of Thomson's atomic model.

RUTHERFORD'S α-PARTICLE SCATTERING EXPERIMENT

Discovery of Nucleus

Ernest Rutherford in 1911 gave the concept of nucleus based on the results of his experiment known as α-**particle scattering experiment**.

Rutherford bombarded a thin gold foil with α-particles. The foil was surrounded by a spherical screen of zinc sulphide. The α-particles were condensed to a narrow beam by passing them through a pair of positively charged parallel plates.

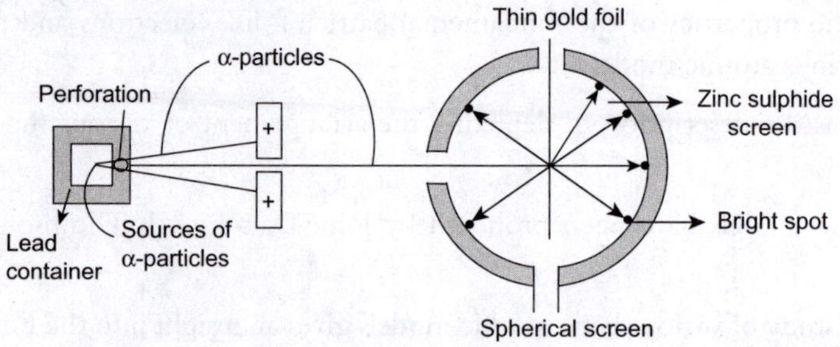

FIGURE 1.9 α-particle scattering experiment

Observations

1. Most of the α-particles passed straight through the gold foil without any deflection.
2. A few α-particles were deflected through small angles and a few were deflected through large angles.
3. Very few (1 in 20,000) α-particles completely rebounded.

On the basis of these observations, Rutherford concluded that Thomson's atomic model could not be correct because of the following reasons:

1. Most of the α-particles passed straight through the gold foil. This proves that atoms must have large empty space.
2. Since very few particles completely rebounded, he concluded that the total positive charge of the atom is concentrated at the centre of the atom. They are not thinly spread in the form of a sphere. The tiny central positively charged core was named as **nucleus**.
3. The large deflection of the α-particles could take place only because of the close encounter of the α-particles with the central positively charged core, i.e., the nucleus.

Rutherford estimated the diameter of the nucleus to be of the order of 10^{-13} cm and that of the atom to be 10^{-8} cm.

Thus, the diameter of the nucleus is about 10^5 times smaller than the diameter of the atom.

Rutherford's Atomic Model

1. Atom consists mostly of empty space.
2. The entire positively charged particles are present in the centre of the atomic sphere. This concentrated positively charged mass within the atom is called **nucleus**.
3. The size of the nucleus is very small compared to the size of the total volume of the atom.
4. The electrons within an atom must revolve around the nucleus at various distances at very high speeds in order to counter balance the electrostatic force of attraction between protons and electrons.

Rutherford's atomic model can be compared with the solar system.

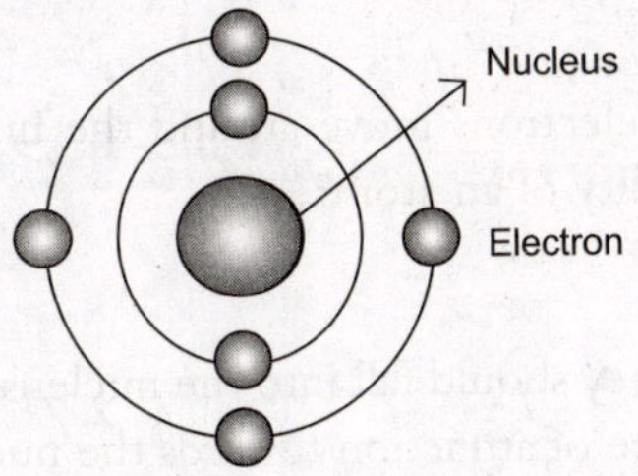

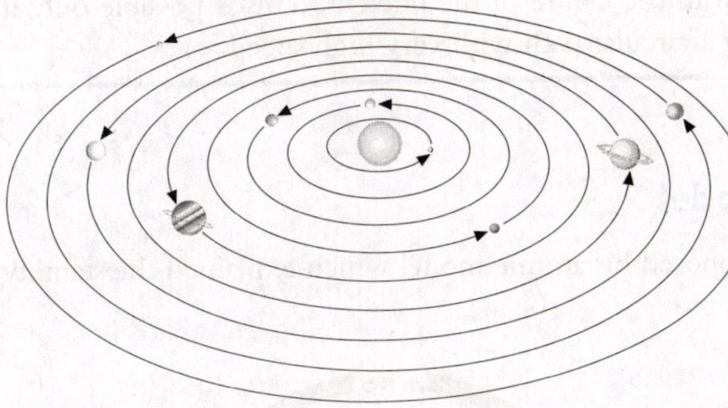

FIGURE 1.10 The solar system

Drawbacks of Rutherford's Atomic Model

Rutherford's model could not explain the stability of an atom. Electron is a charged particle moving around the oppositely charged nucleus. According to classical electrodynamics, an electrically charged particle revolving around in a circular path radiates energy continuously. Hence, an electron revolving around the nucleus should radiate energy and gradually move towards the nucleus. This gives a spiral path for the electron which should finally collide with the nucleus and the atom would collapse. But atoms are quite stable.

EXAMPLE

How did the discovery of isotopes contradict Dalton's atomic theory?

SOLUTION

The discovery of isotopes proved that atoms of the same element may possess different atomic weights, that is atoms of the same element may not be identical in all respects. Hence, discovery of isotopes contradicted Dalton's atomic theory.

EXAMPLE

Why is Rutherford's model called **planetary model**?

SOLUTION

Rutherford's atomic model can be compared with the solar system. Planets revolve round the sun in the solar system. Similarly electrons revolve round the nucleus in an atom. Hence, Rutherford's atomic model is also called planetary model.

EXAMPLE

According to Rutherford, electrons move around the nucleus at very high speed. How did he correlate this with the stability of an atom?

SOLUTION

If the electrons are at rest, they should fall into the nucleus due to electrostatic forces of attraction. In order to balance this force of attraction towards the nucleus, they must be under the action of another force away from the centre of the nucleus. This is possible only if the electrons are in a state of motion along a circular path with very high speed.

Bohr's Atomic Model

In 1913, Neils Bohr proposed his atomic model which explained the stability of an atom.

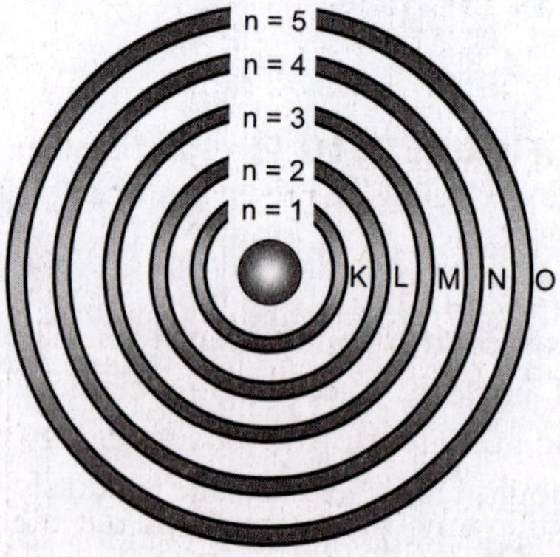

FIGURE 1.11 Bohr's atomic model

Postulates of Bohr's Atomic Model

1. Electrons revolve around the nucleus only in certain permissible circular paths called **orbits** or **shells**.
2. The electron in each orbit has a definite energy.
3. The energy of an electron remains constant as long as it revolves in a particular orbit.

4. An electron moves from a lower-energy level to a higher-energy level when it absorbs energy from an external source.

5. An electron gives out energy while jumping from a high-energy level to a low-energy level.

Discovery of Neutrons

The mass of an atom is concentrated in its nucleus and the mass of the electrons is negligible. Hence, the mass of an atom was expected to be equal to the mass of the protons in it.

Except in the case of hydrogen, the mass of an atom was found to be always greater than the total mass of the protons present inside the atom. Further, the unaccounted mass of atom, i.e., (mass of atom – mass of protons) was either equal to or a multiple of the mass of proton.

Based on the above observation, it was assumed that an atom contains one more kind of particle which has the same mass as that of the proton but without any charge. These particles were named as neutrons and were found to be electrically neutral.

In 1932 James Chadwick proved the existence of neutrons by bombarding beryllium nucleus with alpha particles.

Characteristics of Fundamental Particles

S. No.	Fundamental particles	Charge	Mass	Relative charge
1.	Electron (e)	-1.6×10^{-19} C -4.8×10^{-10} e.s.u.	9.1×10^{-31} kg (or) 0.00055 amu	−1
2.	Proton (p)	$+1.6 \times 10^{-19}$ C $+4.8 \times 10^{-10}$ e.s.u.	1.67×10^{-27} kg (or) 1.0078 amu	+1
3.	Neutron (n)	0	1.72×10^{-27} kg (or) 1.0083 amu	0

Atomic Number and Mass Number

The number of protons present in the nucleus of an atom is called its atomic number and is denoted by the letter Z.

The total number of protons and neutrons present in the nucleus of an atom is called **mass number** and is denoted by the letter A.

For example, a chlorine atom has 17 protons and 18 neutrons in its nucleus. Hence, its atomic number (Z) is 17 and its mass number (A) is 35 and is represented as ${}_{17}Cl^{35}$.

Isotopes

Atoms of an element must have the same atomic number, but their mass number can be different due to the presence of different number of neutrons.

These atoms of an element having different number of neutrons are called isotopes.

For example, hydrogen occurs in nature in three different isotopic forms—protium (${}_1H^1$), deuterium (${}_1H^2$) and tritium (${}_1H^3$).

The atomic number of all the three isotopes is 1, but their mass numbers are 1, 2 and 3, respectively. The percentage of protium is maximum in the natural sample of hydrogen, i.e., 99.98%.

Isobars

These are atoms of different elements having the same mass number.

For example, calcium and argon are found to have the same mass number.

${}_{20}Ca^{40}$ and ${}_{18}Ar^{40}$.

Electronic Configuration of the Atoms

Electrons move around the nucleus in different orbits.

The maximum number of electrons which can be presented in a particular orbit was given by Bohr and Bury. This is known as Bohr–Bury scheme of electronic configuration.

If n represents the shell number, then the maximum number of electrons which can revolve in that particular shell is given by the formula $2n^2$.

Shell numbers	Maximum number of electrons
K-shell ($n = 1$)	$2n^2 = 2 \times 1^2 = 2$
L-shell ($n = 2$)	$2n^2 = 2 \times 2^2 = 8$
M-shell ($n = 3$)	$2n^2 = 2 \times 3^2 = 18$
N-shell ($n = 4$)	$2n^2 = 2 \times 4^2 = 32$

But the maximum number of electrons which can be present in the outermost orbit, i.e., valence shell is 8. The maximum number of electrons that can be present in the penultimate and the anti-penultimate shells is 18 and 32, respectively. An atom is considered to be stable if its outermost orbit contains 8 electrons.

Geometrical Representation of Structure of an Atom

1. The atomic number of carbon is 6 and the mass number of carbon is 12.

   Number of electrons = 6

   Number of neutrons = 6

   Number of protons = 6

2. The atomic number of aluminium is 13 and its mass number is 27.

   Number of electrons = 13

   Number of neutrons = 14

   Number of protons = 13

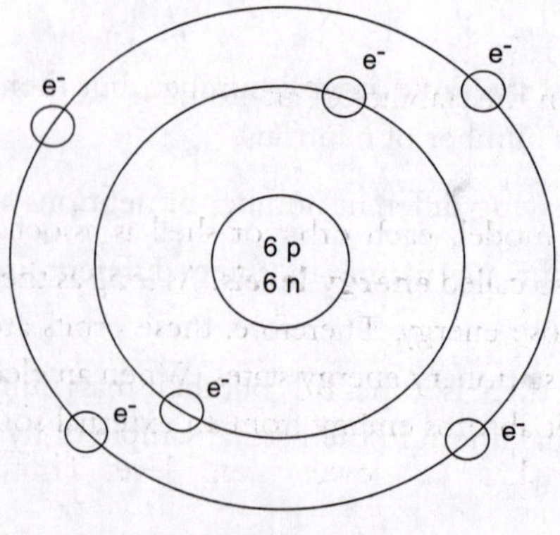

FIGURE 1.12 Geometrical representation of carbon

Valence Shell and Valence Electrons

Valence shell of an element is the outermost shell in an atom.

For example, $_{11}Na^{23}$ – 2, 8, 1 ... Here 1 electron is filled in the last shell, i.e., M-shell. Therefore, M-shell is the valence shell.

The electrons filled in the valence shell are called **valence electrons**. In the above example, there is one valence electron which belongs to the M-shell.

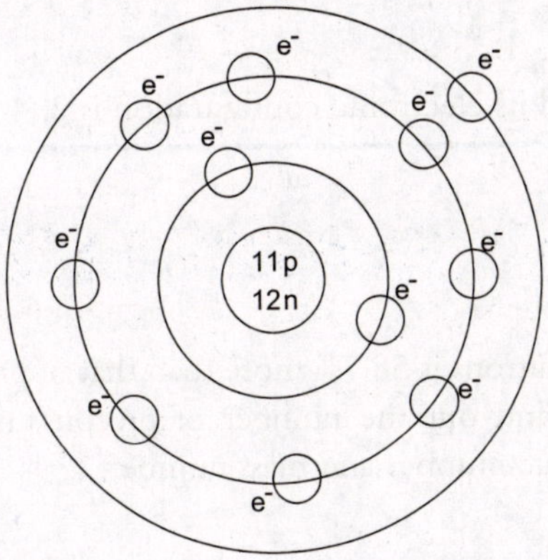

FIGURE 1.13 Geometrical representation of sodium

EXAMPLE

An element X consists of 20 protons and 20 neutrons. Mention the atomic number and mass number and represent the element with atomic number and mass number.

SOLUTION

As X consists of 20 protons ⇒ atomic number, (Z) is 20.

As number of neutrons = 20, mass number, (A) = atomic number + number of neutrons

$\therefore$ A = 20 + 20 = 40

$\therefore$ Mass number, (A) = 40

The element is calcium and can be represented as $_{20}Ca^{40}$.

EXAMPLE

How was Bohr able to explain the stability of an atom?

SOLUTION

According to Bohr's atomic model, each orbit or shell is associated with a definite amount of energy, and hence, they are also called **energy levels**. As long as the electron revolves in a particular orbit, the electron does not lose energy. Therefore, these orbits are called **stationary orbits** and the electrons are said to be in stationary energy states. When an electron moves from lower-energy level to higher-energy level, it absorbs energy from an external source and gives out energy while jumping from a higher-energy level to a lower-energy level. Thus, he explained the stability of an atom.

EXAMPLE

The mass of positively charged particles present in an atom is found to be 11,022 times that of an electron. Identify the element and write its electronic configuration.

SOLUTION

The mass of a proton is 1837 times that of an electron.

$$\text{Number of protons} = \frac{11,022}{1837} = 6$$

Hence, element is carbon and its electronic configuration is 2, 4.

EXAMPLE

In an atom, the number of neutrons is 58.7% more than that of protons. The number of electrons in the neutral atom is 92. Find out the number of protons, neutrons and mass number and represent the atom with atomic number and mass number.

SOLUTION

Since the number of electrons in the neutral atom is 92.

∴ Atomic number (Z) is 92 and number of protons is 92.

Number of neutrons = 92 + (58.7/100) × 92 = 146.

Mass number, (A) = atomic number + number of neutrons.

Mass number = 92 + 146 = 238.

Representation $_{92}X^{238}$.

EXAMPLE

The mass number of an atom is 31. If the atom has 5 electrons in M-shell, calculate the number of neutrons.

SOLUTION

The electronic configuration of the element is 2, 8, 5. Therefore, its atomic number is 15 and the number of neutrons = mass number – atomic number

∴ Number of neutrons = 31 – 15 = 16.

TEST YOUR CONCEPTS

Very Short Answer Type Questions

1. How Rutherford's theory contradicts the laws of electrodynamics?
2. According to Dalton, atoms combine in ________ ratio to form compounds.
3. Which postulate of Dalton's atomic theory is considered to be correct even now?
4. What are the conditions maintained in a discharge tube for the generation of cathode rays?
5. According to Rutherford electrons revolve around the nucleus in ________
6. What are isotopes? Give an example.
7. What is an α-particle?
8. Give the geometrical representations of electronic arrangements of the following elements:

   (a) fluorine (b) phosphorus
9. What is the maximum number of electrons that can be present in the *n*th shell of an atom?
10. What were the comparative values of diameter of nucleus and atom given by Rutherford?
11. When electric field is applied, the cathode rays bend towards ________.
12. Find the number of valence electrons in the following elements by writing the electronic arrangement in their atoms:

    (a) nitrogen (b) sulphur (c) chlorine
13. Why Rutherford's model is called nuclear model?
14. Define atomic number and mass number. How can you represent an atom by using atomic number and mass number? Give two examples.
15. Who discovered neutrons? How was the discovery made?
16. Why is a partially evacuated discharge tube taken for Thomson's experiment?
17. Atoms of different elements having the same mass number are known as ________.
18. The nature of ________ rays depends upon the nature of the gas in the discharge tube.
19. How did Rutherford explain the stability of atom?
20. Name the isotopes of hydrogen and give the number of neutrons present in each of them.
21. What is the relative mass of proton with respect to hydrogen atom?
22. Which experiment led to the discovery of nucleus?
23. Most of the α-particles passed straight through the gold foil. This proved the existence of ________ in an atom.
24. According to Rutherford, ________ force of nucleus is balanced by the high velocity of revolving electrons.
25. The atoms of the same element may differ in the number of ________.
26. The valence shell of an element of atomic number 35 is the ________ shell.
27. Give the mass and charge of an electron, a proton and a neutron in kg and coulombs, respectively.
28. According to Bohr's atomic model, electrons revolve in ________ orbits.

Short Answer Type Questions

29. Explain Thomson's atomic model. What are the drawbacks of this model?
30. An atom X is made up of 20 protons and 20 neutrons. Represent the atom with atomic number and mass number.
31. Why does chlorine have fractional atomic mass?
32. How could Bohr explain the stability of an atom?
33. Give the postulates of Dalton's atomic theory.

34. What are the observations of α-ray scattering experiment? Based on these observations, how did Rutherford disprove Thomson's model?

35. Write the electronic arrangement for the following elements. Also give the geometrical representations.
(a) oxygen
(b) argon
(c) calcium
(d) potassium

36. When different gases are taken in a discharge tube, how do the e/m values of cathode rays and canal rays vary?

37. Give the differences between isotopes and isobars.

38. In J. J. Thomson's experiment, what observations were found when
(a) a small obstruction was placed in the path of cathode rays.
(b) a paddle wheel is placed between cathode and anode.
What were the conclusions drawn on the basis of these observations?

39. Calculate the number of neutrons for the following elements:
(a) $_{11}Na^{23}$
(b) $_{18}Ar^{40}$
(c) $_{17}Cl^{35}$
(d) $_{15}P^{31}$

40. What happens to the cathode rays under a strong magnetic field or an electric field? What is the conclusion made from this?

41. An atom of an element has fourth shell as the valence shell. The difference between electrons present in L- and M-, K- and N-shells are 1 and 0, respectively. Find the atomic number of an element.

42. An atom of an element has one electron in the valence shell and the two inner shells have 8 electrons each. Find the atomic number of that element.

43. Mass of total positive charge present in an atom is 16533 times to that of mass of electron. Find the atomic number of this element.

Essay Type Questions

44. Write down the
(a) electronic configuration,
(b) number of valence electrons,
(c) number of neutrons and
(d) nature of the element for the following:
(1) $_{6}X^{12}$
(2) $_{10}Y^{20}$
(3) $_{19}Z^{39}$

45. Explain how the results of α-ray scattering experiment led to Rutherford's model of atom. Give the postulates and drawbacks of Rutherford's atomic model.

46. State the postulates of Bohr's theory.

47. Find out the maximum number of electrons that can be accommodated in K-shell, L-shell, M-shell and N-shell by using Bohr–Bury scheme.

48. Give the properties of cathode rays in comparison to the properties of canal rays.

For Answer key, Hints and Explanations, please visit: www.pearsoned.co.in/IITFoundationSeries

CONCEPT APPLICATION

Level 1

Directions for questions from 1 to 7

State whether the following statements are true or false.

1. In Thomson's atomic model, positive mass occupies more space than the negative charge in an atom.
2. α-ray scattering experiment proved the presence of neutrons in an atom.
3. Thomson could successfully explain the electrical neutrality of an atom.
4. The e/m ratio of cathode rays is different for different gases.
5. High pressure and low voltage should be maintained in the discharge tube for the production of cathode rays.
6. Mass number is the sum of the number of protons and neutrons in an atom.
7. Cathode rays deflect in the presence of magnetic field.

Directions for questions from 8 to 14

Fill in the blanks.

8. The discovery of ________ proved that atom is divisible.
9. The maximum number of electrons present in fifth shell is ________.
10. Electron present in ________ orbit cannot lose its energy.
11. The fundamental particle present in anode rays produced by $_1H^1$ is ________.
12. The electrode connected to the negative terminal of a battery in a discharge tube is called ________.
13. The specific charge value of anode rays produced by ________ is the maximum.
14. The sum of protons and neutrons is same in ________.

Directions for question 15

Match the entries in Column A with the appropriate ones in Column B.

15.

Column A		Column B
A. Plum pudding model	( )	a. Isobars
B. Planetary model	( )	b. Bohr's atomic model
C. Definite circular paths for electrons	( )	c. Isotopes
D. Fractional atomic weights of elements	( )	d. Rutherford's atomic model
E. Same number nucleons	( )	e. Thomson's of atomic model

Directions for questions from 16 to 30

For each of the questions, four choices have been provided. Select the correct alternative.

16. Certain amount of a gas is enclosed in a discharge tube. The bulb in the arrangement given below can be made to glow when

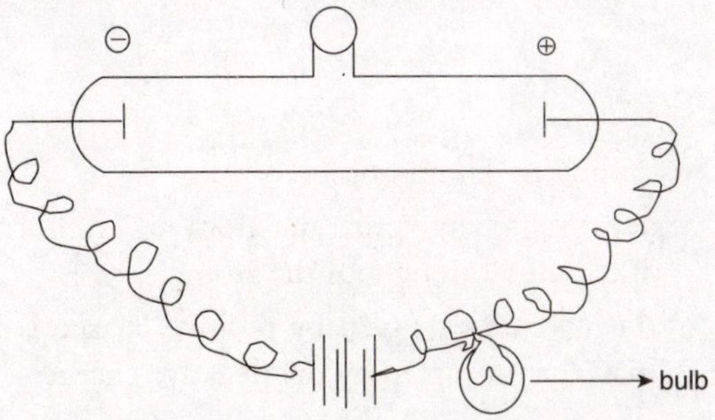

(a) vacuum is created in the discharge tube.
(b) the gas is replaced by the same amount of an easily ionisable gas.
(c) the other gas of low molecular weight is introduced.
(d) the amount of gas in the discharge tube is decreased.

17. Which of the following particles is largely responsible for the chemical behaviour of elements?
(a) proton (b) electron
(c) neutron (d) positron

18. ${}_{8}X^{16}$ and ${}_{8}X^{17}$ represent
(a) isotones (b) isobars
(c) isotopes (d) isosters

19. The isotope with zero neutron is
(a) protium
(b) deuterium
(c) tritium
(d) none of these

20. Two elements X and Y have 6 and 7 electrons in their N- and M-shells, respectively. Find the ratio of atomic numbers of X and Y.
(a) 3 : 4 (b) 1 : 2
(c) 2 : 1 (d) 6 : 7

21. The number of valence electrons in ${}_{4}X^{8}$ atom is
(a) 1 (b) 2
(c) 3 (d) 4

22. The number of valence electrons in ${}^{40}_{20}X$ is
(a) 7 (b) 9
(c) 5 (d) 2

23. Two elements A and B have 14 and 9 electrons in M- and N-shells, respectively. Then the ratio of their atomic numbers is
(a) 2 : 3 (b) 3 : 4
(c) 3 : 2 (d) 1 : 2

24. According to Thomson,
(a) negative charge of an atom is uniformly distributed throughout the atom.
(b) the volume occupied by positive charge is less than that occupied by the negative charge.
(c) electrons are embedded in the positive charge which is spread uniformly.
(d) none of the above

25. ${}^{y}_{x}A$, ${}^{y+1}_{x}A$ are two isotopes of element A. Difference between the number of neutrons in the isotopes is
(a) $1 - 2y$ (b) $1 - x$
(c) 1 (d) $2x - 1$

26. Low pressure is maintained in the discharge tube to
(a) increase the number of molecules
(b) increase ionisation of gas molecules
(c) decrease the velocity of the rays coming from the cathode
(d) all the above

27. If velocity of α-particles increases, then angle of deviation
(a) increases
(b) decreases
(c) remains same
(d) cannot be predicted

28. Which of the following unipositive ions possesses all the three subatomic particles?
(a) helium (b) deuterium
(c) tritium (d) hydrogen

29. The ratio of the number of electrons in the N-shell of A and the M-shell of B with atomic numbers 40 and 32, respectively, is
(a) 5 : 3 (c) 9 : 5
(b) 5 : 9 (d) 5 : 4

30. Total number of electrons present in the penultimate shell of an element with atomic number 36 is
(a) 18 (b) 10
(c) 8 (d) 16

Directions for questions from 31 to 45
Select the correct alternative from the given choices.

31. To draw the geometrical representation for the structure of the oxygen atom the following steps are given. Identify the correct sequence of the steps.
(1) The eight electrons present in the extranuclear part would be distributed in the first two orbits, i.e., K and L. As per the rules, two electrons would occupy the K-orbit and the remaining six electrons occupy the L-orbit.
(2) The atomic number of oxygen is 8.
(3) In the nucleus, 8 protons and 8 neutrons are present and in the extranuclear part, i.e., in the orbits, 8 electrons are present.
(4) Oxygen atom has 8 electrons and 8 protons. The mass number is 16, and hence, the number of neutrons is equal to 8 [${}_{8}O^{16}$].

(a) 2 1 3 4 (b) 3 1 4 2
(c) 2 4 3 1 (d) 3 4 2 1

32. Arrange the following statements in a sequence which involves the calculation of the atomic number and mass number for an atom of an element with 15 electrons and 16 neutrons.

(1) A = Number of protons + Number of neutrons

A = Z + Number of neutrons

A = 15 + 16 = 31

(2) Number of protons and number of electrons are equal in a neutral atom. Hence, the atomic number Z is equal to 15.

(3) Mass number is equal to the total number of protons and neutrons.

(4) Atomic number is 15 and mass number is 31.

(a) 2 4 3 1 (b) 2 3 1 4
(c) 3 2 1 4 (d) 3 2 4 1

33. Many theories and experiments carried out for the study of atom eventually led to the development of its structure. Arrange the given theories or models of atom proposed by different scientists in chronological order.

(1) planetary model
(2) watermelon model
(3) Bohr's atomic model
(4) Dalton's atomic theory

(a) 3 2 1 4 (b) 4 1 2 3
(c) 2 1 4 3 (d) 4 2 1 3

34. Rutherford's α-ray scattering experiment led to the discovery of the nucleus and to the conclusion that an atom consists of large empty space. Arrange the following steps in a sequence which explains the experiment and also the above mentioned conclusions.

(1) To make out the observations a spherical ZnS screen was placed surrounding the gold foil.

(2) The substance which acts as a source of α-particles is taken in a lead container and made to pass through a slit between like charged positive plates.

(3) It was observed that most of the particles passed straight through the gold foil, few were deflected through small angles and very few through large angles. However, very few completely rebounded.

(4) A narrow, condensed beam consisting of α-particles is made to bombard on a thin gold foil.

(a) 1 3 2 4 (b) 2 3 1 4
(c) 4 2 1 3 (d) 2 4 1 3

35. The mass of which of the following fundamental particles is negligible?

(a) electrons (b) protons
(c) neutrons (d) both (1) and (3)

36. Identify the electronic configuration of manganese (Z = 25)

(a) 2, 8, 13, 2 (b) 2, 8, 8, 7
(c) 2, 8, 15 (d) 2, 8, 10, 5

37. Which among the following set of elements contain same number of valence electrons?

(a) ${}^{23}_{11}X$, ${}^{40}_{20}Y$ (b) ${}^{20}_{10}X$, ${}^{39}_{19}Y$
(c) ${}^{23}_{11}X$, ${}^{39}_{19}Y$ (d) ${}^{40}_{18}X$, ${}^{40}_{26}Y$

38. The atoms of the same element may differ in the number of ______

(a) electrons only
(b) protons only
(c) neutrons only
(d) both electrons and protons

39. **Assertion (A)**: Electrons present in ground states of different single electron species (H, He^{+}, Li^{++}) possess different amounts of energy.

Reason (R): Distances of electrons from the nuclei of different single electron species are equal.

(a) Both A and R are correct and R is the correct explanation of A.
(b) Both A and R are correct and R is not the correct explanation of A.
(c) A is correct and R is wrong.
(d) A is wrong and R is correct.

40. Identify the atomic number corresponding to least number of valence electrons

(a) 19 (b) 15
(c) 35 (d) 34

41. An atom of an element has mass number 31. It has 16 neutrons. The valence shell and the number of valence electrons, respectively, could be

(a) M-shell and 6 electrons
(b) M-shell and 5 electrons
(c) N-shell and 5 electrons
(d) L-shell and 6 electrons

42. The number of electrons present in each α-particle is
(a) 2
(b) 3
(c) 0
(d) 1

43. An atom of an element has two electrons in the valence shell and two consecutive inner shells have 8 electrons each. Calculate the atomic number of the element.
(a) 19
(b) 20
(c) 30
(d) 18

44. Rutherford's theory assumed which of the following paths for the electron?
(a) spherical
(b) circular
(c) spiral
(d) not defined

45. If an electron jumps from orbit A to orbit B, it loses energy and if it jumps from C to B, it gains energy. Arrange the orbits in the increasing order of distance from the nucleus.
(a) A < B < C
(b) C < A < B
(c) C < B < A
(d) A < C < B

Level 2

1. A neutral atom of an element has a nucleus with nuclear charge 12 times and mass 24 times that of hydrogen. Calculate the number of electrons, protons and neutrons in its stable positively charged ion.

2. Mass numbers of two isotopes of an element differ by 2 units (A and A + 2). Average atomic mass is 0.5 more than the lower mass number. What could be the ratio of the two isotopes?

3. A stable neutral atom of an element contains three fully filled orbits. Find the atomic number of the element.

4. The percentage abundance of two isotopes of boron in a natural sample are 80 and 20. The first isotope has 6 neutrons in the nucleus. If the actual atomic mass of boron is 11.01, calculate the mass numbers of the two isotopes.

5. A dipositive ion has an electronic arrangement of 2, 8, 8. Find out the number of electrons, protons and neutrons in that element if its mass number is 40.

6. Atoms of two elements P and Q have 5 electrons in the second and third shells, respectively. What could be the geometrical representations of P and Q? What will the atomic numbers of these elements be?

7. Anode rays are also produced along with cathode rays in the discharge tube under low pressure. Justify.

8. Cathode rays are deflected in electric and magnetic fields. But they are made to pass straight in Thomson's experiment. How do you account for this?

9. If the maximum permissible orbits of elements in nature are limited to $n = 4$, what are the number of possible elements?

10. A metallic element forms an ion with unit charge. The ion has 10 electrons and 12 neutrons. What is the number of electrons, protons and neutrons in its neutral atom? Represent the atom with atomic number and mass number.

11. Nuclear charge of an element B is twice that of A. If A has two completely filled orbits and L-shell is its outermost orbit, find out the atomic numbers of A and B.

12. The number of electrons in a dipositive ion of an element X is 18. If the mass number of X is 4 units more than twice the number of electrons of its ion, calculate the number of protons, electron and neutrons in X.

13. Rutherford's α-ray scattering experiment was conducted in order to test the validity of Thomson's model. What results were expected from this experiment?

14. If the average atomic mass of chlorine is 35.5, then find the percentage abundance of the two isotopes of chlorine which have the mass number 35 and 37.

15. The electronic configuration of an atom A is a, $a + b$, $a + 2b$, a and that of B is a, $a + b$, $3a + 2b$, b.
    (a) Write the electronic configurations of A and B.
    (b) Calculate their atomic numbers,
    (c) If the number of neutrons in A is 5b and that in B is 22.5a, calculate their mass numbers.

16. Compare and contrast the angle of deflection of α-rays in α-rays scattering experiment carried out by taking aluminium foil and gold foil, respectively. Justify your results.

17. Why did Thomson assume that electrons are embedded in a positive mass but not the other way round?

18. The ratio of the number of neutrons present in the two elements X and Y is 5 : 7 and the ratio of mass numbers is 10 : 13. The element X attains a stable octet configuration by losing two electrons from the fourth shell. Calculate the number of protons, electrons and neutrons present in X and Y.

19. The dipositive and dinegative ions of different elements possesses an octet configuration in their third shell. Find out the atomic number and number of valence electrons in their neutral atoms.

20. From the following table, identify isotopes and isobars.

Atoms	Number of protons	Number of neutrons
A	X	Z + 2
B	X + 1	Z
C	X − 2	Z + 4
D	X + 1	Z + 1
E	X	Z + 1

21. (i) Element X has two valence electrons in the M-shell.
    (ii) In element Y, the electrons are distributed in the first three shells. It has eight electrons in the M-shell.
    (iii) Element Z has eight electrons in the penultimate shell, i.e., M.

    Based on the information given in the above three statements, answer the following questions.
    (a) Give the electronic configuration of X.
    (b) Which element is stable among X, Y and Z and why?
    (c) In which atom of an element is the number of electrons distributed in all the four shells?
    (d) What is the atomic number of Z in which the number of electrons in the first and the last shell are not the same?
    (e) What are the number of electrons and protons present in Y?

22. In an α-ray scattering experiment what would happen if
    (a) protons are used instead of ?α-particles.

23. An atom of an element has one electron in the valence shell and the two consecutive inner shells have 8 electrons each. Find the atomic number of that element. Write the electronic configuration of preceding and succeeding elements.

Level 3

1. Discharge doesn't take place at normal atmospheric pressure inside the cathode ray tube. Justify.

2. The e/m ratio of cathode rays does not change by changing the gas in cathode ray discharge tube. But the e/m ratio of anode rays changes by changing the gas in the discharge tube. Justify this statement.

3. When the canal ray experiment was conducted by taking helium gas in the discharge tube, e/m value of the particles was found to be less under low voltage and it was found to be more under high voltage. How do you explain this?

4. Different gases can produce different colours in a discharge tube. Explain with reason.

5. Anode rays produced by isotopes and isobars possess same charge when taken in different discharge tubes. Which among the two sets of anode rays show different deflections in the presence of an electric field?

Directions for questions from 6 to 10

Application-based questions

6. If ${}^{y}_{x}A^{+1}$ or ${}^{y-2}_{x-1}B^{+1}$ were to be used instead of a particles in Rutherford's experiment, which would be better and why?

7. According to Bohr's theory, the electrons revolve round the nucleus in definite paths called **orbits.** Do the electrons revolve round with same speed in all orbits? Justify.

8. M-shells of two elements A and B have 18 electrons each. The difference in the number of electrons present in the N-shells of A and B is 8. The M-shell is the penultimate shell in B. Predict the range of probable atomic numbers of A and B.

9. Which postulate of Rutherford's theory is not derived from the results of α-ray scattering experiment? On what basis Rutherford could assume that?

10. Predict the possible atomic number(s) of an atom in which the third shell is incompletely filled and maximum 4 more electrons can be added to that shell of the atom.

PRACTICE QUESTIONS

CONCEPT APPLICATION

Level 1

True or false

1. True
2. False
3. True
4. False
5. False
6. True
7. True

Fill in the blanks

8. Electron
9. 50
10. First
11. Proton
12. Cathode
13. Hydrogen
14. Isobars

Match the following

15. A → e
B → d
C → b
D → c
E → a

Multiple choice questions

16. d
17. b
18. c
19. a
20. c
21. b
22. d
23. a
24. c
25. c
26. b
27. b
28. a
29. c
30. a
31. c
32. b
33. d
34. d

35. Mass of electron is negligible. Hence, correct option is (a).

36. Electronic configuration of manganese is 2, 8, 8, 7. Hence, correct option is (b).

37. ${}^{23}_{11}X$, ${}^{39}_{19}Y$ have one valence electron as they are sodium and potassium with electronic arrangements 2, 8, 1 and 2, 8, 8, 1, respectively. Hence, correct option is (c).

38. The atoms of the same element which have the same atomic number but different mass numbers are called isotopes. Hence, these atoms possess the same number of electrons and protons but differ in the number of neutrons. Hence, correct option is (c).

39. The electrons present in different single electron species possess different amounts of energy due to the difference in the atomic numbers.

The distance of the electrons from the nuclei of different single electron species is different because of difference in atomic number. Hence, correct option is (c).

40. The electronic configuration of an element with atomic number 19 is 2, 8, 8, 1, number of valence electrons is 1; similarly, the electronic configuration of elements with atomic numbers 15, 35 and 34 are 2, 8, 5; 2, 8, 18, 7 and 2, 8, 18, 6, respectively and the valence electrons are, 5, 7 and 6, respectively. So, the atomic number corresponding to least number of valence electrons is 19. Hence, correct option is (a).

41. Mass number = 31. Number of neutrons = 16

Atomic number = 31 − 16 = 15

Electronic arrangement is 2, 8, 5. M-shell is the valence shell and there are 5 electrons in the valence shell. Hence, correct option is (b).

42. α-particles are dipositive helium ions.

$\therefore$ Z = 2 and A = 4

Number of electrons = 0

Helium atom contains two electrons. It loses the two electrons to form He^{+2} ion. Hence, correct option is (c).

43. Electronic configuration of an atom of an element which has two electrons in the valence shell and two consecutive inner shells have 8 electrons each is 2, 8, 8, 2. Hence, atomic number of the element = 20 and the correct option is (b).

44. According to Rutherford, electrons revolve in certain paths around the nucleus.

45.

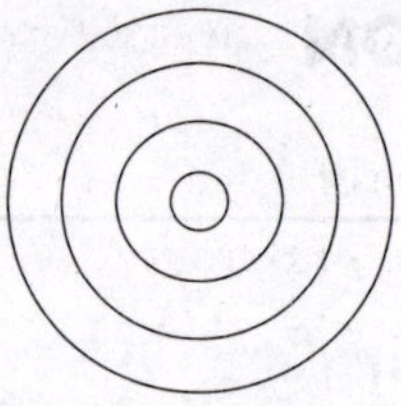

When an electron jumps from a higher orbit to a lower orbit, it loses energy and vice versa.
C is the K-shell near to nucleus.
B is the L-shell followed by C.
A is the M-shell followed by B.
∴ Increasing order of distance from the nucleus is $C < B < A$.

Level 2

1. (a) Number of electrons required to be present in the valence shell of an ion so that the ion becomes stable
   (b) Subatomic particles that cause nuclear charge
   (c) Number of subatomic particles
   (d) Electronic configuration of the stable ion that is formed

2. (a) If the abundance of the isotope with mass number A and A + 2 are n_1 and n_2, respectively, then

$$\frac{n_1 A + n_2 (A+2)}{n_1 + n_2} = A + 0.5$$

   (b) 3 : 1

3. (a) Maximum number of electrons in each orbit
   (b) Number of electrons in valence shell of a stable atom
   (c) Electronic configuration
   (d) 36

4. The mass numbers of the two isotopes is 10.

5. (a) Calculation of the atomic number of the element
   (b) Calculation of the number of electrons in a neutral atom based on the configuration of positive ion
   (c) The atomic number of a neutral atom
   (d) The number of neutrons in a neutral atom based on mass number
   (e) 20, 20, 20

6. (a) Number of valence electrons of P and Q and their electronic configuration
   (b) Calculation of number of electrons in previous shells of P and Q based on the valence shell and the number of electrons in the valence shell

7. (a) Density of gas molecules inside the discharge tube
   (b) The mechanism of production of cathode rays
   (c) The origin of anode rays

8. (a) Effect of equal strengths of electric and magnetic fields
   (b) The effect of electric and magnetic field on cathode rays
   (c) The direction of application of electric and magnetic fields such that there is no

9. (a) Calculation of the maximum number of electrons in each orbit.
   (b) The number of elements that depend on electronic configuration.
   (c) The maximum number of electrons in the valence shell.

10. (a) Metals form cations
    (b) The number of electrons in neutral atom based on the type of ion metals formed
    (c) The atomic number of the metal
    (d) The calculation of mass number from atomic number and number of neutrons

11. (a) Calculation of number of electrons in first two shells
(b) Calculation of atomic number of A
(c) Calculation of atomic number of B from A
(d) 10 and 20

12. (a) Number of electrons in the corresponding neutral atom
(b) Calculation of mass number
(c) Calculation of number of neutrons from mass number and atomic number
(d) 20, 20, 20

13. (a) Basic concept of atom in Thomson's model
(b) Nature of α-particles
(c) Effect of bombardment of α-particles with atom (according to Thomson)

14. (a) If the percentage abundance of Cl-35 is x, then

$$\frac{x \times 35 + (100 - x)37}{100} = 35.5$$

(b) 75% of Cl-35 and 25% of Cl-37.

15. (a) The electronic configuration of A is 2, 8, 14, 2 and that of B is 2, 8, 18, 6.
(b) Their atomic numbers are 26 and 34, respectively.
(c) The number of neutrons in A is $5b = 30$ and that in B = 22.5 a = 45

∴ Their mass numbers are 26 + 30 = 56 and 34 + 45 = 79, respectively.

16. In the normal α-ray scattering experiment, a gold foil is used. In the place of the gold foil, if aluminium foil is used, the angle of deflection will be less. Charge and mass of aluminium nucleus is less than that of gold nucleus. So, the repulsive forces experienced by α-rays and the impact due to the collision with the aluminium nuclei are less. Hence, the angle of deflections will be less in α-ray scattering experiment using aluminium foil instead of gold foil.

17. Thomson assumed that electrons are embedded in a positive mass as it could explain several observations like only electrons are ejected when a metal is heated and never positively charged particles.

18. Element X attains stability by losing two electrons from the fourth shell, its atomic number is 20, element is calcium.

∴ The mass number of Ca is 40.

Let the mass number of Y is a.

$$\therefore \frac{40}{a} = \frac{10}{13} \Rightarrow a = 52$$

∴ Mass number of Y is 52.

Number of neutrons in X is 40 – 20 = 20

Let the atomic number of Y be b.

∴ The number of neutrons in Y be 52 – b

$$\therefore \frac{20}{52 - b} = \frac{5}{7} \Rightarrow 52 - b = 28 \Rightarrow b = 24$$

∴ Element Y's atomic number is 24 and number of neutrons in Y is 28.

Elements	Number of protons	Number of electrons	Number of neutrons
X	20	20	20
Y	24	24	28

19. Electronic configurations of dipositive and dinegative ions are 2, 8, 8 if they contain an octet configuration in their third shell. Electronic configurations of neutral atom of dipositive and dinegative ions are 2, 8, 8, 2 and 2, 8, 6. 2 and 6 are the valence electrons present in the neutral atoms, respectively and atomic numbers are 20 and 16, respectively.

20. A and E are isotopes because they have same atomic number, i.e., X and mass numbers are different. Similarly, B and D are also isotopes. The mass numbers of A, C and D are X + Z + 2, X + Z + 2 and X + Z + 2, respectively and their atomic numbers are X, X – 2 and X + 1.

Therefore, they are isobars.

Similarly, B and E are also isobars.

21. (a) Electronic configuration of X : 2, 8, 2
(b) Element Y is stable due to the presence of 8 electrons (octet) in the valence shell.
(c) In the element Z, the electrons are distributed in four shells because the N-shell (fourth) is the valence shell.
(d) Since 8 electrons are present in the penultimate shell, i.e., M, 1 electron is present in the N-shell

because the number of electrons is not the same in K- and N-shells.

Electronic configuration of Z = 2, 8, 8, 1

Hence, atomic number Z = 19.

(e) Electronic configuration of Y = 2, 8, 8.

Hence, Z = 18 and the number of protons or electrons is 18.

22. If protons are used instead of α-particles, the angles of deflection would be different because the charge of a proton is half of the charge of an α-particle and mass is almost one-fourth of the mass of the α-particle. Angle of deflection depends on both the charge as well as the mass.

23. K-shell → 2 electrons

L-shell → 8 electrons

M-shell → 8 electrons

N-shell → 1

Atomic number = 2 + 8 + 8 + 1 = 19

Preceding element is Ar and electronic configuration is 2, 8, 8, and the succeeding element is Ca and its electronic configuration is 2, 8, 8, 2.

Level 3

1. (a) Number of gaseous molecules present at high pressure

(b) Effect of pressure on velocity of cathode rays

(c) Relation between velocity and discharge

2. (a) Nature of cathode and anode rays

(b) The composition of anode and cathode rays

(c) Factors influencing e/m ratio of anode and cathode rays

(d) Change in e/m with gas for cathode and anode rays

3. (a) The amount of energy required to cause ionisation

(b) Factors affecting e/m values

(c) Charge on helium gas under low pressure and high pressure

(d) The effect of charge on e/m

4. (a) Forces of attraction existing between protons and electrons

(b) Energy required for excitation of electrons

(c) Relation between energy emitted by atom and colour of discharge tube

5. (a) Characteristics of isotopes and isobars

(b) Factors affecting e/m of anode rays

(c) Relation between e/m and deflection

6. The results of Rutherford's α-ray scattering experiment are very clear if the deflections are large. As lighter particles show larger deflections, B^{+1} would be preferable.

7. The electrons revolve round the nucleus at high speed in the orbits in order to counterbalance the nuclear forces of attraction. As nuclear force of attraction decreases with increase in distance from the nucleus, the nuclear force of attraction on the electrons decreases. Therefore, electron revolves with lesser velocity to overcome lesser nuclear force of attraction. Thus, the velocity of electron in orbits decreases in the order K > L > M > N.

8. As the penultimate shell of B is the M-shell which possesses 18 electrons, the valence shell should be the N-shell. The possible electronic configuration of B ranges from 2, 8, 18, 1 to 2, 8, 18, 8.

The atomic numbers of B may range from Z = 29 to Z = 36.

The electronic arrangement of A corresponding to the respective arrangement of B ranges from 2, 8, 18, 9, 2 to 2, 8, 18, 16, 2. The atomic number of A may range from Z = 39 to Z = 46.

9. The postulate that the electrons revolve round the nucleus is not derived from the results of α-ray scattering experiment. The results of α-ray scattering gave the idea that entire positive charge is concentrated in a small part which is known as nucleus.

In order to counterbalance the nuclear forces of attraction, the electrons revolve round the nucleus at very high speeds.

10. The electronic configuration of the element could be

2 8 14 2

or

2 8 4

Hence, its atomic number could be 26 or 14.

Chapter

2

Classification of Matter

Remember

Before beginning this chapter, you should be able to:

- know about the electron, proton and neutron in an atom.
- define matter and states of matter.

Key Ideas

After completing this chapter, you should be able to:

- study kinetic energy of molecules in different states of matter.
- understand the effect of temperature and pressure on the state of matter and changes taking place in the arrangement of molecules.
- classify matter on the basis of chemical composition.
- discuss the properties of elements, compounds and mixtures and their applications.
- learn the different techniques for the separation of mixtures—based on the properties of the constituents.

INTRODUCTION

The objects around us, including air, water, stones, metals, trees, etc., are different varieties of matter. Anything that occupies some space and has mass is called **matter**. The smallest particles of matter which retain all the properties of matter and exist independently are called **molecules**.

On the basis of the forces of attraction existing between the molecules of a substance, matter can be classified as solids, liquids and gases. The characteristics of these three states of matter and the interconversion of a substance from one state to the other represent one aspect of the study of matter.

Matter can also be classified on the basis of chemical composition into three major categories, namely, elements, compounds and mixtures. There are 115 elements discovered till today and these elements are further classified into metals, non-metals and metalloids on the basis of certain characteristic properties. Study of matter also involves study of the properties of various categories of elements. It also includes the study of basic differences between compounds and mixtures and the study of techniques of separation of different types of a mixture.

Molecules are the constituent particles of matter and the characteristics of these molecules and their arrangement in the various states of matter were explained by the kinetic molecular theory of matter.

KINETIC MOLECULAR THEORY OF MATTER

Postulates

1. Every form of matter is composed of small particles called molecules.
2. The empty space (gaps) that exists in between the molecules is called **intermolecular space**.
3. Molecules exert attractive forces, called **intermolecular forces** of attraction, upon one another. These forces decrease with an increase in the distance between the molecules. The force of attraction between similar molecules is called **cohesive force** and that between dissimilar molecules is called **adhesive force**.
4. The molecules possess kinetic energy due to their motion and their movement is ceaseless.

TABLE 2.1 Comparative study of solids, liquids and gases

Parameters	Solids	Liquids	Gases
Packing of molecules	The molecules are closely packed, and therefore, solids have a definite shape, definite volume, high density and negligible compressibility.	The molecules are loosely packed, and hence, liquids do not have definite shape and take the shape of the container. Density of liquids is slightly lesser than solids, and therefore, they are slightly more compressible than solids.	The molecules are very loosely packed, and hence, gases have no definite shape, no definite volume, very low density and very high compressibility.
Intermolecular force of attraction	The molecules have very strong intermolecular force of attraction due to which they are rigid, and expand very less on heating.	The molecules have moderate intermolecular force of attraction which is lesser than solids. These can, thus, flow and expand more than solids when heated.	The molecules have negligible intermolecular force of attraction, and thus, can flow and expand much more than solids and liquids when heated.

Parameters	Solids	Liquids	Gases
Molecular movement	The molecules have only vibratory motion about their mean positions which are fixed. They can, thus, have any number of free surfaces.	The molecules possess translatory and rotatory motions in addition to vibratory motion. The translatory motion is, however, either sideways or downwards. Thus, they have only one free surface and have definite volume.	The molecules possess translatory, rotatory and vibratory motions in all directions randomly. Thus, the gases have no free surfaces and occupy the total volume available for it.
Kinetic energy	The molecules possess very low kinetic energy, and hence, do not diffuse.	The molecules possess higher kinetic energy than in case of solids and can diffuse in certain liquids.	The molecules possess very high-kinetic energy and diffuse spontaneously and rapidly.

On the basis of the above parameters, it can be concluded that the arrangement of molecules is the most important factor which determines the state in which the matter exists. This means that the change in molecular arrangement brings about the conversion of matter from one state to another state. The molecular arrangement in a particular substance, in turn, depends upon the external conditions of temperature and pressure. Hence, the change in molecular arrangement can be brought about by changing the external conditions of temperature and pressure.

EXAMPLE

Conduction of heat is not possible through gases. Explain with respect to kinetic molecular theory.

SOLUTION

Conduction of heat in matter takes place by the transmission of agitation of one molecule to the other, and hence, the molecules should be closely packed. But in gaseous state the molecules are very far from each other. Hence, the heat cannot be transmitted from one molecule to another molecule, and thus, there is no conduction of heat through gases.

EXAMPLE

A given mass of a gas is present in a cylinder of volume 10L which can also be filled in a cylinder of volume 1 L. Explain the above statement with suitable reason/s.

SOLUTION

The force of attraction between the gas molecules is negligible. As a result, the intermolecular spaces between the molecules of the gas is very high. Moreover, the molecules have high kinetic energy. Thus, the molecules are free to move in all directions, and hence, can fill the available space easily, due to which gas can completely occupy a cylinder having volume of 10 L. As intermolecular spaces are large in gas, they can easily be compressed, and hence, the same mass of gas can also be stored in a cylinder with 1-L volume.

EXAMPLE

Gases do not have free surfaces. Explain.

SOLUTION

The molecules of gases possess rotatory, vibratory and translatory motions in all directions at random. Hence, they need to be stored in a closed vessel and have no free surfaces.

INTERCONVERSION OF STATES OF MATTER

The change of matter from one state to another that occurs as a result of a change in external conditions, like, temperature or pressure is called **interconversion of states of matter** or **phase transition**.

The process of phase transition does not produce any change in the mass or composition of the matter. The different processes involving phase transition are given different names on the basis of initial and final states of matter.

Melting

The process which involves the change in state of matter from solid to liquid by heating is called **melting** or **fusion**. The temperature at which a solid changes into a liquid on heating at normal atmospheric pressure is called **the melting point** of that solid.

The heat energy supplied to the solid is absorbed by its molecules. This helps the molecules to overcome the intermolecular force of attraction as a result of which the molecules move apart from each other. The molecules acquire translatory motion in addition to vibratory motion, so, they become free to move, and thus, attain the molecular arrangement of a liquid.

The melting point of solids which expand on melting increases with an increase in pressure while the melting point of solids which contract on melting decreases with an increase in pressure.

Evaporation and Boiling

The slow process involving the change of matter from liquid to gas from the surface of the liquid is called **evaporation**.

The temperature at which a liquid changes into a gas on heating at normal atmospheric pressure is called the boiling point of that liquid and the phenomenon is called **boiling**.

The heat energy which is supplied to the liquid is absorbed by the molecules of the liquid and helps the molecules to overcome the intermolecular forces of attraction almost completely. As a result, the molecules move far apart from each other and start moving in all directions at random. Thus, the liquid attains the molecular arrangement of a gas.

TABLE 2.2 Differences between evaporation and boiling

Evaporation	Boiling
Slow process	Fast process
Surface phenomenon	Bulk phenomenon
It occurs at any temperature	It occurs at a fixed temperature depending on the nature of liquid and external pressure

A decrease in the pressure on the surface of a liquid decreases its boiling point. Soluble impurities present in a liquid increase the boiling point of the liquid.

Condensation

The process which involves the change of matter from gas to liquid on cooling is called **condensation**.

On cooling, the potential energy of the gas molecules is released in the form of heat energy. Consequently, the intermolecular distance between the gas molecules decreases and the intermolecular force increases. As a result, the molecules become less free to move about. Thus, the gas attains the molecular arrangement of a liquid.

Since the gases are highly compressible, they can be liquefied by the application of pressure provided the temperature of the gas is equal to or below its critical temperature and this process is called **liquefaction**.

Critical temperature is the temperature above which the liquefaction of the gas is impossible whatever be the pressure applied on it.

For every gas, there is a specific critical temperature. The gaseous state of matter below its critical temperature is called **vapour**.

Solidification

The process involving the change of matter from liquid to solid on cooling is called **solidification** or freezing. The temperature at which freezing occurs at normal atmospheric pressure is called **freezing point** of that liquid.

On cooling, the potential energy of the liquid molecules is released in the form of heat energy. Consequently, the intermolecular distance decreases and intermolecular force of attraction increases. The molecules lose their translatory movement, rotatory movement and they only vibrate about their fixed mean position. Thus, the molecules of the liquid attain the molecular arrangement of a solid.

Sublimation

The process by which some solid substances directly change into the vapour state on heating without passing through the intermediate liquid state is called **sublimation**.

The solid obtained on cooling the vapour is called **sublimate** and the vapour formed is called **sublime**.

Examples: Camphor and iodine

Kinetic energy of the molecules at the surface of the sublimable substance is high. On the application of external heat and in some cases at normal temperature, the molecules at the surface gain energy and overcome the intermolecular force of attraction. Hence, they directly get converted from solid to vapour states from the surface.

EXAMPLE

How is boiling point related to the vapour pressure of the liquid?

SOLUTION

When the vapour pressure of a liquid becomes equal to the atmospheric pressure, the liquid starts boiling. Hence, the higher the vapour pressure, the lower is the boiling point.

EXAMPLE

Two beakers A and B contain the same amount of alcohol and water at the same temperature, respectively. What is the change in temperature in these two liquids after some time?

SOLUTION

Both alcohol and water evaporate. Alcohol, being more volatile, evaporates more by taking up more amount of heat from the bulk. Thus, the temperature of alcohol is found to be less than that of water.

EXAMPLE

In winter mornings, the exhaled air turns foggy. Explain.

SOLUTION

The exhaled air is warm and consists of mainly of CO_2 and water vapour. As the air outside is very cold in winter morning, the water vapour of the exhaled air condenses to small droplets of water. Hence, the exhaled air turns foggy in winter morning.

EXAMPLE

When a liquid is placed in a closed container, the level of the liquid initially decreases but eventually becomes constant. Give reasons.

SOLUTION

When a liquid is placed in a closed container, initially there is evaporation, and thus, the volume of the liquid decreases. But as time passes, there is an equilibrium attained between the liquid and the vapour, and hence, no further decrease in level of liquid is observed.

EXAMPLE

Some antifreezing substances, like, ethylene glycol are added to the water used as coolant in vehicles. Explain the principle involved.

SOLUTION

Presence of impurities decreases the freezing point and elevates the boiling point of water. Thus, the range of temperature in which water remains in liquid state can be increased. Since the specific heat of water is high, it can be conveniently used as a coolant in presence of antifreeze over a wider range of temperature.

The parameters of various states of matter and their interconversion from one state to the other deal with the study of matter at the molecular level. The study of matter with respect to the molecular composition requires classification into elements, compounds and mixtures.

CLASSIFICATION OF MATTER ON THE BASIS OF CHEMICAL COMPOSITION

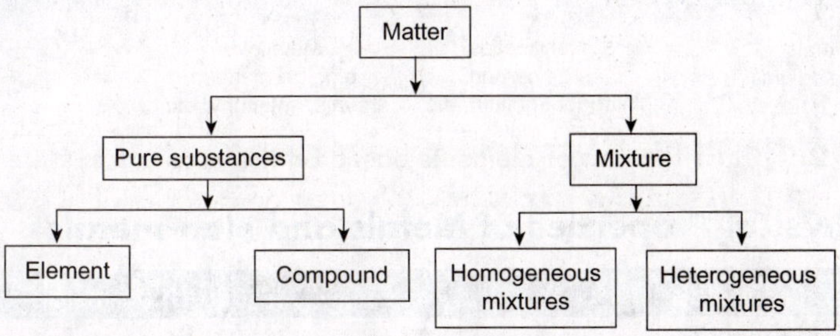

FIGURE 2.1 Classification of matter based on the chemical composition

Pure Substances

Substances which are homogeneous in nature and contain particles (molecules) of only one kind are called **pure substances**. A pure substance is homogeneous in nature and has definite set of properties. The composition of pure substances cannot be changed by physical methods. Pure substances can be further classified as elements and compounds.

Elements

Pure substances in which molecules are composed of only one kind of atoms are called **elements**.

Examples: silver, iron, oxygen, nitrogen, etc.

Atomicity of an Element

The number of atoms present in the molecule of an element is called its atomicity. Based on the atomicity, the elements are classified into three types as listed hereunder.

1. **Monoatomic elements**: The elements each of whose molecules contain only one atom.

   Examples: Cu, Ag and He

2. **Diatomic elements**: The elements each of whose molecules contain two atoms.

   Examples: H_2, O_2 and N_2

3. **Polyatomic elements**: The elements each of whose molecules contain more than two atoms.

   Examples: O_3, P_4 and S_8.

Compounds

Pure substances in which two or more elements combine chemically in a fixed proportion by weight are called **compounds**.

For example, water (H_2O) is considered a pure substance even though it consists of two kinds of atoms, as it has a fixed number of hydrogen and oxygen atoms combined together chemically in a definite proportion by weight. Hydrogen and oxygen combine in a fixed ratio, 1 : 8 by weight, to form water.

Classification of Elements

It was found that there was a wide variation in the properties of elements. Hence, these were further classified into three categories, i.e., metals, non-metals and metalloids based on the properties they exhibit.

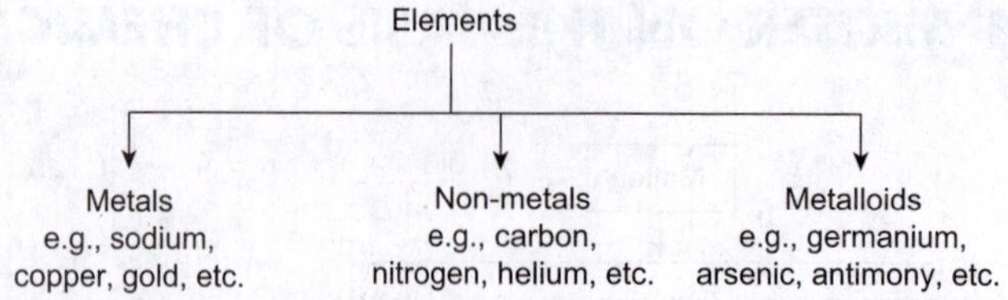

FIGURE 2.2 Classification of elements based on the properties

Comparative Study of Physical Properties of Metals and Non-metals

Properties	Metals	Non-metals
State	Solids at room temperature. Exceptions: Hg and Ga are liquids.	Mostly gases. Exceptions: some of the solid non-metals are C, S, P, I_2, whereas bromine is a liquid non-metal.
Melting and boiling points	Very high melting and boiling points. Exceptions: Na, K, Hg have low melting and boiling points. Ga has a low melting point but a high boiling point.	Low melting and boiling points. Exceptions: C, Si and B have high melting and boiling points.
Hardness	Generally hard. Exceptions: Na and K are soft.	Solid non-metals are brittle. Exception: diamond is the hardest naturally occurring substance.
Density	Have high density. Exception: Li, Na and K have density lower than water (1 g/cm^3).	Have low density. Exception: diamond
Conductivity	Good conductors of heat and electricity. Exceptions: Bi and W are poor conductors of electricity.	Bad conductors of heat and electricity. Exception: graphite and gas carbon are good conductors of electricity.
Lustre	Have lustre.	No lustre. Exceptions: I_2 and graphite
Tensile strength	High tensile strength. Exception: Zn has very less tensile strength	Do not have tensile strength. Exception: carbon fibre, a recently developed allotrope of carbon.
Malleability and ductility	Generally malleable and ductile. Exception: zinc is not malleable and ductile.	Non-malleable and non-ductile. Exception: carbon fibres are ductile.
Sonorousness	Sonorous.	Non-sonorous.
Occurrence	Found in a combined state. Only noble metals are found in a free state.	Found in a free state as well as in the combined state.
Number of electrons in the valence shell	Have 1 to 3 electrons in their valence shells.	Have 4 to 7 electrons in their valence shells. Exceptions: hydrogen has one electron in its valence shell because the first shell is its valence shell.
Formation of ions	Lose electrons from their valence shells to attain stable structures and form cations.	Accept electrons to attain stable structures and form anions.
Formation of oxides	Metals on heating in air or oxygen react to form their respective oxides. The oxides are either basic or amphoteric in nature. Exceptions: metals like Au and Pt do not form oxides.	Non-metals on heating in air or oxygen form their respective oxides. But the oxides are either acidic or neutral in nature.
Reaction with acid and water	Metals, which are more reactive than hydrogen, replace hydrogen from the acid as well as from water.	Generally, non-metals do not react with water. The majority of non-metals do not react with acids.

Location of Metals, Non-metals and Metalloids on Periodic Table

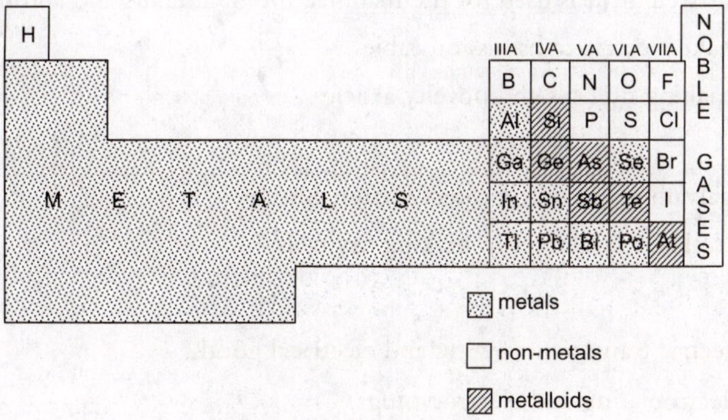

FIGURE 2.3 Periodic chart

Metalloids

Metalloids are elements which show the properties of both metals and non-metals.

Examples: germanium, arsenic, antimony, selenium and tellurium

TABLE 2.3 Some metalliods and their properties

Metalloids	Metallic properties	Non-metallic properties
Germanium	It acts as a semiconductor with rise in temperature	GeO_2 is acidic in nature
Arsenic	Metallic grey arsenic is a fair conductor of electricity	Yellow arsenic forms a hydride, (AsH_3), a weak base
Antimony	Grey-coloured antimony conducts electricity	Yellow antimony forms stibine (SbH_3), a weak base
Selenium	Good conductor of electricity at 475K	It exists in one non-metallic allotropic form
Tellurium	Low electrical conductivity	It resembles sulphur in chemical properties

Uses of Metals

Iron (Fe)

Iron is mainly used in the form of steel, an alloy in which the major component is iron. Steel is used for making buckets, drain pipes, chains, etc., as it is extremely tough and it can withstand stress and has a high melting point.

Lead (Pb)

1. It is used for making containers for corrosive liquids and protective screens for X-ray and other harmful radiations as it is unaffected by impure water, steam or dilute mineral acids and has a low melting point (337°C).
2. It is used in the automobile batteries.

Magnesium

1. It is used in fireworks because it burns with a dazzling white flame.
2. It is used as a reducing agent in the extraction of metals.

Aluminium

1. Due to its light weight, it is used for the manufacture of aircrafts and automobiles.
2. It is used to make electric transmission cables.
3. It is used for making utensils and novelty articles.

Zinc

1. It is used for galvanising iron to protect it from rusting.
2. It is used as a cathode container in making dry cells.

Copper

1. It is used as electric transmission wires and electrical goods.
2. It is used in electroplating and electrotyping.
3. It is used for making printed circuit boards and electronic devices.
4. Copper salts are largely used as insecticides.

Uses of Non-metals

Oxygen

1. It helps in the process of respiration and combustion.
2. It has medical and industrial uses.

Nitrogen

1. It dilutes the activity of oxygen in air.
2. It is used in preserving food and biological specimens.

Sulphur

1. Sulphur powder is an excellent insecticide and fungicide.
2. It is used to make the natural rubber hard for making tyres.

Iodine

1. Iodides are used in medicine and photography.
2. It is used in the manufacture of tincture of iodine.

Hydrogen

1. It is an excellent non-polluting fuel.
2. It is used to fill weather observation balloons and gas bags for airships.

Uses of Noble Metals

Gold

1. Used for covering the mainframe of artificial satellites.
2. It is used for making ornaments and coins.

Silver

1. Silver halides are used for making photographic films.
2. It is used for making ornaments and coins.

Platinum

1. It is used as a catalyst in many chemical reactions.
2. It is used in making jewellery.

Titanium

1. It is completely inert to human body fluids, making it ideal for medical replacement structures, such as, hip and knee implants.
2. Titanium forms a very tenacious surface oxide layer which is an outstanding corrosive inhibitor.

Mixtures

The systematic study of elements is done by categorising them as metals, non-metals and metalloids. The different elements combine with each other to form compounds. The formation of compounds from elements results in change in the molecular composition. Two or more substances, either elements or compounds, can be mixed together in any proportion. The resultant substances are called **mixtures**. Since the formation of a mixture involves only physical process, there is no change in the molecular composition.

Comparative Study of Properties of Compounds and Mixture

Compounds	Mixture
Constituent atoms combine chemically	Constituent substances are mixed physically
Constituents can be separated by chemical methods	Constituents can be separated by physical methods
These are homogeneous	A mixture can be either homogeneous or heterogeneous
It involves significant energy changes	No significant change in the energy

Classification of A Mixture

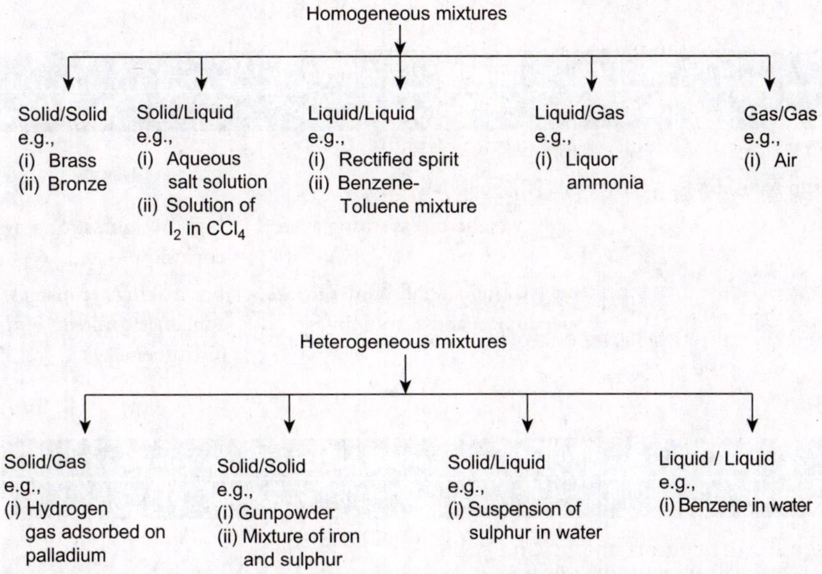

FIGURE 2.4 Classification of homogeneous mixtures and heterogeneous mixtures

Among the various types of a mixture, alloys occupy the most significant position in view of the wide range of applications they find in industry as well as in day-to-day life.

Alloys and Their Uses

Alloy is a homogeneous mixture of two or more metals (or a non-metal). Some important alloys, their composition and uses are listed in the following table:

Major component → Copper (Cu)					
Alloy	Brass	Bronze	Gun metal	German silver	Bell metal
Composition	Cu (60 to 80%) and Zn (20 to 40%)	Cu (80%), Zn (10%) and Sn (10%)	Cu (88%), Sn (10%), Zn (1%) and Pb (1%)	Cu (30 to 60%), Zn (20 to 30%) and Ni (15 to 20%)	Cu (80%) and Sn (20%)
Properties	Lustrous, more malleable and ductile than copper	Hard but brittle, resistant to corrosion, takes very high polish	Very hard, gives a very good cast	White like silver, malleable and ductile	Hard and brittle, produces sonorous sound
Uses	For making shells of ammunition, utensils, electrical switches, statues	For making shells, statues, coins and utensils	For making barrels of guns, gears and bearings	For making imitation silver jewellery, utensils, etc.	For making bells

Major component → Iron (Fe)			
Alloys	Stainless steel	Manganese steel	Tungsten steel
Composition	Fe (83%), C (1%), Cu (15%) and Ni (1%)	Fe (84%), Mn (15%) and C (1%)	Fe (79 to 84%) W(20 to 15%), C(1%)
Properties	Resists corrosion	Very tough and hard	Very very hard
Uses	For making utensils and surgical instruments	For making safes, armour and rock cutter	For making high speed tools

Major component → Aluminium (Al)		
Alloy	Duralumin	Magnalium
Composition	Al (95%), Cu (4%)	
Mn (0.5%) and Mg(0.5%)	Al (95%) and Mg (5%)	
Properties	Light weight and as strong as steel	Light weight, strong, resistant to corrosion
Uses	For making aircraft frames, rockets, speed boats and automobiles	For making aeroplanes, house appliances, mirrors and scientific instruments

Major component → Nickel (Ni)	
Alloy	Monel metal
Composition	Cu (28%), Ni (67%) and Fe (5%)
Property	Resistant to corrosion, malleable and ductile
Uses	Used for making sinks, doors and window screws

EXAMPLE

Why are ornaments prepared by using an alloy of silver with copper and not by pure silver?

SOLUTION

Silver is a soft metal. By alloying with copper it becomes hard. So, ornaments are prepared by alloy of silver with copper and not by pure silver.

EXAMPLE

Copper is used in the form of alloys, like, brass and bronze for making statues and decorative articles, but it is used in the pure form for making electric transmission cable. Give reasons.

SOLUTION

In alloys the physical properties of the metals change to some extent. The properties of copper vary in the alloys, like, brass and bronze. The alloy is harder, stronger and has more shine than the pure metal and due to these properties it is used for making statues and decorative articles. While in electric transmission cables the property exploited is its electrical conductivity and ductility. Both these properties are more prominent in the pure metal than the alloys. Pure copper is, thus, used in making electric transmission cables.

EXAMPLE

Aluminium melts and burns easily whereas alumina is used as a refractory material for making heat resistant bricks. Explain.

SOLUTION

Alumina (Al_2O_3) is a compound of aluminium. It is a compound, and hence, its properties are different from that of aluminium. The melting point of alumina is much higher than that of aluminium and it is highly chemical resistant, hence, it is used as a refractory material.

EXAMPLE

Why is mercury used in thermometer?

SOLUTION

Mercury is used in thermometer because of the following reasons.

(i) It is a shiny viscous liquid.

(ii) It has low thermal expansion, that is, with the increase in temperature the increase in volume of mercury is less compared to other liquids.

(iii) It does not stick to the glass surface because of weak adhensive force between glass and mercury.

Separation of A Mixture

In a mixture, the individual components retain their original properties. This is exploited to separate the mixture into individual components.

Principles Involved

The difference in one or more of the following physical properties of the constituents is utilised to separate the components of a mixture.

1. Physical state
2. Density
3. Melting and boiling points
4. Solubility
5. Magnetic properties
6. Diffusion
7. Ability to sublime
8. Volatility

I. Separation of a Solid–solid Mixture

Techniques	Principles involved	Examples
Solvent extraction	One component of the mixture is soluble and the other is insoluble in a given solvent	(i) Mixture of sulphur (soluble) and sand (insoluble) Solvent: carbon disulphide (CS_2) (ii) Mixture of NH_4Cl (soluble) and I_2 (insoluble) Solvent: water
Magnetic separation	One component of the mixture is a magnetic substance	(i) Mixture of iron ore (magnetic) and sand (ii) Mixture of cobalt (magnetic) and lead
Gravity method	One of the components is heavier and the other one is lighter than a given liquid	(i) Mixture of sand (heavier) and sawdust
Sublimation	One of the components sublimes on heating	(i) Mixture of I_2 (sublimes) and sand (ii) Mixture of NH_4Cl (sublimes) and sand
Fractional crystallisation	Two components soluble in one solvent, but the solubility should be different	(i) Mixture of KNO_3 (more soluble) and NaCl (less soluble)

II. Separation of a Solid–liquid Mixture

Techniques	Principles	Examples
Sedimentation and decantation	The solid component is insoluble and heavier than the liquid component	Mixture of sand and water
Filtration	Separation of insoluble solid component by passing through a porous material, like, filter paper	(i) Mixture of AgCl and H_2O (ii) Mixture of chalk and H_2O
Evaporation	Separation of the mixture by evaporating the liquid component. The solid should be soluble in the liquid and should not sublime.	(i) Mixture of NaCl and H_2O (ii) Mixture of sulphur and CS_2
Distillation	Separation of mixture containing a soluble solid by evaporation followed by condensation. The solid should not sublime.	(i) Mixture of NaCl and H_2O

Distillation is carried out in a special type of apparatus.

Example:
Separation of KCl from a solution of KCl and water

Procedure

The KCl solution is taken in a distillation flask (X).

The flask is carefully heated; the solvent evaporates and the water vapour condenses in Leibig's condenser (Y). KCl remains in the distillation flask and the water is collected in the receiver flask.

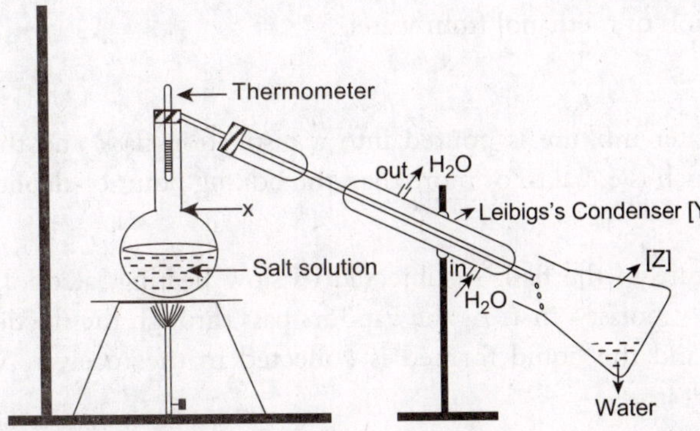

FIGURE 2.5 Separation of components of Ink by paper chromatography

III. Separation of a Liquid–liquid Mixture

(A) Separating funnel

Principle: Separation of immiscible liquid components using a separating funnel where liquids separate out due to different densities.

Example:

Separation of petrol (lighter) from water (heavier)

Procedure

1. The liquid–liquid mixture is poured into a separating funnel clamped vertically and the mixture is allowed to stand. Clear layers of the liquids are formed as the liquid with higher density settles down at the bottom of the flask.
2. The nozzle tap is opened slowly and the heavier component is allowed to trickle down. The lighter component remains in the flask.

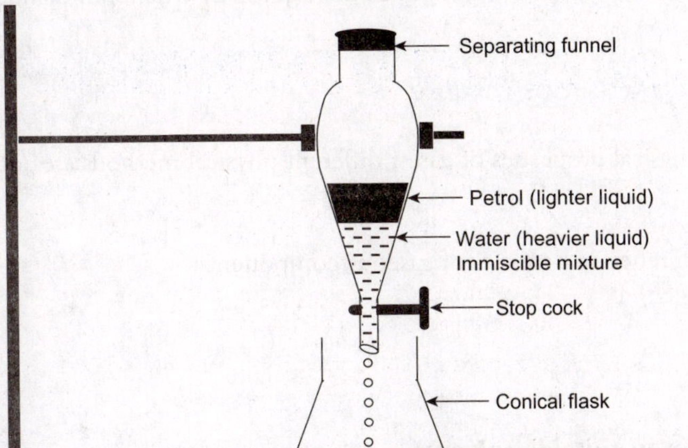

FIGURE 2.6 Separation of immiscible liquids by separating funnel

(B) Fractional distillation

Principle: Separation of two miscible liquid components using a distillation flask with a fractionating column by using the difference in boiling points of the liquid components.

Example:

Laboratory separation of methanol from water

Procedure

1. The alcohol–water mixture is poured into a distillation flask and the flask is heated at a temperature which is equal to or more than the boiling point of alcohol but less than that of water.
2. When the mixture in the flask is subjected to slow heating, alcohol, being more volatile than water, gets vaporised first. As the vapours pass through the fractionating column, they get condensed and the liquid formed is collected in the receiver. Water remains in the distillation flask.

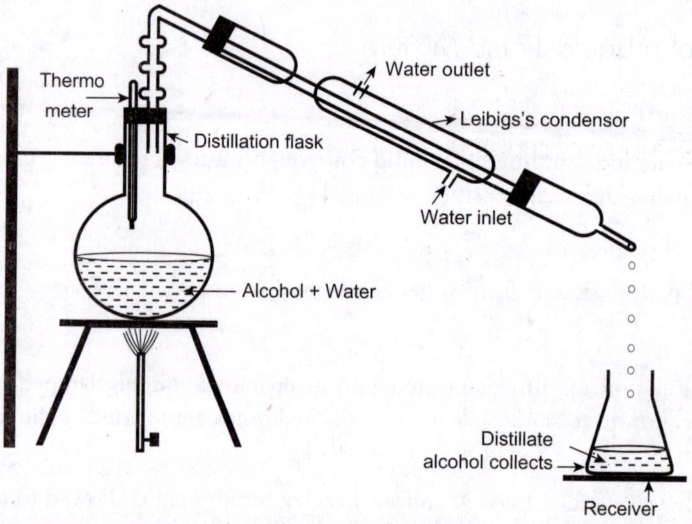

FIGURE 2.7 Separation of miscible liguids by fractional distillataion

IV. Separation of a Gas–gas Mixture

Based on the physical properties of gases, different physical methods are adopted.

(A) Diffusion

Principle: Difference in densities of gaseous components.

Examples:

CO_2 and H_2
SO_2 and N_2

(B) Dissolution in suitable solvents

Principle: When one constituent is soluble in a liquid or reacts chemically with a liquid, it is dissolved in that solvent, from which it can be recovered by a chemical reaction.

Examples:

N_2 (insoluble) and CO_2 (soluble) in KOH
NH_3 (soluble) and N_2 (insoluble) in H_2O
SO_2 (soluble) and O_2 (insoluble) in KOH

(C) Preferential liquefaction

Principle: Employed industrially for the separation of a homogeneous mixture of two gases, one of which liquefies under high pressure, when they are allowed to expand suddenly.

Example:

A mixture of H_2 and NH_3 under very high pressure is allowed to expand suddenly. NH_3 is liquefied and gets separated from H_2.

(D) Fractional evaporation

Principle: This process can be adopted when a mixture of two gases having different boiling points is liquefied by allowing it to expand suddenly under extremely high pressure, followed by evaporating the mixture at the respective boiling points of the constituent gases.

Examples:

N_2 and O_2 (N_2 boils off)

V. Separation of a Liquid–gas Mixture

The solution of a gas in a liquid is called **liquid–gas mixture**.

(A) Separation of a liquid–gas mixture by heating

Principle: The solubility of a gas in a liquid decreases with the rise in temperature.

Example:

1. The liquid–gas mixture (e.g., water–CO_2) is filled in a flask and heated gently so that the solution does not boil.
2. On heating, the solubility of a gas decreases and the dissolved gas is evolved and collected.

(B) Separation of a liquid–gas mixture by releasing pressure

Principle: The solubility of a gas in a liquid can be increased by increasing external pressure and is decreased with the decrease in external pressure.

Example:

CO_2 gas is dissolved in water by applying pressure in aerated drinks and this CO_2 gas comes out with a fizzing sound when the pressure is released.

Chromatography

Definition: It is a technique used for the separation and identification of dissolved constituents of a mixture by adsorbing them over an appropriate adsorbent material.

Principle: This process is based on the difference in adsorption of constituents by a surface of an appropriate adsorbent material or solid medium (stationary phase).The rate of adsorption of a particular constituent depends upon its solubility in the solvent (moving phase) and its affinity for the adsorbing material.

Example:

Separation of coloured constituent in a mixture of ink by paper chromatography.

Procedure

1. A spot of ink is placed at the centre of a base line on a strip of filter paper.
2. The spot is dried and the paper is hung in a glass jar with its lower end immersed in solvent.
3. The solvent flows over the spot and carries the components to distances along the paper indicated by colour spots, which is characteristic of each constituent in the mixture.

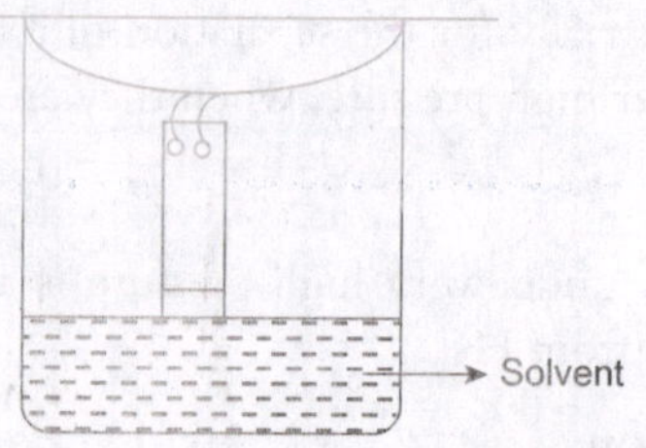

FIGURE 2.8 Separation of components of Ink by paper chromatography

The various methods of separation of mixtures find applications in various fields of industry. One of the most important applications is in metallurgy where different methods of separation have been employed to remove impurities from the ores.

Separation techniques, like, distillation and fractional distillation are utilised in the refining of petroleum, alcohol industry, pharmaceutical and food industry, etc. Solvent extraction is also widely used in the manufacture of medicines.

Chromatography finds applications in research laboratories for the identification of new compounds.

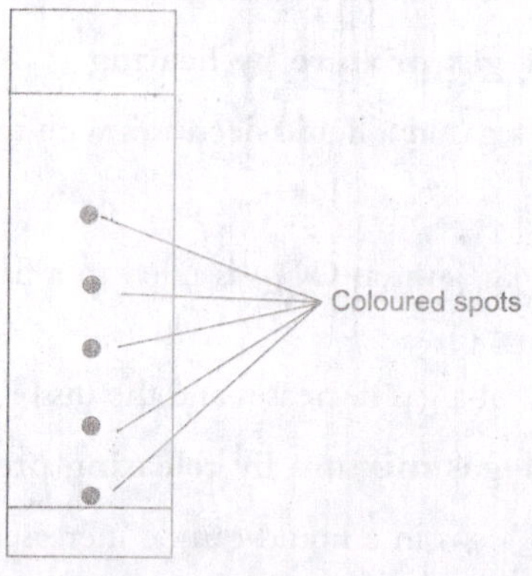

FIGURE 2.9 Chromatogram

EXAMPLE

A mixture of iron and sulphur is taken and heated strongly. Explain what happens if a magnet is brought near it after heating.

SOLUTION

When iron and sulphur are strongly heated, they combine to from a compound called **iron sulphide**. (FeS) This compound FeS does not have the individual properties of iron or sulphur. Thus, the magnetic property of iron is lost and when this is exposed to a magnet, it is not attracted by the magnet.

EXAMPLE

How can a gaseous mixture of CO_2 and SO_2, H_2 be separated?

SOLUTION

The molecular weight of H_2 is much less than CO_2 as well as SO_2 hydrogen gas can be separated from CO_2 and SO_2 by diffusion. Under low-temperature and high-pressure condition CO_2 converts to dry ice, a solid, and thus, can be separated. So, under these conditions, SO_2 converts to liquid state and can be separated.

EXAMPLE

Give the working principle involved in chromatography.

SOLUTION

The particles of a mixture or dye, like, ink are soluble in water. As the water rises on the filter paper, it takes along with it the dye particles. Usually, a dye is a mixture of two or more colours. The coloured components that are more soluble in water, reach to a greater height and in this way the colours get separated.

TEST YOUR CONCEPTS

Very Short Answer Type Questions

1. Define the following terms:
   (i) melting or fusion
   (ii) evaporation
   (iii) condensation
   (iv) solidification
   (v) sublimation
   (vi) melting point
   (vii) boiling point
   (viii) liquefaction
   (ix) freezing point
   (x) critical temperature
   (xi) Matter
   (xii) pure substance
   (xiii) mixture
   (xiv) element
   (xv) compound
   (xvi) metal
   (xvii) non-metal
   (xviii) metalloids
   (xix) alloy
   (xx) noble metals
2. What is corrosion? How does iron get corroded?
3. Blue coloured $CuSO_4$ solution is taken in a beaker. Is the blue solution an element, compound or mixture? Is it homogeneous or heterogeneous?
4. How can rust spots on garments be removed?
5. Coloured dye from ink is separated by the method of ________.
6. How are elements classified based on atomicity? Explain with an example.
7. The process due to which some solid substances directly vaporise on heating and solidify on cooling without becoming a liquid is called ________.
8. Give two examples for the following types of a mixture:
   (i) Solid: solid homogeneous
   (ii) Solid: liquid homogeneous
   (iii) Liquid: gas homogeneous
   (iv) Liquid: liquid homogeneous
   (v) Gas: gas homogeneous
   (vi) Solid: solid heterogeneous
   (vii) Solid: liquid heterogeneous
   (viii) Liquid: liquid heterogeneous
9. Write the products obtained in the following reactions:
   (i) $Na_2O + H_2O \rightarrow$
   (ii) $CO_2 + H_2O \rightarrow$
   (iii) $CO + H_2O \rightarrow$ Nature of reactants
   (iv) $SO_2 + H_2O \rightarrow$
10. What is the principle involved in the following methods of separation of mixtures?
   (i) fractional crystallisation
   (ii) magnetic separation
   (iii) gravity method
   (iv) separating funnel method
   (v) distillation
   (vi) fractional distillation
   (vii) preferential liquefaction
   (viii) chromatography
   (ix) fractional evaporation
11. Mention the allotropic forms of the following metalloids:
   (i) arsenic
   (ii) antimony
   (iii) selenium
12. What is a supernatant liquid?
13. What is the role of platinum in a catalytic converter?
14. In chromatography, the component which has more affinity for the stationary phase appears at the ________ of the paper.
15. Which property of german silver makes it useful for making imitation jewellery?
16. The kinetic energy of the molecules is ________ in solids than in liquids.
17. State one property of germanium which shows its acidic nature.
18. Certain gases dissolve in water by the process of ________.

19. Name the phenomena causing the following events:
    (i) formation of dew
    (ii) disappearance of naphthalene balls
    (iii) drying of wet clothes
    (iv) formation of snow
    (v) formation of cloud

20. Which metal is used in chemical industries for extracting metals?

21. What is meant by the atomicity of an element?

22. What type of ions do the following form?
    (i) a metal
    (ii) a non-metal

23. Give two examples of substances which can be separated by the following methods.
    (i) fractional crystallisation
    (ii) sublimation
    (iii) magnetic separation
    (iv) gravity method
    (v) filtration
    (vi) distillation
    (vii) diffusion
    (viii) solvent extraction
    (ix) dissolution in a suitable solvent

24. The intermolecular forces of attraction between molecules are called ________ and different molecules are called ________.

25. The molecules of a liquid possess_____ types of motions.

26. For the following properties listed below, arrange solids, liquids and gases either in the increasing or decreasing order as indicated against them.
    (i) diffusibility
    (ii) intermolecular spaces
    (iii) thermal expansion
    (iv) intermolecular force of attraction

27. Establish antimony as a metalloid on the basis of its metallic property.

28. Under the normal conditions of temperature and pressure, the metal mercury remains in a ________ state.

29. Thermal expansion in solids is _______ than liquids and gases.

30. The temperature at which a liquid changes into a gas on heating at normal atmospheric pressure is called ________ of that liquid.

Short Answer Type Questions

31. Differentiate between a homogeneous and a heterogeneous mixture.

32. Differentiate the following:
    (a) evaporation and boiling
    (b) gas and vapour
    (c) metals and non-metals
    (d) pure substances and mixture

33. According to the kinetic molecular theory, explain the following:
    (a) Density of a solid is the highest.
    (b) Gases are highly compressible, whereas solids are incompressible.
    (c) Liquids and gases are fluids, whereas solids are rigid.

34. State the uses of the following non-metals:
    (a) oxygen (b) chlorine
    (c) sulphur

35. Explain the procedure for separation of sand water into sand and water.

36. Give examples of noble metals. Why are they called noble metals?

37. Explain the following according to the kinetic molecular theory.
    (a) melting (b) boiling
    (c) condensation (d) freezing

38. Give the characteristics of ________.
    (a) elements (b) compounds
    (c) mixture

39. Give the uses of the following metals:
    (a) Fe (b) Pb
    (c) Cu (d) Zn

40. Explain the separation of charcoal from sulphur.

41. Complete the following table:

Comparative study of the properties of solids, liquids and gases			
Properties	**Solids**	**Liquids**	**Gases**
Mass	Have definite mass		
Volume		Have definite volume	Do not have definite volume
Shape	Have definite shape		
Density	High density		Least density
Compressibility		Slightly compressible	
Rigidity	Rigid (cannot flow)		Fluid (can flow)
Free surfaces			No free surfaces
Thermal expansion diffusion		Higher than solids	
			Gases diffuse spontaneously and rapidly

42. Complete the following table:

Comparative study of molecular arrangement in solid, liquid and a gas			
Parameters	**Solid**	**Liquid**	**Gas**
Packing of molecules	Closely packed		Very loosely packed
Intermolecular space		More space than in solid	Huge intermolecular Space

Comparative study of molecular arrangement in solid, liquid and a gas			
Parameters	**Solid**	**Liquid**	**Gas**
Intermolecular force of attraction	Huge intermolecular force of attraction		
Molecular movement		Molecules possess translatory and rotatory motion in addition to vibratory motion	
Kinetic energy	Molecules have least kinetic energy		

43. Solids have a definite volume and a shape. Explain.

44. How is KNO_3–$KClO_3$ mixture separated by fractional crystallisation?

45. Explain how the following types of a mixture are separated:

(a) NH_4Cl–$NaCl$ mixture

(b) Sand–sawdust mixture

(c) Chalk–water mixture

Essay Type Questions

46. What is the method of separation of

(a) N_2–CO_2 mixture

(b) H_2–O_2 mixture

(c) NH_4Cl, KCl and sand mixture

(d) Ink–water mixture

47. Compare solids, liquids and gases on the basis of their properties.

48. Name the metalloids and state the reasons why they are categorised as metalloids.

49. Write the main postulates of the kinetic molecular theory.

50. Compare metals and non-metals based on their physical properties.

For Answer key, Hints and Explanations, please visit: www.pearsoned.co.in/IITFoundationSeries

CONCEPT APPLICATION

Level 1

Directions for questions from 1 to 7

State whether the following statements are true or false.

1. Gas molecules have higher intermolecular forces of attraction due to larger intermolecular spaces.
2. Non-metals usually form acidic oxides.
3. Boiling occurs throughout the liquid.
4. German silver is an alloy of silver and copper.
5. Distillation is the method used for separation of petrol from water.
6. Glucose–water mixture can be separated by the method of evaporation.
7. Metals form basic oxides or amphoteric oxides.

Directions for questions from 8 to 14

Fill in the blanks.

8. Decrease of pressure ________ the boiling point of a liquid.
9. Rate of evaporation is increased by increasing ________ and ___________.
10. ________ acts as a catalyst during the hydrogenation of vegetable oils.
11. Liquid ________ is used to preserve biological specimens
12. N_2 is ________ in KOH solution while CO_2 is ________.
13. Tincture of iodine is a mixture of _____ and ________.
14. Gases cannot be liquefied above a certain temperature called __________.

Directions for question 15

Match the entries in Column A with the appropriate ones in Column B.

15.

Column A		Column B
A. Mixture of sand and sawdust	( )	a. Separating funnel
B. Mixture of nitre and common salt	( )	b. Heating
C. Mixture of sulphur and CS_2	( )	c. Fractional distillation
D. Mixture of oil and water	( )	d. Fractional crystallisation
E. Mixture of alcohol and water	( )	e. Gravity separation
F. Mixture of CO_2 and water	( )	f. Solvent—KOH
G. Mixture of SO_2 and O_2	( )	g. Evaporation

Directions for questions from 16 to 45

For each of the questions, four choices have been provided. Select the correct alternative.

16. Brass is not suitable for type making because
    (a) brass expands on solidification
    (b) brass contracts on solidification
    (c) brass has less tensile strength
    (d) brass has less ductility
17. Which of the following metals is used to galvanise iron sheets?
    (a) copper (b) aluminium
    (c) tin (d) zinc
18. Iron possesses good casting properties when compared with copper because
    (a) iron contracts on solidification
    (b) iron expands on solidification
    (c) copper expands on solidification
    (d) copper neither contracts nor expands on solidification
19. With the increase in pressure, the boiling point of the liquid ________.
    (a) decreases
    (b) increases
    (c) does not change
    (d) depends on the nature of liquid
20. _______ is used for making photographic films.
    (a) $AgNO_3$ (b) KNO_2
    (c) AgO (d) AgCl
21. Silver tarnishes due to the formation of _____
    (a) oxide layer (b) sulphide layer
    (c) nitride layer (d) hydride layer

22. Which among the pairs are separated by using the principle of dissolution in a suitable solvent?
(a) SO_2 and N_2O_5, KOH as solvent
(b) SO_2 and NO_2, KOH as solvent
(c) SO_2 and N_2O_3, KOH as solvent
(d) SO_2 and NO, KOH as solvent

23. A, B, C and D are four gases. If the order of their critical temperature is as D < B < C < A, then which of the following gases has the highest boiling point?
(a) A (b) B
(c) C (d) D

24. Addition of potassium nitrate to ice results in
(a) increase in melting point
(b) decrease in melting point
(c) change in colour of ice
(d) both (a) and (c)

25. Identify the heterogeneous mixture among the following:
(a) brine solution (b) duralumin
(c) gunpowder (d) liquor ammonia

26. Which of the following is a pure substance?
(a) duralumin (b) magnalium
(c) bell metal (d) magnesium

27. Aluminium foil can be made from aluminium by using
(a) its thermal and electrical conductivities
(b) its malleable property
(c) its sonorous property
(d) all the above

28. Pickles are not stored in steel or aluminium containers because
(a) steel has chromium which is poisonous
(b) aluminium takes up oxygen from pickles and spoils it
(c) pickles have acids which can corrode iron and aluminium making pickles poisonous
(d) none of the above

29. The molecular arrangement of a substance depends upon
(a) temperature (b) concentration
(c) pressure (d) all of these

30. Silver, gold and platinum are called noble metals because ________.
(a) these are costly
(b) these are precious
(c) these have very less reactivity
(d) all of these

31. Which of the following statements is true regarding solids?
(a) Solids are highly compressible.
(b) Solids diffuse rapidly.
(c) Solids possess low density.
(d) Solids possess a number of free surfaces.

32. In which of the following substances, intermolecular force of attraction is the maximum?
(a) iron bar (b) water
(c) air (d) nitrogen

33. Which of the following has maximum compressibility?
(a) iron bar (b) petrol
(c) chlorine (d) bromine

34 On heating, the temperature of the melting solid
(a) increases
(b) decreases
(c) remains constant
(d) may increase or decrease depending upon the nature of the solid

35. Which of the following changes directly from solid to gas on heating?
(a) ammonium chloride (b) sodium chloride
(c) potassium chloride (d) calcium chloride

36. The process of phase transition from solid to liquid involves the following steps. Arrange them in a proper sequence.
(1) Molecules become free to move, and thus, attain molecular arrangement of liquid.
(2) The energy supplied makes the molecules to vibrate more.
(3) During melting, the molecules overcome the forces of attraction between them.
(4) The molecules acquire rotatory motion, translatory motion in addition to vibratory motion.

PRACTICE QUESTIONS

(a) 3 4 1 2 (b) 2 3 4 1
(c) 3 4 2 1 (d) none of these

37. Under the normal conditions of temperature and pressure, the non-metal bromine exists in ______ state.
(a) solid (b) liquid
(c) gaseous (d) ionised

38. Which of the following is not polyatomic?
(a) nitrogen (b) sulphur
(c) ozone (d) phosphorus

39 Which of the following is not a mixture?
(a) Sodium chloride solution
(b) Brass
(c) Bronze
(d) Molten sodium chloride

40. Which of the following elements is used for vulcanisation?
(a) phosphorus (b) sulphur
(c) oxygen (d) nitrogen

41. During the separation of acetone from water by fractional distillation, the following steps are carried out. Arrange the following in a proper sequence.
(1) Water remains in the distillation flask.
(2) The acetone–water mixture is taken in a distillation flask and the flask is heated at a temperature equal to or more than the boiling point of acetone but less than that of water.
(3) As the vapours pass through the fractionating column, they get condensed and the liquid formed is collected in the receiver.
(4) When the mixture in the flask is subjected to slow heating, acetone, being more volatile than water, gets vaporised first.
(a) 2 4 3 1 (b) 2 4 1 3
(c) 3 1 2 4 (d) 3 1 4 2

42. During the separation of immiscible liquid–liquid mixture by a separating funnel, the following steps are followed. Arrange them in a proper sequence.
(1) The nozzle tap is opened slowly and the heavier component is allowed to trickle down.
(2) The liquid–liquid mixture is poured into the separating funnel clamped vertically.
(3) The lighter component remains in the flask.
(4) The mixture is allowed to stand where clear layers of liquids are formed.
(5) The liquid with higher density settles down at the bottom of the flask.
(a) 2 4 1 5 3 (b) 1 2 3 4 5
(c) 2 4 5 1 3 (d) 4 1 2 3 5

43. A student is carrying out distillation process in a lab. Water is boiling in the distillation flask. Water that is collected in the receiver flask is refrigerated and ice cubes are formed. Ice cubes are then kept outside the refrigerator and they started melting. Arrange the following phases of water in the ascending order of their total (PE + KE) energy considering that the mass of water remains the same.
(1) Water collected in the receiving flask.
(2) Water boiling in the distillation flask.
(3) Steam passing through the delivery tube.
(4) Ice cubes formed in the refrigerator.
(a) 4 3 2 1 (b) 4 1 2 3
(c) 3 4 2 1 (d) 4 1 3 2

44. Which among the pairs is separated by using the principle of dissolution in a suitable solvent?
(a) SO_2 and N_2O_5, KOH as solvent
(b) SO_2 and NO_2, KOH as solvent
(c) SO_2 and N_2O_3, KOH as solvent
(d) SO_2 and NO, KOH as solvent

45. In which of the following uses of nitrogen, its characteristic property of inert nature is not exploited?
(a) It is used to preserve biological specimen.
(b) It dilutes the activity of oxygen present in the atmosphere.
(c) It is used to preserve food materials.
(d) Nitrogen is used for the synthesis of ammonia.

Level 2

1. The thermal expansion of solids is the least among solids, liquids and gases. Justify.

2. Explain the method by which CCl_4, H_2O and ethyl alcohol mixture can be separated.

3. For a certain purpose, a liquid having a liquid range from 210°C to 110°C is required in large quantities. What is the suitable liquid for the above purpose and how can it be used?

4. Water is sprayed in orange grooves in very cold countries during winter. Give reasons.

5. Explain the effect of temperature on the electrical conductivity of metals.

6. Why do naphthalene and camphor sublime under normal conditions of temperature and pressure?

7. Two ice cubes can be joined by pressing them together and then by releasing pressure. How do you account for this?

8. Copper in copper oxide does not liberate SO_2 gas while copper in bronze evolves SO_2 gas with conc. H_2SO_4. However, for making statues, copper is used in the form of bronze but not metallic copper or copper oxide. Explain why the same copper has such varied properties.

9. Why are ornaments prepared by using an alloy of Ag with Cu and not by pure Ag?

10. Perfect moulds can be made by using wrought iron but not by using molten copper. Give reasons.

11. In spite of supplying heat, the temperature of the melting solid does not change. Explain with reasons.

12. During the process of soldering, the metal surfaces are cleaned using acids. What purpose does this serve and which separation technique is involved in this?

13. Explain the methods by which the constituents in gunpowder can be separated.

14. Redistillation of nitric acid is carried out in a ferrosilicon vessel but not in an iron vessel. Explain.

15. Deepa and her family on their house-warming ceremony received many bouquets which they kept at the corner of the drawing room. After some time, they felt the fragrance of the flowers all over the drawing room. What could be the reason behind this? Explain with a suitable reason.

16. When a perfume is poured on a palm, a cooling sensation is perceived. Name and explain the phenomenon associated with it.

17. How does liquefaction of a gas depend on critical temperature?

18. What is the principle involved in using brine solution to remove the ice piled on roads in cold regions?

19. Explain why the snow on the mountain peaks does not melt at a temperature slightly above 0°C.

20. A mixture is formed by two kinds of matter, the molecules of which possess only vibratory motion. If the change in solubility of two substances in a given solvent differs widely with the change in temperature, how can these two solids be separated from the solvent?

21. Give the working principle involved in chromatography.

22. When Shashi went to Vizag with his parents, he noticed that all the fishermen store their fish inside a thermally insulated container which is filled with ice and salt. Can you give an explanation for this?

23. Study the following graph and based on that answer the questions with a suitable reason. The graph represents the various stages involved in step-wise change of ice to steam.
    (a) Identify the stages associated with increase in temperature. Give a reason.
    (b) In which stages, the temperature is constant? Why so?

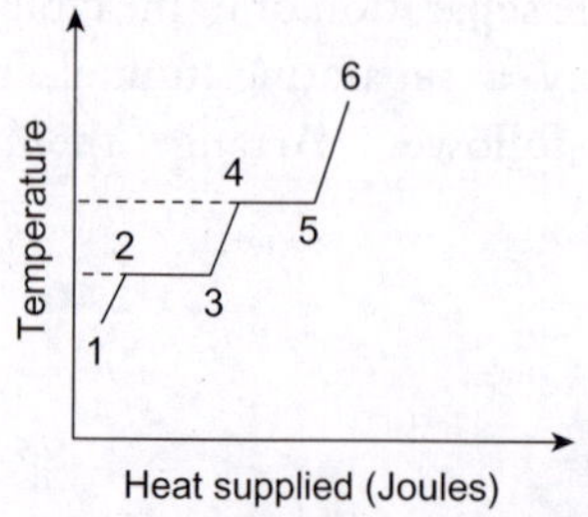

PRACTICE QUESTIONS

Level 3

1. What is the shape of the meniscus observed when water and mercury are taken in two different capillary tubes and why?
2. Evaporation can take place at any temperature, but boiling takes place at a fixed temperature. Give appropriate reasons.
3. Vapour pressure of a liquid A is more that of B. Which of these liquids has higher critical temperature in their gaseous state? Justify.
4. Explain the changes observed when a glass of water is placed on the surface of moon.
5. The surface of the electric bulb with a tungsten filament becomes greyish black after being used for a long period of time. Explain the reason.
6. A test tube filled with water is dipped up to its neck in a boiling water bath. Does the water inside the test tube boil? Justify.
7. Skating on ice is almost impossible at very low temperatures say at around –30°C. Why?
8. How is milk powder made from milk? Explain the principle involved.
9. Discuss the change in energy and arrangement of molecules on increasing the temperature of ice from –5°C to 10°C at 1 atm pressure.
10. If a solution is formed by a combination of solvent A and solid solute B, and decomposition of the solute takes place at the boiling point of solvent; how can we separate these two?

CONCEPT APPLICATION

Level 1

True or false

1. False
2. True
3. True
4. False
5. False
6. True
7. True

Fill in the blanks

8. Decreases
9. Temperature and surface area
10. Nickel
11. N_2
12. Insoluble, soluble
13. Iodine and alcohol
14. Critical temperature

Match the following

15. A → e
B → d
C → g
D → a
E → c
F → b
G → f

Multiple choice questions

16. b
17. d
18. b
19. b
20. d
21. b
22. c
23. a
24. b
25. b
26. c
27. b
28. b
29. c
30. b
31. Due to close packing of molecules in solids, they possess definite shape due to which they have many number of free surfaces.
32. Iron bar is solid, and hence, intermolecular force of attraction is maximum.
33. Since chlorine is a gas at room temperature, it can be compressed to the maximum.
34. During melting the temperature of a solid remains constant, as the external heat energy is utilised to overcome the forces of attraction between the molecules.
35. Ammonium chloride is a sublimable substance which changes directly from solid to gas on heating.
36. (i) The energy supplied makes the molecules to vibrate with more speed.
(ii) During melting, the molecules overcome the forces of attraction between them.
(iii) The molecules acquire rotatory motion, translatory motion in addition to vibratory motion.
(iv) Molecules become free to move, and thus, attain the molecular arrangement of a liquid.
37. Bromine exists in liquid state under normal conditions of temperature and pressure.
38. Nitrogen is a diatomic molecule.
39. Molten sodium chloride is a compound.
40. Sulphur is used for vulcanisation.

41. (i) The acetone–water mixture is passed into the distillation flask and the flask is heated at a temperature equal to or more than the boiling point of acetone but less than that of water.
(ii) When the mixture in the flask is subjected to slow heating, acetone, being more volatile than water, gets vaporised first.
(iii) As the vapours pass through the fractionating column, they get condensed and the liquid formed is collected in the receiver.
(iv) Water remains in the distillation flask.

42. (i) The liquid–liquid mixture is poured into the separating funnel clamped vertically.
(ii) Mixture is allowed to stand where clear layers of liquids are formed.
(iii) The liquid with higher density settles down at the bottom of the flask.
(iv) The nozzle tap is opened slowly and the heavier component is allowed to trickle down.
(v) The lighter component remains in the flask.

43. d a b c
(i) Ice cubes formed in the refrigeration
(ii) Water collected in the receiving flask
(iii) Water boiling in the distillation flask
(iv) Steam passing through the delivery tube

44. Dissolution in a suitable solvent is one of the methods of separation of gas–gas mixture. As SO_2 is acidic in nature, it is dissolved in basic KOH, whereas NO is neutral as it does not dissolve in KOH. So, SO_2 and NO are separated. From the solution SO_2 is separated by chemical means.

45. Nitrogen reacts with hydrogen to form ammonia. Its inert nature is not suitable for this process.

Level 2

1. (i) Effect of external supply of heat energy on molecular arrangement of a substance.
(ii) Comparison of forces acting between the molecules in solids, liquids and gases.
(iii) The effect of heat on the molecular arrangement of a substance.
(iv) Comparison of the effect in solids, liquids and gases.

3. (i) Miscible and immiscible liquids
(ii) The separation of miscible and immiscible liquids
(iii) Comparison of the physical properties of liquid
(iv) Suitable separation procedure based on physical properties

5. (i) Liquid that has liquid range close to −10°C-110°C
(ii) Factors that affect melting and boiling points.
(iii) Changes that can depress freezing point and elevate boiling point.

6. (i) Physical change in water in very cold countries.
(ii) Heat changes during these changes.
(iii) Effect of corresponding heat on plants.
(iv) Conduction of heat through ice.

7. (i) The cause of electrical conductivity in metals.
(ii) The effect of temperature on kinetic energy of metal atoms.
(iii) The effect of temperature on direction of species, conducting electricity.
(iv) Effect of these on conductivity.

8. (i) High vapour pressure.
(ii) The effect of high vapour pressure on sublimation.
(iii) Comparison of the kinetic energy of surface molecules.

9. (i) Effect of pressure on the melting point.
(ii) Changes in the melting point of ice with pressure.
(iii) The application of this in joining two ice cubes.

10. (i) Composition of bronze
(ii) Comparison of chemical properties of constituents of bronze and CuO.
(iii) Comparison of physical properties of constituents of bronze with CuO and Cu.

11. (i) Physical properties of Ag.
(ii) Strength of ornaments made of pure silver.
(iii) Change in properties on the addition of Cu.

12. (i) Generally density in a solid state is higher than that in a liquid state.
(ii) Requisites for a good mould.
(iii) Comparison of the volumes on the solidification of iron and copper.

13. (i) At the melting point, molecules of a solid move apart.
(ii) Different energies possessed by molecules.
(iii) Energy which is affected while heating.
(iv) Energy which is affected during change in phase.

14. (i) The phenomenon of soldering.
(ii) Composition of metal surface.
(iii) Effect of addition of acid to metals.
(iv) Process of separation.

15. (i) Composition of gunpowder.
(ii) Identification of suitable solvents.
(iii) Extraction of the components from respective solutions.

16. Nitric acid is a strong oxidizing agent. It reacts with iron to form ferric oxide. Ferrosilicon, an alloy of iron is less reactive when compared to iron and does not react with nitric acid. Thus, the redistillation process is carried out in a ferrosilicon vessel.

17. The molecules which cause fragrance diffused into the air from the bouquets and that's how travel from one corner of the room to another. So, Deepa and her family after sometime felt the fragrance of the flowers all over the room.

18. Perfume is a highly volatile liquid. When it rapidly evaporates from the palm, it absorbs heat energy from the palm. This gives a cooling sensation.

19. Liquefaction of a gas by application of pressure is possible only at or below critical temperature. At low temperature the intermolecular forces of attractions are considerably high. This makes the conversion of gaseous state to liquid state feasible on application of pressure.

20. The ice piled on roads in the cold regions is removed by melting process. For this process brine solution is used because this decreases the melting point of ice. Thus, ice melts below 0°C and can be removed.

21. The atmospheric pressure on the mountain peaks is low. As ice contracts on melting, with the decrease in pressure its melting point increases. Thus, the snow does not melt slightly above 0°C.

22. Solids possess the molecules which have only vibratory motion. Thus, both the substances are solids. As their solubility in a particular solvent differs in a particular range of temperature, they can be separated by fractional crystallisation.

23. The particles of a mixture or dye, like, ink are soluble in water. As the water rises on the filter paper, it takes along with it the dye particles. Usually, a dye is a mixture of two or more colours. The coloured components that are more soluble in water, reach to a greater height and in this way the colours get separated.

24. Salt added to ice (freezing mixture) is a better refrigerant than ice as adding some impurity (salt) to the ice decreases its melting point. During melting of ice, it takes away a lot of heat from the substance(s) which is in contact with it. That's why the fishermen store their fish inside a thermally insulated container which is filled with ice and salt.

25. (a) In the graph, parts 1 to 2, 3 to 4 and 5 to 6 show heating of solid, liquid and gas, respectively which increases kinetic energy, and hence, there is rise in temperature.
(b) The parts 2 to 3 and 4 to 5 represent melting of solid and boiling of liquid. At these points the heat energy supplied is utilised for decreasing the intermolecular force of attraction, and hence, there is no change in temperature.

Level 3

1. (i) Type of forces between Hg molecules and Hg–glass molecules.
(ii) Type of forces between water molecules and water–glass molecules.
(iii) Effect of these forces on the shape of meniscus.

2. (i) Differences between evaporation and boiling.
(ii) Comparison of the part of the liquid from where evaporation and boiling take place.
(iii) Condition at which boiling starts in a liquid.

3. (i) Relation between critical temperature and intermolecular forces of attraction of a gas.

   (ii) Relation between vapour pressure and intermolecular forces of attraction.

   (iii) Relation between intermolecular force of attraction and boiling point.

   (iv) Relation between boiling point and critical temperature.

4. (i) Relative pressure on the surface of the moon.

   (ii) Effect of pressure on evaporation of water.

5. Change in state.

6. The water in the test tube becomes hot but does not boil. The water in the tube gets the heat from the water outside. As the maximum temperature of water in the container outside is 100°C, the water inside the test tube attains 100°C temperature, but immediately the transmission of heat stops due to thermal equilibrium, and hence, the water inside the test tube cannot boil.

7. Skating on ice is possible because ice contracts on melting. So, on applying pressure, the melting point of ice decreases and the ice below the skates starts to melt and because of the formation of thin water film skating is possible on the ice But when temperature is around −30°C, the pressure exerted by body mass is not sufficient to melt the ice below the skates. Hence, skating on ice is not possible at around −30°C.

8. Milk is heated under low pressure conditions. This decreases the boiling point of milk, and thus, the water present in the milk evaporates. This concentrated milk is then sprayed in a hot dry chamber where the evaporation of the leftover water is instant and concentrated milk turns to milk powder.

9. On heating ice at −5°C, its temperature increases up to 0°C, i.e., the kinetic energy of the molecules increases. At 0°C, the ice starts to melt. During this period the energy supplied is taken up to increase the potential energy of the molecules and the arrangement of molecules changes. Once the ice cube melts, the heat energy supplied is again used to increase the temperature of water due to increase in kinetic energy of the molecules. However, from 0°C to 4°C, the molecules of water come closer and above 4°C the molecules move farther away.

10. At the temperature at which solvent A boils, the solute B decomposes. Hence, it is not possible to separate the solute B from solvent A by distillation under normal atmospheric pressure. As the pressure decreases, the boiling point decreases. Thus, by decreasing the external pressure in the above distillation processes, the boiling point of solvent A can be decreased. At this temperature solute B does not decompose and can be separated from the liquid.

Chapter

3

Language of Chemistry and Transformation of Substances

Remember

Before beginning this chapter, you should be able to:

- explain the interconversion of states of matter.
- classify matter based upon physical and chemical properties.

Key Ideas

After completing this chapter, you should be able to:

- distinguish between physical and chemical changes.
- learn Berzelius system of writing symbols of elements and formulae of elements and compounds.
- know the naming of binary compounds, acids, bases and salts.
- understand valencies of elements with respect to hydrogen, chlorine and oxygen.
- represent chemical changes by using chemical equations and understand different laws of chemical combination and their experimental verifications.
- learn trial and error method and partial equation method for balancing chemical equations.
- study classification of chemical reactions based on the nature of reaction, the energy changes and into oxidation – reduction reactions.

INTRODUCTION

Chemistry is the branch of science which deals with the study of matter. The study of matter can have different aspects, such as, preparation, composition and properties. Since preparation and properties of a substance invariably depend on the composition of the matter, the study of composition of matter is of prime importance. On the basis of composition, the matter can be classified into elements, compounds and types of a mixture. In nature, every substance has an inherent tendency to undergo transformation which may or may not be associated with the change in composition, and hence, properties.

PHYSICAL AND CHEMICAL CHANGE

The transformations which are associated with the change in the properties of the matter are considered as chemical changes in contrast to the physical changes in which the matter retains its identity. The innumerable chemical changes occurring in nature can conveniently be represented in the form of chemical equations. For the sake of convenience and universal application, the 118 elements discovered so far have been assigned unique symbols. The molecules formed by the combination of the various elements are represented by distinct formulae. The study of symbols, formulae and chemical equations comes under the purview of language of chemistry.

The transformation which involves a change in the structure or composition of a substance is called **chemical change**.

Comparative Study of Characteristics of Physical and Chemical Changes

Physical change	Chemical change
No change in molecular composition takes place. Hence, no new substances are formed. ***Example:*** When water is cooled to 0°C, it changes to solid form, i.e., ice but no new product is formed in this process. $\underset{(\text{liquid } H_2O)}{\text{Water}} \xrightarrow{0°C} \underset{(\text{solid } H_2O)}{\text{Ice}}$	Molecular composition changes. Hence, new substances are formed. ***Example:*** When calcium carbonate is heated, calcium oxide and carbon dioxide are formed.
Physical change is temporary and easily reversible. ***Example:*** Water on cooling to 0°C is converted to ice. Hence, ice on heating can be converted back to water. $\underset{(\text{Liquid})}{\text{Water}} \underset{\text{heating}}{\overset{\text{cooling}}{\rightleftharpoons}} \underset{(\text{solid})}{\text{Ice}}$	Chemical change is permanent and not easily reversible. ***Example:*** Sugar on heating is converted to carbon (black residue) and steam but the sugar cannot be obtained by cooling the products. $\text{Sugar} \xrightarrow{\Delta} \text{Carbon} + \text{Steam}$
There is no net gain or loss of energy. ***Example:*** In the conversion of 5 g of water to water vapour some energy is absorbed, and the same amount is released in converting back to water. $\text{Water} \underset{\text{Energy absorbed}}{\overset{\text{Energy absorbed}}{\rightleftharpoons}} \text{water vapour}$ ***Examples:*** (i) Conversion of water into steam (ii) Magnetisation of an iron bar (iii) Liquefaction of any gas (iv) Melting of ice	There is a gain or loss of energy in the form of heat, light or electricity, etc. ***Example:*** During the formation of ammonia from nitrogen and hydrogen, there is a loss of 22 kcal of energy. ***Examples:*** (i) Rusting of iron (ii) Formation of curd from milk (iii) Burning of paper (iv) Blackening of silverware

Processes Involving both Physical and Chemical Changes

Processes	Physical changes involved	Chemical changes
Heating of ammonium chloride	Ammonium chloride sublimes	Decomposition to ammonia and hydrogen chloride
Heating of sodium nitrate	Sodium nitrate melts	Decomposition to sodium nitrite and oxygen

REPRESENTATION OF CHEMICAL CHANGES

Every chemical change can be conveniently represented in the form of a chemical equation. This is because describing a chemical change with the names of the substances becomes cumbersome. The elements and compounds are, therefore, given shorthand notations of symbols and formulae.

Symbols are the shorthand notations representing a single atom of an element and generally consist of a letter or combination of letters derived from the name of the element.

In 1814, Berzelius suggested a simple system of writing symbols to represent an atom of an element in the following ways:

1. In most cases the first letter of the name of the element in capital letter is used as the symbol of the element.

Element	Symbol
Boron	B
Carbon	C
Fluorine	F
Hydrogen	H
Iodine	I
Nitrogen	N
Oxygen	O
Phosphorous	P
Sulphur	S
Vanadium	V
Uranium	U

2. When the names of two or more elements have the same initial letter (e.g., carbon and calcium), another letter from the name of the element is written in a small letter along with the initial letter written in capital.

Element	Symbol
Aluminium	Al
Arsenic	As
Argon	Ar
Barium	Ba
Beryllium	Be
Bromine	Br
Bismuth	Bi
Calcium	Ca

Element	Symbol
Cadmium	Cd
Chromium	Cr
Chlorine	Cl
Cobalt	Co
Palladium	Pd
Platinum	Pt
Selenium	Se
Silicon	Si
Strontium	Sr

3. For some elements the symbols are derived from their Latin or Greek names.

Name of the elements	Latin names	Symbols
Sodium	Natrium (Greek)	Na
Potassium	Kalium	K
Iron	Ferrum	Fe
Copper	Cuprum	Cu
Silver	Argentum	Ag
Gold	Aurum	Au
Mercury	Hydrargyrum (Greek)	Hg
Lead	Plumbum	Pb
Tin	Stannum	Sn
Antimony	Stibium (Greek)	Sb
Tungsten	Wolfram	W

Just as an atom is represented by a symbol, a molecule of an element or a compound is represented by means of a formula. The formula represents the number of atoms of each element present in the molecule.

Examples:

Hydrogen : H_2
Chlorine : Cl_2
Ozone : O_3
Water : H_2O
Sulphuric acid : H_2SO_4

The compounds are formed by the combination of atoms of different elements.

During the formation of the molecules of the compounds, atoms combine in certain fixed proportions. This is due to the fact that different atoms have different combining capacities. The combining capacity of an atom is known as its valency.

The valency of a hydrogen atom is taken as one and is selected as the standard. Valencies of the other elements are expressed in terms of hydrogen.

Valency of an element can also be defined as the number of hydrogen atoms which combine with one atom of it.

TABLE 3.1 Valencies of elements with respect to hydrogen

Molecules	Description	Valencies of the elements
HCl Hydrogen chloride	One hydrogen atom combines with one chlorine atom	1 (chlorine)
H_2O Water	Two hydrogen atoms combine with one oxygen atom	2 (oxygen)
NH_3 Ammonia	Three hydrogen atoms combine with one nitrogen atom	3 (nitrogen)
CH_4 Methane	Four hydrogen atoms combine with one carbon atom	4 (carbon)

Since most of the elements do not combine with hydrogen, the valency or the combining capacity of the element is also defined in terms of other elements, like, chlorine or oxygen. This is because almost all the elements combine with chlorine and oxygen.

Valency with respect to chlorine: Since valency of chlorine is one, the number of chlorine atoms with which one atom of an element can combine is called its valency.

Example: NaCl ⇒ Valency of Na = 1

Valency with respect to oxygen: In another way, valency can be defined as double the number of oxygen atoms with which one atom of an element can combine since valency of oxygen is two.

Example: MgO ⇒ Valency of Mg = 2

Certain metals exhibit more than one valency, i.e., they can exhibit variable valency.

IONS OR RADICALS

An atom or a group of atoms, when they either lose or gain electron(s), gets converted into ions (or radicals). Ions formed by the loss of electron(s) are positively charged and are called **cations** or positive radicals and the ions formed by the gain of electron(s) are negatively charged and are known as **anions** or **negative radicals**.

An ion or radical is classified as monovalent, divalent, trivalent or tetravalent when the number of charges over it is 1, 2, 3 or 4, respectively. A list of ions and their charges is given below:

TABLE 3.2 Positive radicals

Radical	Nature
Sodium (Na^+)	Monovalent
Potassium (K^+)	Monovalent
Lithium (Li^+)	Monovalent
Ammonium ($NH_4{}^+$)	Monovalent
Hydrogen (H^+)	Monovalent
Barium (Ba^{+2})	Divalent
Calcium (Ca^{+2})	Divalent
Zinc (Zn^{+2})	Divalent
Magnesium (Mg^{+2})	Divalent
Nickel (Ni^{+2})	Divalent
Cobalt (Co^{+2})	Divalent
Aluminium (Al^{+3})	Trivalent
Chromium (Cr^{+3})	Trivalent

Some metallic elements show variable valency (more than one valency) and form positive ions with different charges. In that case, the ion with lower charge gets 'ous' suffix and the ion with higher charge gets 'ic' suffix or the value of charge of an ion is shown by Roman numerals (such as, I, II, III, IV, etc.) in parentheses which is followed by the name of the metal.

Examples:

Elements	Cations formed	Names
Copper	Cu^{+}	Cuprous or copper (I)
	Cu^{+2}	Cupric or copper (II)
Iron	Fe^{+}	Ferrous or iron (II)
	Fe^{+3}	Ferric or iron (III)
Tin	Sn^{+2}	Stannous or stannum (II)
	Sn^{+4}	Stannic or stannum (IV)
Mercury	Hg^{+}	Mercurous or mercury (I)
	Hg^{+2}	Mercuric or mercury (II)
Lead	Pb^{+2}	Plumbous or lead (II)
	Pb^{+4}	Plumbic or lead (IV)

Negative radicals	
Radicals	Nature
Hydride (H^{-})	Monovalent
Hydroxide (OH^{-})	Monovalent
Bisulphite (HSO_3^{-})	Monovalent
Bisulphate (HSO_4^{-})	Monovalent
Fluoride (F^{-})	Monovalent
Chloride (Cl^{-})	Monovalent
Hypochlorite (ClO^{-})	Monovalent
Chlorite (ClO_2^{-})	Monovalent
Chlorate (ClO_3^{-})	Monovalent
Perchlorate (ClO_4^{-})	Monovalent
Bromide (Br^{-})	Monovalent
Dihydrogen phosphate $(H_2PO_4)^{-1}$	Monovalent
Nitrate $(NO_3)^{-}$	Monovalent
Nitrite $(NO_2)^{-}$	Monovalent
Iodide (I^{-})	Monovalent
Oxide (O^{-2})	Divalent
Peroxide (O_2^{-2})	Divalent
Sulphide (S^{-2})	Divalent
Sulphite (SO_3^{-2})	Divalent
Sulphate (SO_4^{-2})	Divalent
Biphosphate (HPO_4^{-2})	Divalent
Phosphate (PO_4^{-3})	Trivalent
Phosphide (P^{-3})	Trivalent
Nitride (N^{-3})	Trivalent

Derivation of Formulae of Compounds

Chemical formulae of the compounds are derived by considering the number of charges on ions.

Certain basic rules are followed for writing formulae of compounds as listed hereunder:

1. The positive radical or cation is written first and then it is followed by the negative radical or anion.
2. The molecule of any compound being electrically neutral, the total positive charge on the positive radical or cation should be equal to the total negative charge on the negative radical or anion.

Examples:

1. **To form a compound between A^+ and X^-:** To form a neutral compound with A^+ and X^-, the total number of positive charges should be equal to the total number of negative charges. As the number of charges on A and X is the same, one atom of A combines with one atom of X to form the neutral compound AX.

   Example: Compound with Na^+ and Cl^-.

   Molecular formula of the compound is NaCl.

2. **To form a compound between A^+ and X^{2-}:** To make a neutral compound by combining these two, two atoms of A compensate the two negative charges on X. The compound formed is of the kind A_2X.

   Example: Compound with H^+ and S^{-2} and molecular formula is H_2S.

3. **To form a compound between A^{+2} and X^{-3}:** One atom of A cannot compensate for all the negative charges of X. Two atoms of A have a total of +4 charges while X has only −3.Two atoms of X have a total of 6 charges which are to be compensated by 3 atoms of A. The compound formed is A_3X_2.

   Examples:

$$Al^{+3}SO_4^{-2} \longrightarrow Al_2(SO_4)_3$$

$$Si^{+4}O^{-2} \longrightarrow SiO_2$$

$$Ca^{+2}CO_3^{-2} \longrightarrow CaCO_3$$

The above methods for writing formulae of a compound can be simplified with the help of criss-cross method.

Criss-cross Method

Step I

The symbol of the cation or positive radical is written on the left side and the symbol of the anion or negative radical on the right side.

Examples:

1. H S
2. Ca F

Step II

The number of charges on the ion or radical is indicated.

Examples:

1. H^{+1} S^{-2}
2. Ca^{+2} F^{-1}

Step III

The value of the charge on the ion or radical is interchanged and shifted to the lower right side of the ion or radical (the values of the charges are criss-crossed).

Examples:

1. $H^{+1}\ \ S^{-2} \longrightarrow H_2S$
2. $Ca^{+2}\ \ F^{-1} \longrightarrow CaF_2$

If the charge on any one ion or radical or both the ions and radicals is 1, then no number is required to be written after they are interchanged and shifted to the lower right side.

Examples:

1. $K^{+1}\ \ Cl^{-1} \longrightarrow KCl$
2. $NH_4^{+1}\ \ Cl^{-1} \longrightarrow NH_4Cl$

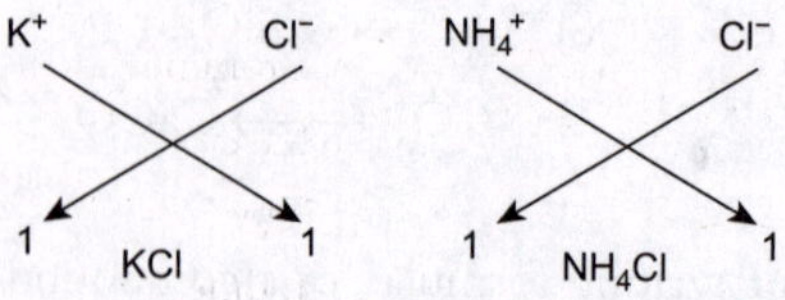

In case the charge on both the ions or radicals is the same, no number is needed to be written.

Examples:

1. $Fe^{+2}\ \ O^{-2} \longrightarrow FeO$
2. $Al^{+3}\ \ N^{-3} \longrightarrow AlN$

If one of the combining species or both the combining species are polyatomic, then the radical(s) are written within parentheses in case the number of radical(s) present in one molecule of the compound is more than 1.

Examples:

1. Ca^{+2} $NO_3^{-1} \longrightarrow Ca(NO_3)_2$

2. NH_4^{+1} $SO_4^{-2} \longrightarrow (NH_4)_2SO_4$

In case the charge of both the ions or radicals has some highest common factor (greater than 1), then both these numbers have to be divided by the highest common factor and the value of the quotient is used.

Examples:

1. Si^{+4} $O^{-2} \longrightarrow SiO_2$

2. Mn^{+4} $O^{-2} \longrightarrow MnO_2$

Atomic Weight or Atomic Mass

An individual atom is very small, negligible in weight and cannot be weighed directly. Hence, the mass of the atom is calculated indirectly by comparing its mass with that of hydrogen atom which is taken as the standard atomic mass. Later one-twelfth mass of ${}^{12}_{6}C$ isotope is considered to be the standard for comparing atomic masses of other elements.

The **relative atomic mass** is defined as the number that represents how many times an atom of an element is heavier than one-twelfth of the mass of ${}^{12}_{6}C$ atom.

TABLE 3.3 Atomic weights of some common elements

Elements	Atomic mass	Elements	Atomic mass
Hydrogen	1	Calcium	40
Lithium	7	Chromium	52
Boron	11	Manganese	55
Carbon	12	Iron	56
Nitrogen	14	Copper	63.5
Oxygen	16	Zinc	65.5
Fluorine	19	Bromine	80
Sodium	23	Silver	108
Magnesium	24	Tin	119
Aluminium	27	Iodine	127
Phosphorous	31	Barium	137
Sulphur	32	Platinum	195
Chlorine	35.5	Mercury	200
Potassium	39	Lead	207

One-twelth of the mass of a $^{12}_{6}C$ atom is called **atomic mass unit**, abbreviated as amu. Hence, atomic weights of the elements are expressed in amu.

Example: Atomic weight of oxygen is 16 amu.

The relative atomic mass or atomic weight of an element expressed in grams is called **gram atomic weight** or **gram atom**.

Example: As the atomic weight of oxygen is 16 amu, gram atomic mass of oxygen is 16 g.

Molecular Weight

Molecular weight is calculated by adding the atomic weights of all the constituent atoms.

Examples:

1. Molecular weight of $NaHCO_3$

   The atomic weight of Na = 23 amu

   H = 1 amu

   C = 12 amu and

   O = 16 amu

   Therefore, the molecular weight of $NaHCO_3 = 23 + 1 + 12 + (16 \times 3) = 84$ amu

2. Molecular weight of $Ca(OH)_2$

   The atomic weight of Ca = 40 amu

   O = 16 amu

   H = 1 amu

   Therefore, the molecular weight of $Ca(OH)_2 = 40 + (16 \times 2) + (1 \times 2) = 74$ amu

The molecular weight expressed in grams is called **gram molecular weight**.

Example:

Molecular weights of O_2 and H_2O are 32 amu and 18 amu, respectively. Hence, gram molecular weights of O_2 and H_2O are 32 g and 18 g, respectively.

NAMING OF BINARY COMPOUNDS

The compounds that are formed by the combination of two elements are called **binary compounds**.

In naming of the binary compounds, the electropositive atom (generally metal) is specified first by giving its ordinary English name. The name of the second element which is generally a non-metal is obtained by adding the suffix 'ide' to its name.

Examples:

$MgCl_2$	Magnesium chloride
$CaCl_2$	Calcium chloride
BaO	Barium oxide
H_2S	Hydrogen sulphide

In case of metals showing **variable valency**, it is necessary to specify which of the positive ions are present.

Examples:

FeO	Ferrous oxide or iron (II) oxide
Fe_2O_3	Ferric oxide or iron (III) oxide
$CuCl$	Cuprous chloride or copper (I) chloride
$CuCl_2$	Cupric chloride or copper (II) chloride

For binary covalent compounds, generally formed by two non-metallic elements, it is required to specify the number of atoms of more electronegative element with the help of a meaningful prefix.

Number of atoms	Prefix
One	Mono
Two	Di
Three	Tri
Four	Tetra
Five	Penta
Six	Hexa
Seven	Hepta
Eight	Octa
Nine	Nona
Ten	Deca

The less electronegative element is specified first, followed by the more electronegative element.

The prefix is generally added to the more electronegative element to specify its number of atoms.

SO_2	Sulphur dioxide
N_2O_5	Dinitrogen pentoxide
SF_6	Sulphur hexafluoride
PCl_3	Phosphorus trichloride
CO	Carbon monoxide

Naming of Acids, Bases and Salts

1. **Binary acids**: Binary acids are named as hydro…….ic acid.

   Examples:

HCl	Hydrochloric acid
HBr	Hydrobromic acid

2. **Oxyacids**: Oxyacids are named without mentioning hydrogen. Often an element (non-metal) is able to form more than one oxyacid. In naming such acids, the one with the greater number of oxygen atom is given the suffix 'ic' and the one with the lesser number of oxygen atoms is given the suffix 'ous.'

   Examples:

HNO_2	Nitrous acid
HNO_3	Nitric acid
H_2SO_4	Sulphuric acid
H_2SO_3	Sulphurous acid

When a non-metal forms more than two oxyacids, the prefix '**hypo**' is used for the acids containing lesser number of oxygen than '**ous**' acids and '**per**' is used for acids containing more oxygen atoms than '**ic**' acids.

Examples:

$HClO$	Hypochlorous acid
$HClO_2$	Chlorous acid
$HClO_3$	Chloric acid
$HClO_4$	Perchloric acid

3. **Bases**: For naming bases, the name of the metal (or positive radical) is specified first and then hydroxide due to the presence of hydroxyl radical.

Examples:

KOH	Potassium hydroxide
$Ca(OH)_2$	Calcium hydroxide
$Fe(OH)_2$	Iron (II) hydroxide
$Fe(OH)_3$	Iron (III) hydroxide
NH_4OH	Ammonium hydroxide

4. **Salts**

Salts of binary acids are written with '**ide**' suffix, i.e., the name of the metallic radical (or positive radical) is written first and it is then followed by the name of the negative radical.

Examples:

$NaCl$	Sodium chloride
K_2S	Potassium sulphide
$MgBr_2$	Magnesium bromide
CaF_2	Calcium fluoride

Salts of oxyacids are derived from their corresponding oxyacids. The salts which come from the oxyacids with 'ous' suffix are given the suffix 'ite' and those from 'ic' suffix are given the suffix 'ate.'

Examples:

$ZnSO_3$	Zinc sulphite
$FeSO_4$	Iron (II) sulphate
$NaNO_2$	Sodium nitrite
$Cu(NO_3)_2$	Copper (II) nitrate
$NaOCl$	Sodium hypochlorite
$Ca(OCl)_2$	Calcium chlorite
$KClO_3$	Potassium chlorate
$KClO_4$	Potassium perchlorate

EXAMPLE

Calculate the total positive charge present on the positive radicals in the following compounds:

(a) Calcium phosphide **(b)** Magnesium nitrate

(c) Zinc sulphide **(d)** Sodium zincate

SOLUTION

(a) Calcium phosphide → $Ca^{+2}P^{-3} \Rightarrow Ca_3P_2$

∴ Total positive charge is 6.

(b) Magnesium nitrate → $Mg^{+2}\ NO_3^{-1}$

∴ Total positive charge is 2.

(c) Zinc sulphide → $Zn^{+2}S^{-2} \Rightarrow ZnS$

∴ Total positive charge is 2.

(d) Sodium zincate → $Na^{+}\ ZnO_2^{-2} \Rightarrow Na_2ZnO_2$

∴ Total positive charge is 2.

EXAMPLE

An oxyacid contains three hydrogen atoms one phosphorus atom and four oxygen atoms.

(a) Name the acid.

(b) Name the different salts that can be formed by the acid on reaction with sodium hydroxide.

(c) Calculate the molecular masses of the above salts.

SOLUTION

(a) The acid is phosphoric acid (H_3PO_4)

(b) NaH_2PO_4 → Sodium dihydrogen phosphate

Na_2HPO_4 → Sodium biphosphate

Na_3PO_4 → Sodium phosphate

(c) Molecular mass of $NaH_2PO_4 = 23 + 2 + 31 + 64 = 120$

Molecular mass of $Na_2HPO_4 = 46 + 1 + 31 + 64 = 142$

Molecular mass of $Na_3PO_4 = 69 + 31 + 64 = 164$

EXAMPLE

The valency of a metal 'M' is 2 and its atomic weight is 24. Calculate the molecular masses of its

(a) sulphite (b) chloride (c) chlorate

SOLUTION

Valency of metal M is 2 and atomic mass is 24

(a) Formula of sulphite of metal is $MSO_3 \Rightarrow$ Molecular mass $= 24 + 32 + 48 = 104$

(b) Formula of metal chloride is $MCl_2 \Rightarrow$ Molecular mass $= 24 + (2 \times 35.5) = 95$

(c) Formula of metal chlorate is $M(ClO_3)_2 \Rightarrow$ Molecular mass $= 24 + 2\ (35.5 + 48) = 191$

EXAMPLE

(a) In an acid-base neutralisation reaction, the salt produced contains one metal atom (M), two nitrogen atoms and four oxygen atoms. Give the formulae of the acid and the base.

(b) A molecule of a binary salt contains two metal atoms and one sulphur atom. Determine the number of metal atoms present in one molecule of the binary salt formed by that metal and nitrogen? Give reasons in support of your answer.

SOLUTION

(a) The salt produced from the acid-base neutralisation reaction is $M(NO_2)_2$

Thus, the valency of metal is 2 as valency of NO^-_2 radical is 1.

The acid used for the formation of this salt is HNO_2 and the base is $M(OH)_2$.

$M(OH)_2 + 2HNO_2 \longrightarrow M(NO_2)_2 + 2H_2O$

(b) A molecule of a binary salt contains two metal atoms and one sulphur atom. Hence, the formula of the salt is M_2S and valency of the metal is 1. Valency of nitride is 3. According to criss-cross method, the formula of binary salt containing metal and nitrogen is M_3N.

Chemical Equation

By using various symbols and formulae, it is possible to present a chemical change by means of a chemical equation.

The substances (elements, compounds or both) which take part in the chemical change are called **reactants**.

The new substances (elements, compounds or both) which are formed from the reactants during the reaction are called **products**.

The reactants are written on the left-hand side and the products on the right-hand side of the arrow.

Examples:

$$NaOH + H_2SO_4 \longrightarrow Na_2SO_4 + 2H_2O$$

$$KClO_3 \longrightarrow KCl + O_2$$

All the chemical reactions are bound by certain laws, which are called **laws of chemical combination**.

Laws of Chemical Combination

1. **Law of conservation of mass:** The law states that mass can neither be created nor destroyed. This law is found applicable to all chemical reactions. This means that during a chemical reaction no change in the mass of the substances takes place. The total mass of the reactants is always equal to the total mass of the products.

   Example:

$$Na_2SO_3 + CuCl_2 \longrightarrow 2NaCl + CuSO_3$$

   Mol. wt of Na_2SO_3 = 126 g Mol. wt of NaCl = 58.5 g
   Mol. wt of $CuCl_2$ = 134.5 g Mol. wt of $CuSO_3$ = 143.5 g
   Total mass of reactants = 260.5 g
   Total mass of products = 117 + 143.5 = 260.5 g

2. **Law of definite proportions:** When two or more elements combine to form a compound, they combine in a fixed ratio of their weights irrespective of the method of preparation.

Example:

Carbon dioxide can be obtained by three processes as listed hereunder:

(a) By the decomposition of metallic carbonates.

(b) By burning carbon.

(c) By the reaction of metallic carbonates with acids.

When the three samples of CO_2 produced by the three different methods are analysed, the ratio by weight of carbon and oxygen has been found to be the same, i.e., 12 : 32 or 3 : 8.

3. Law of multiple proportions: When two elements combine in different ratios to give more than one type of a product, the ratio of the masses of the element that combines with a fixed weight of the other element always bears a simple integral ratio.

Example: Nitrogen and oxygen combine and form compounds, like, N_2O, NO, NO_2, etc.

N_2O: 28 g of nitrogen combines with 16 g of oxygen
Therefore, 14 g of nitrogen combines with 8 g of oxygen
NO: 14 g of nitrogen combines with 16 g of oxygen
NO_2: 14 g of nitrogen combines with 32 g of oxygen

If we analyse the ratio of oxygen that is combining with fixed mass of nitrogen in all the three compounds, it bears a simple integral ratio, i.e., 1 : 2 : 4.

A quantitative relationship exists between the reactants and products in a chemical reaction. If specific amount of reactants are taken, then definite quantity of products are formed. Hence, it is required to balance all the chemical equations with respect to the number of atoms of various elements involved in the equation.

Balanced Chemical Equation

A balanced chemical equation is one in which the number of atoms of each element of the reactants which are there on the left-hand side of the reaction is equal to that of atoms of each element of the products present on the right-hand side of the reaction.

The number of molecules of the reactants and that of the products is written as coefficients.

Examples:

$$2NaOH + H_2SO_4 \longrightarrow Na_2SO_4 + 2H_2O$$

$$2KClO_3 \longrightarrow 2KCl + 3O_2$$

Balancing of a Chemical Equation (Trial and Error Method)

Initially the number of times (frequency) an element occurs on both sides of the skeleton equation should be counted. An element with the least frequency is balanced first. When two or more elements have the same frequency, the metallic element (if present) is balanced first in preference to the non-metallic element(s).

Example:

Skeleton equation:

$$Fe_2O_3 + C \longrightarrow Fe + CO$$

Process of balancing:

$Fe_2O_3 + C \longrightarrow 2Fe + CO$

$Fe_2O_3 + C \longrightarrow 2Fe + 3CO$

$Fe_2O_3 + 3C \longrightarrow 2Fe + 3CO$

Balanced equation:

$Fe_2O_3 + 3C \longrightarrow 2Fe + 3CO$

Example:

Skeleton equation:

$HNO_3 + S \longrightarrow H_2SO_4 + NO_2 + H_2O$

Process of balancing:

$4HNO_3 + S \longrightarrow H_2SO_4 + NO_2 + H_2O$

$4HNO_3 + S \longrightarrow H_2SO_4 + 4NO_2 + H_2O$

$6HNO_3 + S \longrightarrow H_2SO_4 + 6NO_2 + 2H_2O$

Balanced equation:

$6HNO_3 + S \longrightarrow H_2SO_4 + 6NO_2 + 2H_2O$

Example:

Skeleton equation:

$K_2Cr_2O_7 + HCl \longrightarrow KCl + CrCl_3 + H_2O + Cl_2$

Process of balancing:

$K_2Cr_2O_7 + HCl \longrightarrow 2KCl + 2CrCl_3 + H_2O + Cl_2$

$K_2Cr_2O_7 + 2HCl \longrightarrow 2KCl + 2CrCl_3 + H_2O + Cl_2$

$K_2Cr_2O_7 + 14HCl \longrightarrow 2KCl + 2CrCl_3 + 7H_2O + Cl_2$

Balanced equation:

$K_2Cr_2O_7 + 14HCl \longrightarrow 2KCl + 2CrCl_3 + 7H_2O + 3Cl_2$

Writing a balanced chemical equation does not necessarily imply that the reaction takes place inevitably at all conditions. For every chemical reaction to take place, certain specific conditions are required.

Conditions Required for A Chemical Reaction

1. **Physical contact:** Chemical reaction takes place only when the reactants are brought in contact with each other.

   Example:

   $$CaO + H_2O \longrightarrow Ca(OH)_2$$

   Calcium hydroxide is formed only when calcium oxide comes in contact with water.

2. **Solution:** Some chemical reactions take place only when the reactants are taken in the form of solutions.

Example: There is no reaction between silver nitrate and sodium chloride when they are in solid state. Reaction takes place only when they are dissolved in water.

$$AgNO_3 + NaCl \longrightarrow AgCl + NaNO_3$$

3. Heat: A large number of chemical reactions take place by the absorption of heat. These are called **thermochemical reactions**.

Example:

(a) $2KClO_3 \xrightarrow{\Delta} 2KCl + 3O_2$

(b) $Fe + S \xrightarrow{\Delta} FeS$

On simple mixing of iron fillings and sulphur, no reaction takes place; they combine and form iron sulphide only on heating.

4. Light: There are certain reactions which take place only in the presence of light. These are called **photochemical reactions**.

Example: Photosynthesis

$$6CO_2(g) + 6H_2O(\ell) \xrightarrow{sunlight} C_6H_{12}O_6(s) + 6O_2(g)$$

Photosynthesis does not take place in the absence of light.

5. Electricity: Some reactions take place only by the passage of electric current. These are called **electrochemical reactions**.

Example:

(a) Decomposition of water into hydrogen and oxygen:

$$\xrightarrow{\text{Electric current}} 2H_2 + O_2$$

(b) Decomposition of molten Al_2O_3 into aluminium and oxygen:

$$2Al_2O_3 \longrightarrow 4Al + 3O_2$$

6. Sound: Certain reactions take place by the absorption of sound energy.

Example:

Decomposition of acetylene into carbon and hydrogen:

$$C_2H_2 \xrightarrow{\text{Sound energy}} 2C + H_2$$

7. Pressure: Certain chemical reactions take place only when pressure is applied.

Example:

Formation of ammonia from nitrogen and hydrogen takes place at high pressure:

$$N_2 + 3H_2 \xrightarrow[\text{pressure}]{} 2NH_3$$

8. **Catalyst:** A chemical substance which alters the rate of reaction without undergoing any net change in its chemical composition at the end of the chemical reaction is called **catalyst**.

The rates of some chemical reactions are influenced by the catalysts and such reactions are called **catalytic reactions**.

Positive catalyst

The catalyst which accelerates the rate of a reaction is called **positive catalyst**.

Example: The rate of decomposition of $KClO_3$ is more in the presence of MnO_2:

$$2KClO_3 \xrightarrow{MnO_2} 2KCl + 3O_2$$

Negative catalyst or inhibitor

The catalyst which retards the rate of reaction is called **negative catalyst**.

Example: The rate of decomposition of hydrogen peroxide decreases in the presence of alcohol or ether:

$$2H_2O_2(\ell) \xrightarrow[\text{(or) ether}]{\text{Alcohol}} 2H_2O(\ell) + O_2(g)$$

Since the number of chemical reactions is large, the study of these reactions can be made easier by classifying them. All the chemical reactions are classified into four broad categories depending on the way the product is formed.

EXAMPLE

Two oxides of a metal contain 25.8% and 41.02% of oxygen by weight, respectively. Find the ratio of weights of metal combining with fixed weight of oxygen?

SOLUTION

Assume the weight of each oxide is 100 g.

	Weight of metal	Weight of oxygen
Oxide - I	74.2	25.8
Oxide - II	58.98	41.02

25.8 g of oxygen reacts with 74.2 g of metal.

1 g of oxygen reacts with $= \dfrac{1 \times 74.2}{25.8} = 2.87$ g of metal

41.02 g of oxygen reacts with 58.98 g of metal.

1 g of oxygen reacts with $= \dfrac{1 \times 58.98}{41.02} = 1.437$ g of metal

$\therefore$ The ratio of weight of the metal in the two oxides is 2.87 : 1.437 = 2 : 1 (approx)

EXAMPLE

For each of the following reactions identify the products formed and balance the reaction.

(a) $BaCl_2 + Na_2SO_4 \longrightarrow$ **(b)** $2CuS + 3O_2 \longrightarrow$

(c) $Na + H_2O \longrightarrow$ **(d)** $2KI + Cl_2 \longrightarrow$

SOLUTION

(a) $BaCl_2 + Na_2SO_4 \longrightarrow BaSO_4 + 2NaCl$

(b) $2CuS + 3O_2 \longrightarrow 2CuO + 2\,SO_2$

(c) $2Na + 2H_2O \longrightarrow 2NaOH + H_2$

(d) $2KI + Cl_2 \longrightarrow 2KCl + I_2$

CLASSIFICATION OF CHEMICAL REACTIONS

All chemical reactions can be broadly classified into four types depending upon the nature of the reaction.

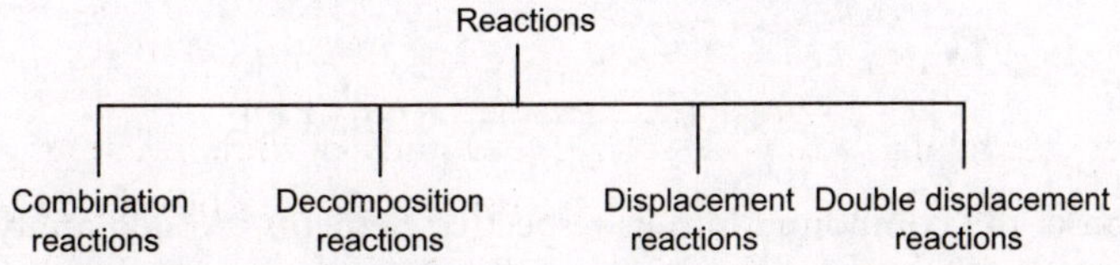

FIGURE 3.2 Classification of reactions based on nature

1. **Combination reaction:** A chemical reaction in which two or more substances combine to form a single new substance is called **combination reaction**.

Representation: $A + B \longrightarrow AB$

Examples:

(a) Element–element combination reaction. The formation of a compound from its constituent elements is called **synthesis**.

$$H_2 + Cl_2 \longrightarrow 2HCl$$

(b) Element–compound combination reaction.

$2CO + O_2 \longrightarrow 2CO_2$

$2NO + O_2 \longrightarrow 2NO_2$

(c) Compound–compound combination reaction.

$CaO + CO_2 \longrightarrow CaCO_3$

2. **Decomposition reaction:** The reaction in which a single compound splits into two or more simpler substances is known as decomposition reaction.

Representation: $AB \longrightarrow A + B$

Examples:

(a) $2Pb(NO_3)_2 \longrightarrow 2PbO + 4NO_2 + O_2$

(b) $2Al_2O_3 \longrightarrow 4Al + 3O_2$

If the decomposition of a substance takes place by the absorption of heat, it is called **thermal decomposition**.

Examples:

(a) $CaCO_3 \xrightarrow{\Delta} CaO + CO_2$

(b) $2HgO \xrightarrow{\Delta} 2Hg + O_2$

If the decomposition of a substance takes place in the presence of light, it is called **photolytic decomposition (photolysis)**.

Example:

$$2HOCl \xrightarrow{\text{Sunlight}} 2HCl + O_2$$

If the decomposition of a substance takes place by the passage of electricity, it is called **electrolytic decomposition (electrolysis)**.

Example:

$$2NaCl \xrightarrow{\text{Electric current}} 2Na + Cl_2$$

Decomposition of the compound into its respective elements is called **analysis**.

3. **Displacement reaction:** In a displacement reaction the more reactive element displaces the less reactive element from its compound.

Representation:

$$AB + C \longrightarrow CB + A$$

$$XY + Z \longrightarrow XZ + Y$$

The ability of an element to displace another element is known by its relative position in the reactivity series.

TABLE 3.4 Metal reactivity series

Potassium	K	(most reactive metal)
Sodium	Na	
Calcium	Ca	
Magnesium	Mg	
Aluminium	Al	
Zinc	Zn	Reactivity decreases
Iron	Fe	
Nickel	Ni	
Tin	Sn	
Lead	Pb	

Hydrogen	H	
Copper	Cu	
Mercury	Hg	
Silver	Ag	
Gold	Au	
Platinum	Pt	↓ (least reactive metal)

The more reactive metal displaces the less reactive metal from its compound.

Example:

$$Fe + CuSO_4 \longrightarrow FeSO_4 + Cu$$

(copper sulphate) (ferrous sulphate)

As iron is more reactive than copper, it displaces copper from copper sulphate solution, thereby forming ferrous sulphate.

Halogen Reactivity Series

(Most reactive halogen)

F_2

Cl_2

Br_2

I_2

↓ Reactivity

(Least reactive halogen)

The more reactive halogen displaces the less reactive halogen from its compound.

Example:

$$2NaBr + Cl_2 \longrightarrow 2NaCl + Br_2$$

Chlorine is more reactive than bromine, hence, it displaces bromine from sodium bromide and a reddish brown bromine gas is formed.

4. **Double decomposition/double displacement reaction:** The chemical reaction in which two reactants (compounds) combine to form two new substances by exchanging their radicals is called **double decomposition**.

   Representation: $AB + CD \longrightarrow AD + CB$

   Examples:

   (a) $2NaNO_3 + CuSO_4 \longrightarrow Na_2SO_4 + Cu(NO_3)_2$

   (b) $NaOH + HCl \longrightarrow NaCl + H_2O$

   (c) $K_2SO_4 + Cu(NO_3)_2 \longrightarrow 2KNO_3 + CuSO_4$

   If the reaction takes place between an acid and a base, it is called **neutralisation reaction**. Salt and water are formed in this reaction.

   Examples:

   (a) $NaOH + HCl \longrightarrow NaCl + H_2O$

   (b) $2NH_4OH + H_2SO_4 \longrightarrow (NH_4)_2SO_4 + 2H_2O$

In a double decomposition reaction, if one of the products gets precipitated, the reaction can be called **precipitation reaction**.

Examples:

(a) $KCl + AgNO_3 \longrightarrow KNO_3 + AgCl\downarrow$

(b) $BaCl_2 + Na_2SO_4 \longrightarrow 2NaCl + BaSO_4\downarrow$

All the chemical reactions that take place fall under any one of the above categories.

In addition to the above categories, some chemical reactions are categorised as redox reactions as they involve oxidation and reduction reactions.

Oxidation

It is defined as addition of oxygen or electronegative element or removal of hydrogen or electropositive element from a compound.

Reduction

It is defined as the addition of hydrogen or electropositive element or removal of oxygen or electronegative element from a compound.

Oxidation and reduction are simultaneous processes taking place in a reaction. That is why those reactions are called **redox reactions**. In a redox reaction, one substance undergoes oxidation and the other substance undergoes reduction.

The substance which undergoes oxidation by itself is called **reducing agent** and the substance which undergoes reduction by itself is called an **oxidising agent**.

Example:

$$H_2S + Cl_2 \longrightarrow 2HCl + S$$

H_2S loses hydrogen, and hence, is said to undergo oxidation. Chlorine adds hydrogen, and hence, is said to undergo reduction. Therefore, H_2S is called **reducing agent** and chlorine an oxidising agent.

Example:

$$2HgCl_2 + SnCl_2 \longrightarrow Hg_2Cl_2 + SnCl_4$$

A more electropositive element, mercury, is added to $HgCl_2$. It is, therefore, said to be reduced. A more electronegative element (chlorine) is added to $SnCl_2$. It is, therefore, said to be oxidised. $HgCl_2$ acts as the oxidising agent and $SnCl_2$ acts as the reducing agent.

Chemical reactions can also be classified on the basis of energy changes associated with the reactions.

EXOTHERMIC REACTIONS

A chemical reaction associated with evolution of heat energy is called an **exothermic reaction**.

Representation

Reactants $\longrightarrow$ Products + Q kcal

(or)

Reactants – Q kcal $\longrightarrow$ Products

Q = heat energy released

Example:

$$C + O \longrightarrow CO_2 + 94 \text{ kcal}$$
$$C + O_2 - 94 \text{ kcal} \longrightarrow CO_2$$

For the formation of CO_2 from carbon and oxygen, the bonds between oxygen atoms in oxygen molecules should be broken. For the breaking of this bond, some amount of energy is absorbed. At the same time, some amount of energy is released during the formation of new bonds between carbon and oxygen.

If energy released is more than the energy required during the reaction, the difference in energy is released as heat energy.

ENDOTHERMIC REACTIONS

A chemical reaction which proceeds with the absorption of heat energy is called an **endothermic reaction.**

Representation

Reactants + Q kcal $\longrightarrow$ Products

or

Reactants $\longrightarrow$ Products – Q kcal

Q = heat energy absorbed

Example:

$$N_2 + O_2 \longrightarrow 2NO - 44 \text{ kcal}$$
$$N_2 + O_2 + 44 \text{ kcal} \longrightarrow 2NO$$
$$C + 2S + 22 \text{ kcal} \longrightarrow CS_2$$

For the formation of nitric oxide from nitrogen and oxygen, some amount of energy is required to break the bonds between nitrogen and oxygen atoms present in the respective molecules. Some amount of energy is released during the formation of bonds between nitrogen and oxygen. In this case, the energy absorbed is more than the energy released. Hence, the difference in energy is absorbed as heat energy during the reaction.

EXAMPLE

Nitric acid turns yellow on long standing. Explain.

SOLUTION

On long standing, HNO_3 undergoes photolytic decomposition and gives NO_2 which is a brown coloured gas. Hence, HNO_3 appears yellow.

$$4HNO_3 \xrightarrow{h\nu} 4NO_2 + 2H_2O + O_2$$

EXAMPLE

Silver ware tarnishes on exposure to polluted atmosphere. Give reason.

SOLUTION

Silver ware tarnishes in the polluted atmosphere because of the presence of H_2S gas. Silver reacts with H_2S present in atmosphere to form silver sulphide which is black in colour.

$$4Ag + 2H_2S + O_2 \longrightarrow 2Ag_2S + 2H_2O$$

EXAMPLE

The complete combustion of a hydrocarbon gives CO_2 and H_2O. In the balanced chemical equation, the coefficients of CO_2 and H_2O are 3 and 4, respectively. Find out the formula of the hydrocarbon.

SOLUTION

Hydrocarbons on complete combustion give CO_2 and H_2O. Coefficients of CO_2 and H_2O are 3 and 4, respectively. The hydrocarbon must contain 3 carbon atoms and eight hydrogen atoms as the hydrocarbon is composed of carbon and hydrogen. Thus, the formula of hydrocarbon must be C_3H_8.

$$\text{Balanced equation is } C_3H_8 + 5O_2 \longrightarrow 3CO_2 + 4H_2O$$

EXAMPLE

In the welding of railway tracks, a proper proportion of aluminium powder and iron (III) oxide are made to react with each other at high temperature. Explain the type of reaction involved and also identify the reducing and the oxidising agents.

SOLUTION

At high temperature aluminium reacts with iron (III) oxide.

$$2Al + Fe_2O_3 \longrightarrow Al_2O_3 + 2Fe + \text{Heat}$$

It is a displacement and exothermic reaction.

Al acts as reducing agent as it undergoes oxidation while Fe_2O_3 acts as oxidising agent as it undergoes reduction.

EXAMPLE

Mercury loses its lusture and sticks to the walls of the glass in the presence of ozone. Write the reasons and the possible reaction for this change.

SOLUTION

When ozone is passed through mercury, the mercury loses its lusture and sticks to the glass tube. This is called **tailing of mercury** and is due to the formation of mercurous oxide.

$$2Hg + O_3 \longrightarrow Hg_2O + O_2$$

TEST YOUR CONCEPTS

Very Short Answer Type Questions

1. In the following table some commonly used positive and negative radicals are listed. Use the criss-cross method to obtain the formulae of the compound that is formed using the given radicals. Name the compound, thus, obtained.

S. No.	Positive radicals	Negative radicals	Formulae	Name of the compounds
1.	Na^+	Cl^-		
2.	Na^+	CO_3^{-2}		
3.	Al^{+3}	PO_4^{-3}		
4.	Zn^{+2}	PO_4^{-3}		
5.	Ca^{+2}	NO_3^{-1}		
6.	Al^{+3}	CO_3^{-2}		
7.	K^{+1}	SO_4^{-2}		
8.	NH_4^{+1}	SO_4^{-2}		
9.	Ni^{+2}	S^{-2}		
10.	Al^{+3}	C^{-4}		
11.	Ag^{+2}	Br^{-1}		
12.	Ca^{+2}	F^{-1}		
13.	Li^{+1}	H^{-1}		
14.	Al^{+3}	N^{-3}		
15.	Fe^{+3}	O^{-2}		
16.	Na^+	I^{-1}		
17.	K^{+1}	MnO_4^{-1}		
18.	H^{+1}	ClO_3^{-1}		
19.	Ca^{+2}	HSO_4^{-1}		
20.	H^{+1}	NO_2^{-1}		
21.	H^{+1}	SO_3^{-2}		
22.	Ca^{+2}	P^{-3}		
23.	K^{+1}	OH^{-1}		
24.	H^{+1}	NO_3^{-1}		
25.	H^{+1}	SO_4^{-2}		
26.	H^{+1}	S^{-2}		
27.	Cu^{+1}	S^{-2}		
28.	Cu^{+2}	Cl^{-1}		
29.	Hg^{+2}	Cl^{-1}		
30.	Na^+	PO_3^{-3}		
31.	Ba^{+2}	PO_4^{-3}		
32.	Ca^{+2}	HCO_3^{-1}		
33.	NH_4^{+1}	OH^{-1}		
34.	NH_4^{+1}	HPO_4^{-2}		
35.	K^{+1}	$H_2PO_4^{-1}$		
36.	H^{+1}	Cl^-		
37.	H^{+1}	ClO^{-1}		
38.	H^{+1}	ClO_4^{-1}		
39.	H^{+1}	ClO_2^{-1}		
40.	K^{+1}	CrO_4^{-2}		
41.	K^{+1}	$Cr_2O_4^{-2}$		
42.	Sn^{+4}	S^{-2}		
43.	Cr^{+3}	SO_4^{-2}		
44.	NH_4^{+1}	$Cr_2O_4^{-2}$		
45.	Fe^{+3}	OH^{-1}		
46.	Pb^{+4}	Cl^{-1}		
47.	Mn^{+2}	O^{-2}		
48.	Ba^{+2}	CO_3^{-2}		
49.	Na^+	ZnO_2^{-2}		
50.	Pb^{+2}	NO_3^{-1}		

2. Why is the burning of LPG a chemical change?
3. The formula of ammonium bisulphate is ________.
4. Balance the following chemical equations:
   (i) $As + HNO_3 \longrightarrow NO_2 + H_3AsO_4 + H_2O$
   (ii) $Cl_2 + SO_2 + H_2O \longrightarrow H_2SO_4 + HCl$
   (iii) $Zn + HNO_3 \longrightarrow Zn(NO_3)_2 + NO_2 + H_2O$
   (iv) $NH_3 + Br_2 \longrightarrow N_2 + NH_4Br$

PRACTICE QUESTIONS

(v) $KI + H_2SO_4 + MnO_2 \longrightarrow KHSO_4 + MnSO_4 + H_2O + I_2$

(vi) $C_3H_8 + O_2 \longrightarrow CO_2 + H_2O$

(vii) $CO_2 + H_2O \longrightarrow C_6H_{12}O_6 + O_2$

(viii) $Fe_3O_4 + H_2 \longrightarrow Fe + H_2O$

(ix) $Pb(NO_3)_2 \longrightarrow PbO + NO_2 + O_2$

(x) $Pb_3O_4 \longrightarrow PbO + O_2$

(xi) $CuO + NH_3 \longrightarrow Cu + H_2O + N_2$

(xii) $HNO_3 + C \longrightarrow CO_2 + H_2O + NO_2$

(xiii) $Na_2O_2 + H_2O \longrightarrow NaOH + O_2$

(xiv) $H_2S + FeCl_3 \longrightarrow FeCl_2 + HCl + S$

(xv) $NaOH + Cl_2 \longrightarrow NaCl + NaClO_3 + H_2O$

(xvi) $K_2Cr_2O_7 + HCl \longrightarrow KCl + CrCl_3 + H_2O + Cl_2$

(xvii) $Ca(OH)_2 + NH_4Cl \longrightarrow CaCl_2 + H_2O + NH_3$

(xviii) $FeCl_3 + SO_2 + H_2O \longrightarrow FeCl_2 + HCl + H_2SO_4$

(xix) $NH_3 + O_2 \longrightarrow NO + H_2O$

(xx) $FeS_2 + O_2 \longrightarrow Fe_2O_3 + SO_2$

(xxi) $Ca_3(PO_4)_2 + SiO_2 + C \longrightarrow CaSiO_3 + P_4 + CO$

(xxii) $KMnO_4 + SO_2 + H_2O \longrightarrow K_2SO_4 + MnSO_4 + H_2SO_4$

(xxiii) $Sn + HNO_3 \longrightarrow Sn(NO_3)_2 + H_2O + NH_4NO_3$

(xxiv) $Al_2(SO_4)_3 + NaOH \longrightarrow Na_2SO_4 + NaAlO_2 + H_2O$

(xxv) $Al_4C_3 + H_2O \longrightarrow Al(OH)_3 + CH_4$

(xxvi) $HI + HIO_3 \longrightarrow I_2 + H_2O$

(xxvii) $Ca_3P_2 + H_2O \longrightarrow Ca(OH)_2 + PH_3$

(xxviii) $S + HNO_3 \longrightarrow H_2SO_4 + NO_2 + H_2O$

(xxix) $I_2 + HNO_3 \longrightarrow HIO_3 + NO_2 + H_2O$

(xxx) $Na_2O_2 + KMnO_4 + H_2SO_4 \longrightarrow Na_2SO_4 + MnSO_4 + K_2SO_4 + H_2O + O_2$

5. Plumbous ion is represented as ________.

6. What is the difference between photochemical and thermochemical reactions?

7. The suffix for salts of 'ous' oxyacids is ________.

8. What is an inhibitor? What is the inhibitor used in the preparation of H_2SO_4?

9. In the following table, some compounds are listed. In each case identify the positive and negative radicals present in the compound.

S. No.	Compounds	Positive radicals	Negative radicals
(i)	SiO_2		
(ii)	CuS		
(iii)	H_2O_2		
(iv)	BaO_2		
(v)	MgS		
(vi)	$NaAlO_2$		
(vii)	MnO_2		
(viii)	LiH		
(ix)	$KMnO_4$		
(x)	$CaSiO_3$		
(xi)	CaF_2		
(xii)	$HOCl$		
(xiii)	$Ca(OCl)_2$		
(xvi)	H_2SO_3		
(xv)	KH_2PO_4		
(xvi)	K_2HPO_4		
(xvii)	H_2S		
(xviii)	H_2SO_3		
(xix)	$Mn(ClO_4)_2$		
(xx)	$Ba(OH)_2$		

10. The compound SF6 is named as ________.

11. For each of the following reactions identify the products formed and balance the reaction.

(i) $NaCl + AgNO_3 \longrightarrow$

(ii) $KOH + H_2SO_4 \longrightarrow$

(iii) $H_2CO_3 \xrightarrow{\Delta}$

(iv) $KNO_3 + H_2SO_4 \longrightarrow$

(v) $HgO \xrightarrow{\Delta}$

(vi) $C_4H_{10} + O_2 \longrightarrow$

(vii) $Na_2CO_3 + HCl \longrightarrow$

(viii) $Zn + HCl \longrightarrow$

(ix) $Ca(OH)_2 + H_2CO_3 \longrightarrow$

(x) $AgNO_3 + Cu \longrightarrow$

(xi) $BaCl_2 + Na_2SO_4 \longrightarrow$

(xii) $CuS + O_2 \longrightarrow$

(xiii) $PbSO_4 + Na_2CO_3 \longrightarrow$

(xiv) $Na + H_2O \longrightarrow$

(xv) $KI + Cl_2 \longrightarrow$

(xvi) $CaCO_3 \xrightarrow{\Delta}$

(xvii) $NaBr + Cl_2 \longrightarrow$

(xviii) $NaOH + HCl \longrightarrow$

(xix) $Fe + Cl_2 \longrightarrow$

(xx) $KCl + O_2 \longrightarrow$

12. Why is a physical change reversible?

13. What is the difference between synthesis and analysis?

14. The reaction $Fe + S \longrightarrow FeS$ represents ________.

15. Why is the action of heat on iodine a physical change?

16. What is meant by oxidation and reduction?

17. What is the change that takes place when common salt is dissolved in water?

18. Stibnum is the Latin name of ________.

19. Define an exothermic reaction. Give an example.

20. $Ag + CuSO_4 \longrightarrow Cu + AgSO_4$

Is this reaction possible? Explain.

21. Why do chemical reactions involve loss or gain of energy?

22. What is meant by oxidation and reduction?

23. When Fe^{+2} combines with O^{-2}, the compound obtained is ________.

24. What is a displacement reaction?

25. What is chemical decomposition? Give one example.

26. What are catalytic reactions? Give an example.

27. Define an endothermic reaction. Give one example.

28. $N_2 + 3H_2\ 2NH_3 + X$ kcal/mole, then the formation of NH_3 involves ________ of energy with respect to reactants.

29. The symbols of carbon and cobalt are ________ and ________, respectively.

30. The symbol S stands for ________.

Short Answer Type Questions

31. Sugar, on being treated with H_2SO_4, forms a black residue. If we observe the weights of sugar and the residue, we find a difference in weights. Why?

32. Burning of candle is an example of both physical and chemical changes. Justify your answer.

33. What is a chemical equation? Write the steps involved in writing a chemical equation.

34. Write the differences between reduction and oxidation.

35. To obtain hydrogen and oxygen from water, what are the conditions to be maintained?

What are the different names that can be given to this reaction?

36. Why are the double decomposition reactions also called double displacement reactions?

37. Write the steps in naming a binary compound formed by two non-metallic elements, except hydrogen, with the help of an example.

38. Write the steps in naming a base.

39. $Fe_3O_4 + 4H_2 \longrightarrow 3Fe + 4H_2O$

$2Na + Cl_2 \longrightarrow 2NaCl$. Identify the oxidising and reducing agents in the given reactions.

40. Photolysis comes under which type of chemical reaction? Explain it with an example.

41. Classify the following equations into combination, displacement, decomposition and double displacement.

(i) $NH_4Cl \longrightarrow NH_3 + HCl$

(ii) $2NO + O_2 \longrightarrow 2NO_2$

(iii) $ZnCO_3 \longrightarrow ZnO + CO_2$

(iv) $Ag_2SO_4 + 2FeSO_4 \longrightarrow Ag + Fe_2(SO_4)_3$

(v) $2NH_3 \longrightarrow N_2 + 3H_2$

(vi) $AgNO_3 + HCl \longrightarrow AgCl + NaNO_3$

(vii) $2SO_2 + O_2 \longrightarrow 2SO_3$

42. Write the characteristics of a chemical reaction.

43. Classify the following into physical and chemical changes.

(i) freezing of water
(ii) fermentation of alcohol
(iii) burning of coal
(iv) breaking of glass
(v) glowing of an electric bulb

44. Why do we need to use formulae?

45. Write the steps in naming oxyacids:
(i) with greater number of oxygen atoms and
(ii) with less number of oxygen atoms.

Essay Type Questions

46. Explain the law of definite proportions with an example.

47. Give the differences between oxidation and reduction in terms of oxygen, hydrogen, electropositive element and electronegative element.

48. What is a decomposition reaction? Explain different decomposition reactions with equations.

49. What is a chemical combination reaction? Explain the different types of combination reactions.

50. Explain the law of multiple proportions with an example.

For Answer key, Hints and Explanations, please visit: www.pearsoned.co.in/IITFoundationSeries

CONCEPT APPLICATION

Level 1

Directions for questions from 1 to 7
State whether the following statements are true or false.

1. Formula for potassium biphosphate is $KHPO_4$.

2. The compounds H_2O and D_2O follow law of multiple proportions.

3. A_2X is comprised two divalent negative radicals and one monovalent positive radical.

4. Formation of sodium nitrite and oxygen by thermal decomposition of sodium nitrate involves only a chemical change.

5. The reaction $C + O_2 \longrightarrow CO$, follows the law of conservation of mass.

6. Valency of sulphur in SO_2 is 2.

7. In exothermic reactions, the energy of products is more than the energy of reactants.

Directions for questions from 8 to 14
Fill in the blanks.

8. The valencies of sulphur in hydrogen sulphide and sulphur dioxide are ______ and ______, respectively.

9. When 58 g of $Mg(OH)_2$ reacts with 98 g of H_2SO_4, it gives 36 g of H_2O and ________ of $MgSO_4$.

10. If the molecular weight of a compound $Na_x\ SO_Y$ is 142, then the values of X and Y are, respectively, ________ and ________.

11. In $Sn + HNO_3 \longrightarrow Sn(NO_3)_2 + H_2O + NH_4NO_3$, the valencies of Sn are ______.

12. In binary compounds, the suffix ________ is added to the second element.

13. The symbol of the element ________ is F.

14. The reverse reaction of neutralisation is ________.

Directions for question 15
Match the entries given in Column A with appropriate ones in Column B.

15.

Column A		Column B
A. 2H	( )	a. 9 Nitrogen atoms
B. 3CO	( )	b. 9 Sodium atoms
C. 4 H_2O	( )	c. 5 Hydrated copper sulphate molecules
D. $2H_2$	( )	d. 4 Water molecules
E. 9Na	( )	e. 3 Cobalt atoms
F. $8Cl^{-1}$	( )	f. 2 Hydrogen atoms
G. 9 N	( )	g. 3 Carbon monoxide molecules
H. $9Na^{+1}$	( )	h. 2 Hydrogen molecules
I. 3Co	( )	i. 8 Chloride radicals
J. $5CuSO_4\ 5H_2O$	( )	j. 9 Sodium ions

PRACTICE QUESTIONS

Directions for questions from 16 to 45

For each of the questions, four choices have been provided. Select the correct alternative.

16. Which of the following is not a physical change?

(a) dissolution of oxygen in water

(b) dissolution of carbon dioxide in water

(c) dissolution of alcohol in water

(d) dissolution of salt in water

17. Which of the following double displacement reactions is correct?

(a) AB + CD $\longrightarrow$ AC + BD

(b) AB + CD $\longrightarrow$ AD + BC

(c) AB + CD $\longrightarrow$ CA + BD

(d) AB + CD $\longrightarrow$ AD + CB

18. The formula of the phosphate of an element R is RPO_4, then the formulae of its hydroxide and sulphide, respectively, are ______ and ______.

(a) $R(OH)_3$ and R_3S_2

(b) $R(OH)_2$ and R_2S_3

(c) $R(OH)_2$ and R_3S_2

(d) $R(OH)_3$ and R_2S_3

19. The molecular weight of a compound which contains a total number of five radicals is 160, then it is

(a) Ca_3P_2 (b) Fe_2O_3

(c) Al_2O_3 (d) Mg_3N_2

20. Removal of CO_2 and H_2O from atmospheric air by using KOH and anhydrous $CaCl_2$ is an example of ______ and ______ changes, respectively.

(a) chemical, chemical

(b) physical, physical

(c) chemical, physical

(d) physical, chemical

21. Which of the following reactions is a synthesis reaction?

(a) When steam is passed over red hot coke, a mixture of carbon monoxide and hydrogen is formed.

(b) Sodium reacts with water to form sodium hydroxide and hydrogen.

(c) When the milk of lime (calcium hydroxide) is added to hot sodium carbonate solution, sodium hydroxide is obtained and calcium carbonate separates out as mud.

(d) Stannic chloride is prepared by passing chlorine into molten tin.

22. $Pb(NO_3)_2 + Fe_2(SO_4)_3 \longrightarrow Fe(NO_3)_3 + PbSO_4$

Coefficients of lead sulphate and ferric nitrate in the balanced equation of the above reaction are

(a) 3, 4 (b) 3, 3

(c) 3, 2 (d) 2, 3

23. The names of the salts formed by the reaction of
(i) Ca and HNO_3 and
(ii) Ca and H_2SO_3 are

(a) (i) calcium nitrate (ii) calcium sulphate

(b) (i) calcium nitrite (ii) calcium sulphite

(c) (i) calcium nitrate (ii) calcium sulphite

(d) (i) calcium nitrite (ii) calcium sulphate

24. A, B and C are the elements such that A on reaction with air produces a dazzling white flame, B is used in rubber industry for hardening and C acts as a conductor with rise in temperature. Then A, B and C are

(a) metals

(b) metal, and non-metal, respectively

(c) non-metal, metal and metalloid, respectively

(d) metal, non-metal and metalloid, respectively

25. In the preparation of H_2SO_4 the catalyst and the inhibitor, respectively, are

(a) platinum, molybdenum

(b) iron, arsenic oxide

(c) platinum, arsenic oxide

(d) iron, molybdenum

26. $Fe_2O_3 + 3C \longrightarrow 2Fe + 3CO$, in this reaction

(a) Fe undergoes oxidation and C undergoes reduction

(b) Fe undergoes reduction and C undergoes oxidation

(c) both Fe and C undergo reduction

(d) both Fe and C undergo oxidation

27. Arrange the elements Zn, Sn, Ca and Al in the increasing order of their reactivity for replacing Cu from $CuSO_4$ solution:

(a) Zn > Sn > Ca > Al

(b) Ca > Al > Zn > Sn

(c) Ca > Al > Sn > Zn

(d) Ca > Sn > Zn > Al

28. The valency of sulphate radical is equal to the valency of

(a) phosphate radical
(b) hydrogen phosphate radical
(c) dihydrogen phosphate radical
(d) phosphide radical

29. The ratio of oxygen atoms present in one molecule of cupric nitrite and ferric sulphite is

(a) 4 : 9 (b) 2 : 3
(c) 1 : 2 (d) 1 : 3

30. Which of the following statements is false?

(a) A catalyst is highly specific.
(b) The percentage of yield of products can be influenced by a catalyst.
(c) All catalysts have a large surface area.
(d) Composition of a catalyst changes during the reaction.

31. Which one of the following is the salt of a binary acid?

(a) calcium sulphate
(b) magnesium bromide
(c) zinc phosphate
(d) sodium carbonate

32. Which of the following is a salt of 'ous' acid?

(a) Na_2SO_4 (b) $NaNO_3$+
(c) $NaClO_2$ (d) $NaClO_4$

33. Arrange the following compounds in the order of valency of a positive radical.

(i) $A(H_2PO_4)_2$
(ii) B_2O
(iii) $C_2(SO_4)_3$

(a) (iii) > (i) > (ii)
(b) (iii) > (ii) > (i)
(c) (ii) > (i) > (iii)
(d) (i) > (ii) > (iii)

34. The name of a substance is given to a student. He was asked to write its formula. What is the systematic method to be followed to derive the formula? Arrange the given statements in a proper sequence to obtain the formula.

(1) Symbol of positive ion or radical should be placed to the left-hand side and symbol of negative ion should be placed to the right-hand side.
(2) Place the valency with charge of respective radicals on the top right hand corner of their symbols.
(3) Write the symbols of the respective ions or radicals present in the given compound.
(4) Criss-cross the valency on the lower right hand side of ions/radicals.
(5) A radical consisting of more than one element has to be enclosed within the brackets if the respective number attained in criss-cross is more than one.
(6) No space should be left in between oppositely charged ions while writing the formula.

(a) 3 1 2 4 5 6 (b) 4 3 6 2 5 1
(c) 4 1 3 2 4 6 (d) 5 6 4 2 1 3

35. The different samples of CO_2 were found to contain carbon and oxygen in the same ratio of their mass. This illustrates

(a) law of conservation of mass
(b) law of definite proportions
(c) law of multiple proportions
(d) law of reciprocal proportions

36. When the reaction, $Pb(NO_3)_2 \rightarrow PbO + NO_2 + O_2$ is balanced, the coefficients of $Pb(NO_3)_2$, PbO and NO_2 are ______, ______ and ______, respectively.

(a) 2, 2 and 2 (b) 2, 4 and 4
(c) 4, 2 and 4 (d) 2, 2 and 4

37. The reaction $Hg + S \rightarrow HgS$ represents a ______ as well as a ______ reaction.

(a) combination, synthesis
(b) combination, analysis
(c) decomposition, analysis
(d) decomposition, synthesis

38. The reaction $NaOH + HCl \rightarrow NaCl + H_2O$

(a) follows law of conservation of mass
(b) is a neutralisation reaction
(c) is a precipitation reaction
(d) both (1) and (2)

39. The formation of sulphur trioxide from sulphur dioxide and oxygen is an ______ reaction.

(a) endothermic as well as redox
(b) endothermic as well as precipitation
(c) exothermic as well as redox
(d) exothermic as well as precipitation

40. The valency of nitride ion is same as the valency of ______ ion

PRACTICE QUESTIONS

(a) ferric (b) plumbic
(c) zinc (d) calcium

41. Removal of CO_2 and H_2O from atmospheric air by using KOH and anhydrous $CaCl_2$ is an example of _______ and _______ changes, respectively.
(a) chemical, chemical
(b) physical, physical
(c) chemical, physical
(d) physical, chemical

42. Reaction between barium chloride and aluminium sulphate is an example of
(a) neutralisation reaction
(b) displacement reaction
(c) precipitation reaction
(d) combination reaction

43. Which among the following salts produces maximum number of metal ions per molecule when dissolved in a suitable solvent?
(a) aluminium phosphate, $AlPO_4$
(b) magnesium phosphate, $Mg_3(PO_4)_2$
(c) sodium biphosphate, Na_2HPO_4
(d) aluminium dihydrogen phosphate, $Al(H_2PO_4)$

44. A series of chemical reactions were carried out in a laboratory in the following way. At first zinc granules reacted with H_2SO_4 to form H_2 gas. Then hydrogen gas reacted with chlorine gas under diffused sunlight to form hydrogen chloride gas. Hydrogen chloride gas produced in this process was dissolved in water to form hydrochloric acid. Hydrochloric acid reacted with sodium hydroxide to form sodium chloride and water. Sodium chloride, thus, produced is first melted and then electricity is passed through it. Due to the passage of electricity through sodium chloride, sodium metal and chlorine gas are obtained.

Rahul was asked to arrange the above reactions in the order of combination, decomposition, displacement and double decomposition.

His answer is given below.
(1) formation of H_2 gas
(2) formation of hydrogen chloride gas
(3) formation of sodium and chlorine from sodium chloride
(4) formation of sodium chloride

Which among the following orders given below is correct, according to you?
(a) 3 4 2 1 (b) 2 3 1 4
(c) 1 2 3 4 (d) 2 3 4 1

45. Arrange the following reactions in the given order, i.e., compound–element combination, compound–compound combination and element–element combination.
(1) Coke is burnt in an inadequate supply of air.
(2) The product formed in the reaction (a) is again burnt in the presence of oxygen.
(3) The product formed in the reaction (b) is treated with water.
(a) 1 3 2 (b) 2 3 1
(c) 2 1 3 (d) 3 1 2

Level 2

1. An oxide X of carbon on treatment with oxygen gives Y which turns lime water milky and blue litmus to red. Predict the valencies of carbon in X and Y and what is the composition of milky precipitate formed?

2. One molecule of a binary acid contains two hydrogen atoms and a negative radical X. What will be the formula of the salts when it reacts with bases, like, M(OH), $M(OH)_2$ and $M(OH)_3$? Explain with reasons.

3. The formula of hydrogen phosphate of a metal M is $MHPO_4$.

Give the formula of its
(a) chloride
(b) bicarbonate
(c) sulphite

4. Write the balanced chemical equation for the following:
(i) Potassium bromide on treatment with manganese dioxide and sulphuric acid gives manganese and potassium sulphates, bromine and water.
(ii) In the preparation of phosphate fertilisers, calcium phosphate in phosphate rock is converted into phosphoric acid and calcium sulphate.

(iii) Sodium nitrite is produced by the reaction of the oxides of nitrogen in which nitrogen shows valency 2 and 4 in a solution of sodium carbonate.

5. Nitrogen and oxygen react to produce nitric oxide. What is the weight of oxygen required to convert 4.9 g of nitrogen to nitric oxide?

6. The salt of an oxyacid of metal M contains two sulphur and six oxygen atoms. What will be the formula of the base formed by the metal and why?

7. The molecular weight of a salt of oxyacid of chlorine of a divalent metal which contains more number of oxygen atoms than its corresponding 'ic' acid is 239. What will be the molecular weights of its (i) phosphate, (ii) iodide and (iii) bisulphate?

8. Given below are three chemical equations. Study the equations and identify the elements that show variable valency? Give reasons in support of your answer. ('M' and 'N' stand for different metals.)

(i) $MS + ZnSO_4 \longrightarrow MSO_4 + ZnS$

(ii) $3MCl_2 + N_2(SO_4)_3 \longrightarrow 3MSO_4 + 2NCl_3$

(iii) $NS + H_2SO_4 \longrightarrow NSO_4 + H_2S$

9. Blue-coloured $CuSO_4$ is taken in two test tubes A and B. Zinc granules are added to test tube A and small iron pieces are added to test tube B. Explain the observations in each case by giving reasons.

10. How do you account for the following?

(a) Nitric acid is colourless but on long standing it turns yellow.

(b) Hydrochloric acid can be concentrated by conc. H_2SO_4 but not by phosphorous pentoxide (or) quick lime.

11. In the welding of railway tracks, a proper proportion of aluminium powder and iron (iii) oxide are made to react with each other at high temperature. Explain the type of reaction involved and also identify the reducing and the oxidising agents.

12. The valency of a metal is 2 and its atomic weight is 24. What will be the molecular weight of its

(a) sulphite

(b) chloride

(c) chlorate?

13. While balancing a chemical equation, only the coefficients of the formulae are changed, but the subscripts are not changed. Give reasons.

14. The chemical X is a hydroxide of a divalent metal. On treating this hydroxide with CO_2, a milky white precipitate of Y is formed. The precipitate turns to colourless solution by the excess passage of CO_2. This colourless solution again gives milky white precipitate Y on heating. Identify X and Y and also give necessary equations.

15. A hydrocarbon on complete combustion produces 176 g of carbon dioxide and 90 g of water. What will x the formula of hydrocarbon be? Also give balanced chemical equation of combustion of hydrocarbon.

16. Heating and subsequent cooling of certain substances are given below. Classify them into either physical or chemical change.

(a) lead nitrate

(b) bluish green copper carbonate

(c) yellow coloured lead oxide

(d) White powdered zinc oxide

17. Arrange the following radicals in the increasing order of total number of constituent atoms present in the respective radicals.

(a) hydroxide

(b) nitride

(c) chromate

(d) sulphite

(e) dihydrogen phosphate

18. Two beakers A and B contain water. Glucose is added to beaker A and ammonia gas is passed through beaker B. What types of changes (physical or chemical) take place in the beakers? Justify.

19. Oxide of a metal on treatment with water produces a hissing sound and energy. The product (Y) formed on treatment with hydrochloric acid gives a solid X. Identify the oxide, the product (Y) and X. Also write all the balanced chemical equations and calculate molecular masses of the oxide, the product (Y) and X.

20. A non-metal X forms two oxides, A and B. The ratio of weight of the element X to the weight of oxygen in A and B is 7 : 20 and 7 : 16, respectively. If the molecular mass of the oxide, A is 108, identify A and B.

21. Electrolysis of molten sodium chloride produces sodium and chlorine. Is this reaction a redox reaction? Give reasons in support of your answer.

22. Express the following chemical changes in the form of chemical equations and identify what types of chemical reactions they are.
   (a) A copper coin is placed in a solution of corrosive sublimate, mercuric chloride. The products obtained are cupric chloride and mercury.
   (b) A piece of (a) sulphur and (b) charcoal burns vigorously when dropped in molten potassium nitrate, because potassium nitrate decomposes to form potassium nitrite and oxygen and this oxygen helps to burn charcoal and sulphur giving out carbon dioxide and sulphur dioxide, respectively.
   (c) Aqueous ammonium hydroxide solution is made to react with aqueous copper sulphate solution and a bluish white precipitate of cupric hydroxide and ammonium sulphate are formed.

23. (a) Decomposition reactions are always initiated with the supply of energy. Give appropriate reasons.
   (b) Generally, burning or combustion reactions are exothermic. Justify.

24. In the welding of railway tracks, a proper proportion of aluminium powder and iron (III) oxide are made to react with each other at high temperature. Explain the type of reaction involved and also identify the reducing and the oxidising agents.

Level 3

1. What is the role of ultraviolet rays in the purification of water in modern water purifiers?
2. Under which condition does Bunsen burner produce a luminous flame and a non-luminous flame? Give reasons in support of your answer.
3. Anhydride of an acid X contains 2 phosphorous atoms and 5 oxygen atoms. If this acid X is made to react with bases, like, sodium hydroxide, calcium hydroxide and aluminium hydroxide, what will be the formulae of the corresponding normal salts formed?
4. A compound X of silver on treatment with barium chloride gives the respective products Y and Z. X on treatment with sodium hydroxide gives A and B where A can also be obtained when silver is attacked by ozone and B is the salt of an oxyacid of nitrogen which ends with the suffix 'ate.' Identify and give the chemical formulae of the substances X, Y, Z, A and B.
5. The salt of hypohalous acid is prepared from the respective components, namely, halogen and the corresponding metallic hydroxide. The metal is the one which possesses the number of electrons in the ratio of 1 : 4 : 4 : 1 which corresponds to, namely, K, L, M and N shells, respectively, and the halogen is a greenish-yellow colour gas which can displace bromine from magnesium bromide. Identify the salt and the respective components.
6. The molecular masses of sulphate and hydroxide of a metal M are 142 and 40, respectively. Calculate atomic mass and valency of the metal.
7. What are the changes observed when moist sugar is treated with anhydrous calcium chloride and concentrated H_2SO_4, respectively?
8. Identify the type of chemical change that silver chloride undergoes in photogrey lenses.
9. Blue-coloured gas X having a characteristic fishy odour, can restore the colour of lead paintings. This gas can also be used for sterilizing water. Identify the gas X. Mention the type of reaction(s) involved.
10. Fluorine is very reactive and attacks all metals but still a copper vessel is used in the preparation of fluorine gas. Why?

CONCEPT APPLICATION

Level 1

True or false

1. False 2. True 3. False 4. False 5. False
6. False 7. False

Fill in the blanks

8. 2, 4 9. 120 g 10. 2, 4
11. 0 and 2 12. ide 13. fluorine
14. hydrolysis

Match the following

15. A →f D →h G →a J →c
B →g E →b H →j
C →d F →i I →e

Multiple choice questions

16. b 17. c 18. c
19. b 20. c 21. c
22. c 23. c 24. c
25. c 26. b 27. b
28. b 29. a 30. b

31. Magnesium bromide is a salt formed from magnesium hydroxide ($Mg[OH]_2$) and hydrobromic acid (HBr).
Hydrogen bromide is a binary acid. Hence, magnesium bromide is a salt of binary acid.

32. $NaClO_2$ is the sodium salt of chlorous acid ($HClO_2$)

33. (i) $A[H_2PO_4]_2$ A^{+2}
(ii) B_2O B+1
(iii) $C_2(SO_4)_3$ C+3
iii > i > ii

34. (i) Write the symbols of the respective ions or radicals present in the given compound.
(ii) Symbol of positive ion or radical should be placed to the left-hand side and symbol of negative ion should be placed to the right-hand side.
(iii) Place the valency with charge of respective radicals on the top right hand corner of their symbols.
(iv) Criss-cross the valency on the lower right hand side of ions/radicals.
(v) A radical consisting of more than one element has to be enclosed within the brackets if the respective number attained in criss-cross is more than one.
(vi) No space should be left between oppositely charged ions while writing the formula.

35. Law of definite proportions states that when two or more elements combine to form a compound, they combine in a fixed ratio of their weights irrespective of the method of preparation.

36. $2Pb(NO_3)_2 \rightarrow 2PbO + 4NO_2 + O_2$

37. It is a combination as well as a synthesis reaction. Element–element combination reaction is called **synthesis reaction**.

38. $NaOH + HCl \rightarrow NaCl + H_2O$

It is a neutralisation reaction because it involves the formation of neutral substances, i.e., salt and water. It follows law of conservation of mass as it is balanced.

39. $2SO_2 + O_2 \rightarrow 2SO_3$ + heat

It is an exothermic as well as a redox reaction. Since oxidation and reduction takes place simultaneously, it is a redox reaction.

40. Nitride: N^{3-}

Ferric: Fe^{3+}

However, others are Pb^{+4}, Zn^{+2} and Ca^{+2}

41. By passing atmospheric air through KOH it will react with CO_2 and forms K_2CO_3 and H_2O which is an acid–base or neutralisation reaction. It is an example of a chemical change. $CaCl_2$ will absorb the water vapour from the atmospheric air. So, it is an example of a physical change.

42. $3BaCl_2 + Al_2(SO_4)_3 \rightarrow 3BaSO_4 + 2AlCl_3$

The above reaction is an example of precipitation reaction because in this case we will get $BaSO_4$ as a precipitate.

43. Formulae of compounds are

(a) $AlPO_4$

(b) $Mg_3(PO_4)_2$

(c) Na_2HPO_4

(d) $Al(H_2PO_4)_3$

$Mg_3(PO_4)_2$ will produce maximum number of metal ions by dissolving in a suitable solvent.

44. $Zn + H_2SO_4 \rightarrow ZnSO_4 + H_2$, displacement reaction

$H_2 + Cl_2 \rightarrow 2HCl$ is a combination reaction.

$HCl + NaOH \rightarrow NaCl + H_2O$ is a double displacement reaction.

$2NaCl \rightarrow 2Na + Cl_2$ decomposition reaction

Hence, the order is (b), (c), (a) and (d),

(i) formation of hydrogen chloride gas

(ii) formation of sodium and chlorine from sodium chloride

(iii) formation of H_2 gas

(iv) formation of sodium chloride

45. $2C$ (coke) + $O_{2\,(inadequate)} \rightarrow 2CO$ is element–element combination

$2CO + O_2 \rightarrow 2CO_2$ is compound–element combination

$CO_2 + H_2O \rightarrow H_2CO_3$ is compound–compound combination

(i) The product formed in reaction (a) is again burnt in the presence of oxygen.

(ii) The product formed in reaction (b) is treated with water.

(iii) Coke is burnt in an inadequate supply of air.

Level 2

1. (i) identification of Y from the given data
(ii) identification of X from Y
(iii) predicting the valencies of carbon in X and Y
(iv) reaction between Y and lime water
(v) composition of the above product

2. (i) formula of the binary acid
(ii) valency of X
(iii) valency of M in each case
(iv) derivation of the formulae of salts produced

3. (i) valency of M
(ii) identification of the valency of metal M
(iii) derivation of the formula of chloride, bicarbonate and sulphite from its valency

4. (i) reactants on left-hand side and products on right-hand side
(ii) balancing the equations by keeping appropriate coefficients on either side of the reaction.

5. (i) law of definite proportions
(ii) determination of the weight of nitrogen and oxygen which combine to form nitric oxide
(iii) calculation of the weight of oxygen from the weight of nitrogen given
(iv) 5.6 g

6. (i) negative radical in an oxyacid
(ii) Identification of the types of negative radicals formed from sulphur and oxygen
(iii) derivation of the formula of the salt
(iv) derivation of the formula of the base formed by the metal

7. (i) identification of negative radical of the given oxyacid
(ii) identification of salt of an oxyacid from the given molecular weight
(iii) calculation of atomic weight of metal and identification of metal
(iv) Writing formulae of the divalent metal with corresponding negative radicals
(v) calculation of molecular weights of the above salts
(vi) 58

8. (i) Calculate valency of M and N (metals) present in the reactants and products
(ii) valencies of M and N in their respective equations
(iii) identification of the element with variable valency

9. (i) reactivity series of metals
(ii) reactivity of metals according to metal reactivity series
(iii) reactions taking place
(iv) change in property of the solution due to the reaction

10. (i) changes that take place in nitric acid on long standing
(ii) effect of the product on nitric acid solution
(iii) reactivity of HCl towards concentrated H_2SO_4, P_2O_5 and quick lime

11. (i) Give the formula of iron (III) oxide.
(ii) reaction between Al and iron (III) oxide
(iii) Based on the above chemical reaction, predict the type of reaction.
(iv) Identification of oxidising and reducing agents.

12. (i) formulae of salts based on valency of metal
(ii) derivation of formulae of the compounds based on the valency of the metal
(iii) calculation of its corresponding molecular weight

13. significance of coefficient and subscripts associated with the formula

14. formula of the white precipitate

15. (i) general balanced chemical equation for combustion of hydrocarbon
(ii) calculation of the coefficients of carbon dioxide and water using the formula
(iii) coefficient of

$$CO_2 = \frac{\text{Amount of } H_2O \text{ produced}}{\text{Molecular weight}}$$

(iv) Coefficient of

$$H_2O = \frac{\text{Amount of } H_2O \text{ produced}}{\text{Molecular weight}}$$

(v) chemical formula of hydrocarbon from the coefficients of carbon dioxide and water

16. Physical changes are heating of yellow coloured lead oxide and white powdered zinc oxide. Chemical changes are heating of lead nitrate and bluish green copper carbonate.

17.

	Name of the radicals	Formulae	No. of constituents
a.	Nitride	N^{-3}	1
b.	Hydroxide	$\bar{OH}$	2
d.	Sulphite	SO_3^{-2}	4
c.	Chromate	CrO_4^{-2}	5
e.	Dihydrogen phosphate	$H_2PO_4^{-1}$	7

18. When glucose is added to beaker A containing water, dissolution takes place. It is a physical change. When ammonia gas is passed through beaker B containing water, formation of NH_4OH takes place. This is a chemical change.

19. Calcium oxide on treatment with water produces hissing sound and energy.

$CaO + H_2O \rightarrow Ca(OH)2$
Product (Y)
$Ca(OH)_2 + 2HCl \rightarrow CaCl_2 + 2H_2O$
(X)
Molecular mass of CaO = 40 + 16 = 56
Molecular mass of $Ca(OH)_2$ = 40 + 2(17) = 74
Molecular mass of $CaCl_2$ = 40 + 2(35.5) = 111

20. In 108 g of A, $\frac{7}{27}\times 108 = 28\,g$ of A is present.

Since the valency of oxygen is 2, we can consider the formula of A as $X_2\,O_a$.

$\therefore\ a = \frac{108-28}{16} = 5$ and the formula of A is X_2O_5.

Atomic weight of X = 28/2 = 14

∴ Element X is nitrogen, and A is N_2O_5.

Let the formula of B is N_2O_b Since the ratio of N and O in B is 7 : 16, the number of oxygen atoms present in B is 4 [∴ 28 g of nitrogen combines with 64 g of oxygen].

∴ Formula of B is N_2O_4 (or) NO_2

21. During electrolysis of molten sodium chloride, sodium is deposited at cathode and chlorine is liberated at anode. Since removal of more electronegative element from NaCl gives sodium, the process is called **reduction**. Since removal of more electropositive element from NaCl gives chlorine, the process is called **oxidation**. Therefore, the electrolysis of molten sodium chloride is called **redox reaction.**

22. (a) $Cu + HgCl_2 \rightarrow CuCl_2 + Hg$

Copper displaces mercury from mercuric chloride and forms cupric chloride and mercury. This is a displacement reaction.

(b) $2KNO_3 \rightarrow 2KNO_2 + O_2 \rightarrow$ (1)

$S + O_2 \rightarrow SO_2 \rightarrow$ (2)

$C + O_2 \rightarrow CO_2 \rightarrow$ (3)

The first reaction represents the decomposition of potassium nitrate to form potassium nitrite and oxygen. Oxygen liberated helps burn sulphur and charcoal to give sulphuric dioxide and carbon dioxide as given in reactions (2) and (3). Reaction (1) is a decomposition reaction, whereas reactions (2) and (3) are combination reactions.

(c) $2NH_4OH + CuSO_4 \rightarrow Cu(OH)_2 \downarrow + (NH_4)_2SO_4$

This is a double displacement reaction.

23. (a) Since the atoms are bonded within the molecule by certain forces of attraction, energy is required to dissociate the molecules. In a decomposition reaction, breaking of bond takes place. To break bonds, energy is required. Hence, the energy needs to be supplied to initiate most of the decomposition reactions.

(b) Burning or combustion is a combination of a substance with oxygen and new bonds are formed with oxygen. As formation of bonds involves release of energy, combustions are generally exothermic.

24. At high temperature, aluminium reacts with iron (III) oxide.

$$2Al + Fe_2O_3 \longrightarrow Al_2O_3 + 2Fe + Heat$$

It is a displacement as well as an exothermic reaction. Al acts as a reducing agent as it undergoes oxidation while Fe_2O_3 acts as an oxidising agent as it undergoes reduction.

Level 3

1. (i) oxygen remains in the dissolved state in water
(ii) conversion of oxygen to another allotropic form
(iii) condition required for the conversion
(iv) role of that allotropic form in the purification of water

2. (i) difference between luminous and non-luminous flame
(ii) reactions taking place in luminous and non-luminous flame.
(iii) conditions required for these reactions

3. (i) identification of X from the respective anhydride
(ii) predicting the formulae of the bases based on nomenclature
(iii) Nature of reaction between acid X and respective bases
(iv) Predicting the valency of negative radical in X
(v) predicting the valency of sodium, calcium and aluminium, respectively
(vi) applying criss-cross method to determine formulae of the corresponding salts

4. (i) identification of A from the product formed by the reaction of silver with ozone
(ii) identification of X from B
(iii) identification of Y and Z from X

5. (i) identification of the metal from the given ratio
(ii) identification of halogen based on colour
(iii) identification of chemical formula of salt of oxyacid

6. Let the valency of metal be x and atomic weight be m.

$\therefore$ Metal sulphate is $M^{+x}SO_4^{-2} \Rightarrow M_2(SO_4)_x$

$\therefore$ Metal hydroxide is $M^{+x}\bar{OH}_4^{-2} \Rightarrow M(OH)_x$

$\therefore$ Molecular weight of metal sulphate is

$$2m + 96x = 142 \rightarrow \quad (1)$$

Molecular weight of metal hydroxide is $m + 17x = 40$

$$\Rightarrow 2m + 34x = 80 \rightarrow \quad (2)$$

From (1) and (2)

$$\Rightarrow \quad 2m + 96x = 142$$

$$\Rightarrow \quad 2m + 34x = 80$$

$$(-) \quad (-) \quad (-)$$

$$62x = 62$$

$$\Rightarrow x = 1$$

$\therefore$ From (1) $\Rightarrow 2m + 96(1) = 142$

$$\Rightarrow 2m = 142 - 96 = 46 \Rightarrow m = 23$$

$\therefore$ Valency and atomic weight of the metal are 1 and 23, respectively.

7. When moist sugar is treated with anhydrous $CaCl_2$, it removes the moisture from the moist sugar due to its deliquescent nature. The chemical composition of sugar does not change in this process. Hence, it is a physical change. When sugar reacts with concentrated H_2SO_4, it is converted to black residue called **sugar charcoal**. Concentrated H_2SO_4, due to its dehydrating nature, removes the hydrogen and oxygen present in the compound as water and the chemical composition of sugar changes. Hence, it is a chemical change.

8. Silver chloride present in the photogrey lenses undergoes photolysis and gives silver and chlorine.

$$2AgCl \xrightarrow{\text{Sunlight}} 2Ag + Cl_2$$

It is a decomposition reaction as well as a redox reaction as silver loses an electronegative element, i.e., chlorine. Silver undergoes reduction while chlorine undergoes oxidation.

9. Since X is a gas which is used in sterilizing water and has a characteristic fishy odour, it is O_3. O_3 combines with black lead sulphide to give lead sulphate. It is a redox reaction.

$$PbS + 4O_3 \rightarrow PbSO_4 + 4O_2$$

10. Fluorine attacks all metals including copper. In the preparation of fluorine gas electrolysis is carried out in the copper vessel. Copper reacts with fluorine to form stable copper fluoride. This copper fluoride so formed acts as a protective layer against further corrosion of copper.

Chapter

4

Air and Oxygen

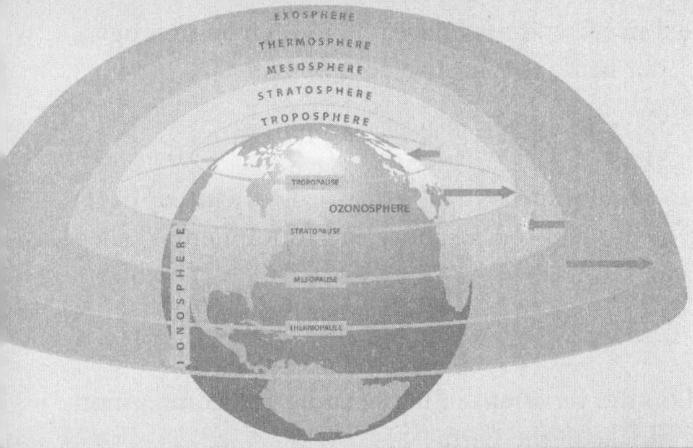

Remember

Before beginning this chapter, you should be able to:

- name different layers of atmosphere.
- understand the importance of common gases in nature and their uses.

Key Ideas

After completing this chapter, you should be able to:

- study about the composition and characteristics of air.
- explain different layers of atmosphere and their importance.
- learn different methods of preparation and properties of oxygen.
- Understand the importance of oxygen in nature and its uses.
- study the causes, effects and different measures to curb air pollution.

INTRODUCTION

Nature provides us with all the basic necessities of life, like, air, water, food, fire, etc. Among all these, air plays the most important role in several processes taking place in nature. Since all processes in nature are associated with air, we cannot imagine life without air. Though it is invisible, the presence of air is felt in every activity in nature.

The study of air and its importance dates back to the 15th century until when air was considered to be an element. Later, in 1674, Mayoco for the first time predicted the presence of two components in air, namely, the active component and the inactive component. Since then, air is no more considered to be an element. In the later years, Lavoisier also found the ratio of the active and inactive components of air to be 1 : 4 by volume.

The later studies and experiments have revealed major components to be oxygen and nitrogen, the former being the active component and the latter being the inactive component.

ATMOSPHERE

The layer of air that surrounds the Earth up to an altitude of 300 km is called **atmosphere**. Above this altitude, the region is absolutely free of air. This region above the atmosphere is called **space**.

Layers of Atmosphere

The atmosphere is divided into four layers based on the variations in temperature and composition of different regions at different altitudes from the surface of the Earth.

1. **Troposphere**: The layer of atmosphere which is in contact with the Earth's surface is called troposphere. The range of temperature in this layer is close to that of the Earth since it is just above the Earth's surface. In this layer, the temperature decreases with increase in altitude up to about –50°C. It lies between 0 km and 10 km above the Earth's surface and contains the maximum percentage of the total mass of the atmosphere.
2. **Stratosphere**: The layer of atmosphere above the troposphere is called stratosphere. In this layer, temperature range does not alter up to a height of about 25 km. Above this, the temperature gradually decreases up to a range of 0°C–10°C. It lies between 10 km and 50 km above the surface of the Earth.
3. **Mesosphere**: The layer succeeding the stratosphere is called mesosphere. In this layer, the range of temperature is lower than that of the layers below it. It lies between 50 km and 80 km above the surface of the Earth.
4. **Thermosphere**: This is the topmost layer of atmosphere and it is called so due to the very high temperatures prevailing there. The basic reason for this is that the atmosphere in this layer absorbs the intense solar radiation.

The composition of air is not uniform throughout the atmosphere. It varies from one layer to the other layer.

Significance of Atmosphere

The atmosphere plays an important role in all natural phenomena taking place. These are:

1. Formation of clouds
2. Occurrence of rain
3. Formation of snow
4. Preventing the harmful radiations reaching the earth
5. Formation of winds

Since the atmosphere is associated with all these natural processes, the study of atmosphere helps in making weather forecasts regarding cyclones, floods and droughts. They further help in taking proper steps to protect the life from these natural disasters.

Atmospheric Pressure

The atmosphere in any layer is composed of air, which exerts a downward pressure, and this downward pressure exerted by air due to its weight on the surroundings is called **atmospheric pressure**.

Since pressure is defined as the force exerted per unit area, it is expressed in Newtons/metre^2 which is called **pascal**. Hence, the SI unit of pressure is pascal (Pa) or kilopascal.

Measurement of the Atmospheric Pressure

Since the composition and also the density of air vary with the altitude, the pressure exerted by air also varies. The atmospheric pressure decreases with an increase in the altitude. It is due to this reason that the atmospheric pressure is measured at sea level where it is maximum.

The instrument used to measure the atmospheric pressure is called **barometer**. Two types of barometers are in use for this purpose:

1. mercury barometer and
2. aneroid barometer

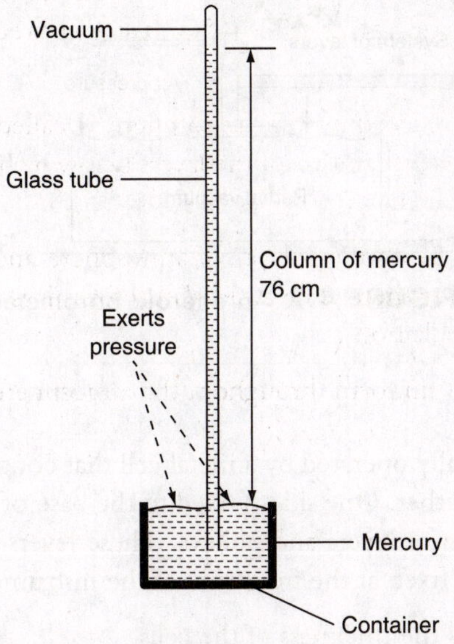

FIGURE 4.1 A mercury barometer

1. **Mercury barometer:** This is the most common type of barometer used.

   Principle: Mercury is a liquid which has high density (13.6 g/cc). Hence, it can rise as a short column when the pressure exactly balances the atmospheric pressure. Moreover, mercury does not stick to the walls of the glass tube due to weak adhesive forces between them.

Construction and Working

A graduated glass tube of about 840 mm length which is closed at one end and open at the other end is taken. This tube is filled completely with mercury and then inverted into a trough full of mercury. Depending on the external pressure, some mercury from glass tube comes out and stands at a certain height. This height is measured. Above this column, there is almost vacuum and it is called **torricellian vacuum**.

At normal atmospheric pressure at sea level, the height of the mercury column falls to about 760 mm of Hg. Hence, this is taken as the standard value of atmospheric pressure.

1 atm = 760 mm of Hg = 760 torr = 101.3 kilopascals

The pressure can be calculated by substituting the height of the mercury column in the formula $P = hdg$, where '*h*' is the height of the mercury column, '*d*' is the density of the mercury and '*g*' is the acceleration due to gravity.

2. **Aneroid barometer:** This barometer does not contain any liquid. It is convenient to use because it is very light in weight and portable.

   Principle: Balancing the atmospheric pressure by the elasticity of the metal.

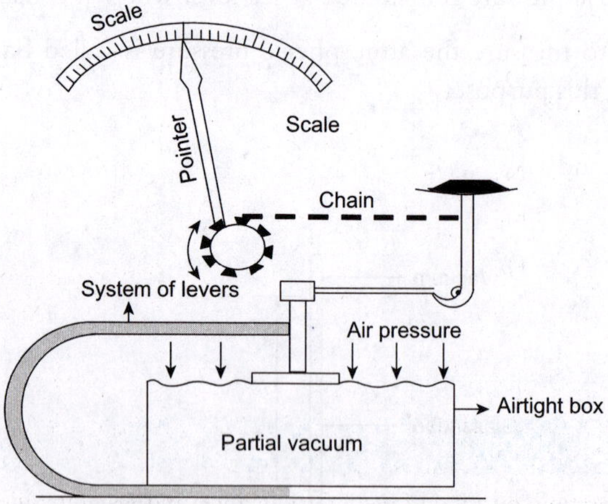

FIGURE 4.2 An aneroid barometer

Construction and Working

The aneroid barometer is basically operated by a metal cell that contains very small amount of air or a series of such cells joined together. One side is fixed to the base of the instrument while the other side is connected with a system of levers and pulleys. These levers and pulleys are connected to a pointer that moves over a scale fixed at the front side of the instrument.

Any change in pressure alters the thickness of the cells.

Characteristics of Air as a Mixture

1. Variable composition of air in different places on earth,
2. No heat change is involved in the mixing up of gases in air,
3. No definite boiling point for liquid air,
4. Separation of air into various components can be done by physical methods,
5. The properties of different gases are retained in the air,
6. Air has no definite chemical formula
7. Air does not exhibit definite chemical properties of its own.

Components of Air

Oxygen and nitrogen are the major components of air. Apart from these two, some other gases, like, carbon dioxide, water vapour and inert gases are present in the atmosphere.

The various components of air including inert gases can be separated by the fractional distillation of liquid air. This is based on the principle that different components of air boil at different temperatures.

TABLE 4.1 Boiling points of components of air

Gases	Boiling points
CO_2	–78.5°C
Xe	–108°C
Kr	–153°C
O_2	–183°C
Ar	–186°C
N_2	–196°C
Ne	–246°C
He	–269°C

Functions of Different Components of Air

Components	Functions
Oxygen	Respiration, burning of fuels, fermentation and decomposition of organic matter
Nitrogen	Growth of plants and animals. Slows down the activity of oxygen in the atmosphere
CO_2	Photosynthesis and greenhouse effect
H_2O	Moisture for growth of plants and animals. Prevention of excess evaporation from living cells
Helium	Weather balloons and for diluting oxygen carried by scuba divers
Neon	Advertisement sign boards and lighting in aerodromes
Argon	Electric bulbs

Composition of Air

Though the composition of air varies from place to place and time to time, the average composition by weight and by volume are determined.

Components	Percentage by weight	Percentage by volume
Oxygen	23.1	21
Nitrogen	75.5	78
CO_2	0.03	0.03 to 0.04
Water vapour	Variable	Variable (up to a maximum of 4%)
Inert gases	1	0.95%

Apart from these, other gases and dust particles are also present in air in trace amounts.

EXAMPLE

Why does atmospheric pressure decrease with an increase in altitude?

SOLUTION

The atmospheric pressure decreases with increase in altitude. This is due to the decrease in density of air with increase in altitude. The percentage of heavier components of air is more near the surface of earth due to higher gravitational force of attraction.

EXAMPLE

Atmospheric air contains a large amount of oxygen and traces of hydrogen. Why do they not react and cause explosion?

SOLUTION

To react and cause an explosion, the percentage of hydrogen in atmosphere should be more. Moreover high energy is required to initiate the reaction between hydrogen and oxygen. Hence, the trace amount of hydrogen present in atmosphere cannot give a reaction with oxygen.

EXAMPLE

Why is the temperature high in thermosphere?

SOLUTION

Molecules present in thermosphere absorb the Sun's radiation directly. Since very few molecules are there in thermosphere, these molecules easily get ionised by absorbing intense solar radiation. During this process the kinetic energy of the particles increases which in turn increases their temperature.

Oxygen

Oxygen is one of the major components of air. Nitrogen, the other major component is present in greater proportions in air. As nitrogen is an inactive component, most of the properties of air are attributed to the presence of oxygen in air. As oxygen is responsible for carrying out the vital processes of nature, such as, respiration and burning; oxygen is considered to be the supporter of life on earth.

Historical Aspects

A Swedish chemist, Carl Scheele for the first time prepared oxygen by heating potassium nitrate and mercuric oxide. Since this gas was found to support combustion, he named it as 'fire air' or 'vital life.'

Later on, an English chemist, Joseph Priestley prepared oxygen by focusing intense sun rays using a short focus convex lens on a test tube containing mercuric oxide.

The fact that oxygen is an element was proved by Lavoisier. Assuming that oxygen is invariably present in all acids, he named it as 'oxygen' which means 'acid former.' Lavoisier also proved that oxygen constitutes 21% by volume in air.

Occurrence

Oxygen is the most abundant element on earth's crust. It occurs both in free and in combined states.

1. **Free state:** Oxygen is present in a free state in the atmospheric air. It comprises about 21% by volume and about 23% by mass of the total air. Water in oceans and other water bodies also contains some amount of oxygen in dissolved state. Due to the presence of this dissolved oxygen in water, all aquatic species are able to survive in water.
2. **Combined state:** Water is the most important compound which contains oxygen in combined state. Plants and animals also contain 50%–70% of oxygen in the combined state. Further, 50% of oxygen is present in the form of silicates, carbonates, limestone and other ores.

   Oxygen is a diatomic element. Its symbol is O and formula is O_2. Its atomic number is 8, and hence, the electronic configuration is 2, 6. Its atomic weight is 16 and molecular weight is 32. The valency of oxygen is 2. It has an allotropic form, i.e., ozone (O_3).

General Methods of Preparation

Methods	Equations	Observations
Heating of oxides On heating, mercuric and silver oxides decompose to form their respective metals and oxygen gas	(a) $2HgO \xrightarrow{\Delta} 2Hg + O_2$ (b) $2Ag_2O \longrightarrow 4Ag + O_2$	(a) Forms mirror-like surface near the cooler parts of the test tube (b) Silvery white globules are formed
Thermal decomposition of heavy oxides Heavy metal oxides decompose to give oxygen and lower oxides	(a) $2Pb_3O_4 \longrightarrow 6PbO + O_2$ (b) $2PbO_2 \longrightarrow 2PbO + O_2$	(a) Reddish brown residue turning yellow on cooling is called **litharge** (b) Chocolate brown PbO_2 turns to yellow litharge
Thermal decomposition of nitrates Alkali metal nitrates on heating decompose to give metal nitrites and oxygen	(a) $2KNO_3 \longrightarrow 2KNO_2 + O_2$ (b) $2NaNO_3 \longrightarrow 2NaNO_2 + O_2$	

Laboratory Methods of Preparation

1. From hydrogen peroxide

Principle: Hydrogen peroxide undergoes catalytic decomposition in the presence of manganese dioxide to give water and oxygen at room temperature.

$$2H_2O_2 \xrightarrow{MnO_2} 2H_2O + O_2$$

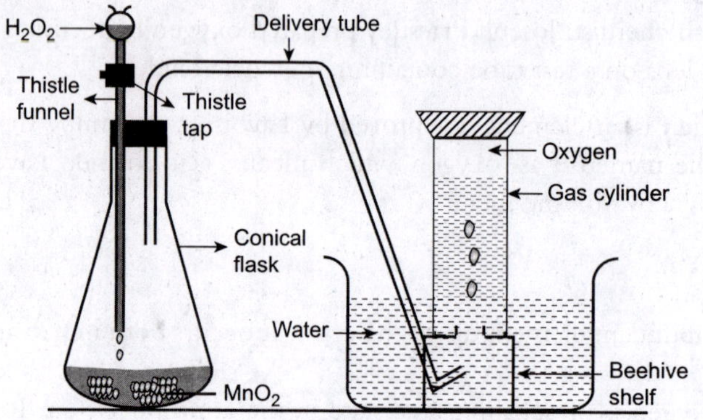

FIGURE 4.3 Laboratory preparation of oxygen from H_2O_2

Experiment I

MnO_2 is taken in a flat-bottomed flask. A solution of H_2O_2 is added dropwise to MnO_2 in the flask through a thistle funnel.

Observation: Effervescence starts with the evolution of oxygen gas. The gas rekindles a glowing splinter.

$$2KClO_3 \xrightarrow[MnO_2]{\Delta} 2KCl + 3O_2$$

Precautions

(a) no heating is required,

(b) MnO_2 used should be pure

2. From potassium chlorate

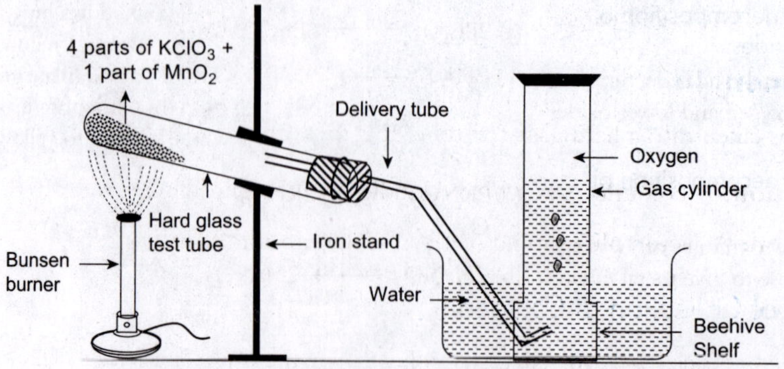

FIGURE 4.4 Preparation of oxygen from $KClO_3$

Principle: Potassium chlorate on heating strongly decomposes to give potassium chloride and oxygen. MnO_2 acts as a catalyst for this reaction.

Experiment II

A mixture of potassium chlorate and MnO_2 in the ratio of 4: 1 is taken in a hard glass test tube. The test tube is fixed to a stand in a slightly slanting position. The mixture is heated.

Observation: A colourless gas is evolved which rekindles the burning candle.

Role of MnO_2

MnO_2 reduces the melting point of potassium chlorate from 350°C to 327°C. The decomposition temperature is also brought down to 350°C from 370°C. It also acts as a positive catalyst for the reaction.

Precautions

$$2KMnO_4 \xrightarrow{\Delta} K_2MnO_4 + MnO_2 + O_2$$

(a) The delivery tube is removed from the trough before the burner is taken out after the experiment.
(b) MnO_2 used should be free of carbon.

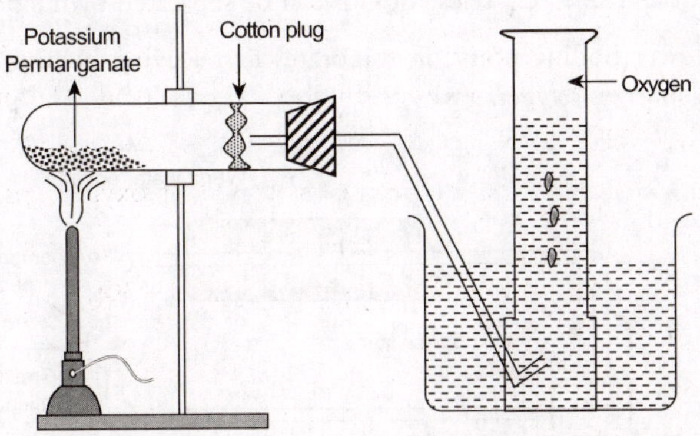

FIGURE 4.5 Laboratory preparation of oxygen

3. From potassium permanganate.

Principle: On heating, potassium permanganate decomposes to give potassium manganate, manganese dioxide and oxygen.

Experiment III

$KMnO_4$ is taken into a hard glass test tube. It is then heated with a Bunsen burner.

Observation: A colourless gas which rekindles the glowing splinter is evolved.

Precaution: A cotton plug should be fixed at the mouth of the test tube.

Method of Collection of Oxygen

In all the methods, the evolved gas is collected in the same method. A glass jar is inverted over the water tank in a trough and oxygen gas is collected in the glass jar by the downward displacement of water.

III Industrial Methods of Preparation

Air and water being the resources in which oxygen is abundantly available, oxygen is prepared in a large scale from these natural resources.

1. Fractional distillation of liquid air: The various steps involved are given below:

(a) Removal of dust particles: Air should be first free from dust particles. This is done by passing air either through filters or through electric precipitators.

(b) Removal of water vapour: The air free of dust particles is passed through conc. H_2SO_4, or anhydrous calcium chloride.

(c) Removal of CO_2: The dry air is passed through caustic soda or caustic potash.

(d) Liquefaction of air: A high pressure of 100 atm–200 atm range is applied to dry air. Then air is allowed to expand by pumping it through a fine jet. This sudden expansion results in cooling. The same process is repeated a number of times so that the temperature is decreased and air is converted to liquid state. Liquid air is obtained at −200°C.

(e) Fractional distillation of liquid air: Liquid air mainly contains liquid nitrogen and liquid oxygen. Liquid nitrogen has a boiling point of −95°C and liquid oxygen has a boiling point of −182.9 °C. These liquids can be separated by fractional distillation.

As nitrogen has a lower boiling point, it evaporates first leaving behind liquid oxygen. Gentle heating of liquid oxygen gives oxygen gas.

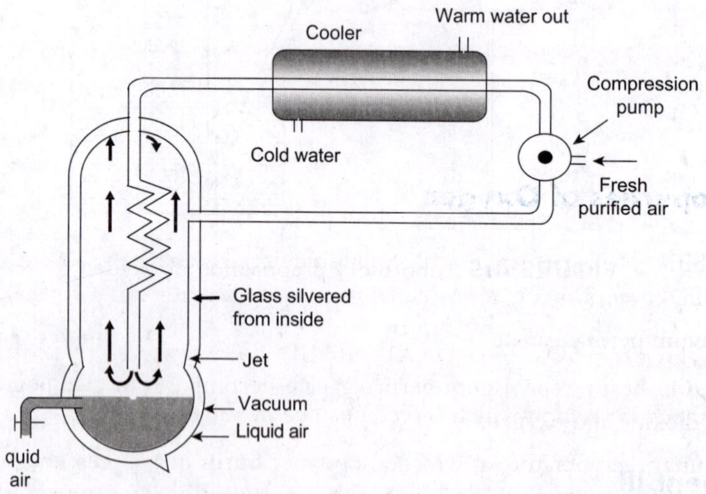

FIGURE 4.6 Liquefaction of air

2. Electrolysis of water: If a little amount of sulphuric acid is added to water, the water then is called **acidulated water**. When this is subjected to electrolysis, water decomposes to give hydrogen and oxygen. Hydrogen is liberated at the cathode and oxygen is liberated at the anode.

$$2H_2O \xrightarrow{\text{Electric current}} 2H_{2(g)} + O_{2(g)}$$

Experiment IV

Advantages: Acidulated water is taken in a rectangular tank. Platinum plates are inserted into the tank, which are connected to the opposite terminals of the battery. When a high voltage is passed through the tank, water electrolyses to give hydrogen gas at the cathode and oxygen gas at the anode.

(a) The process is comparatively economical and can be used especially in places where the electricity is available at cheaper rates.

(b) Hydrogen gas is obtained as a by-product.

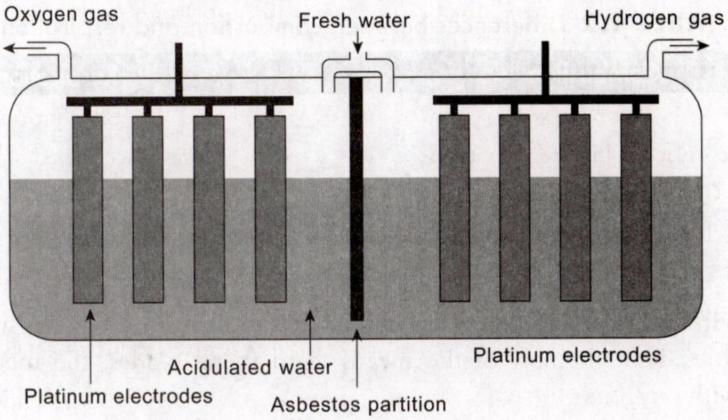

FIGURE 4.7 Industrial electrolysis of water

Oxygen is a colourless, odourless, tasteless and a non-poisonous gas. Its vapour density is 16. Boiling and freezing points of O_2 are –183°C and –218°C, respectively. Oxygen is slightly soluble in water.

Chemical Properties of Oxygen

1. **Combustibility:** Oxygen is a no n-combustible gas as it does not burn on its own. It is a supporter of combustion as it allows combustion of other substances.

Example: $C_6H_{12}O_6 + 6O_2 \longrightarrow 6CO_2 + 6H_2O + \text{Energy}$

It is an exothermic reaction which is accompanied by the evolution of heat.

The minimum temperature at which a substance burns in the presence of oxygen is called its **ignition temperature**. When the ignition temperature of a substance is around room temperature, the substance burns in air at ordinary temperature without being heated.

Example: phosphorus

A combustible substance which has an ignition temperature close to the room temperature is called an **inflammable substance**. These substances are used as fuels, e.g., petrol, kerosene, hydrogen.

The substances which do not undergo combustion are called **incombustible substances**, e.g., silica, calcium carbonate, etc.

Respiration: The process of respiration taking place in plants and animals is also a slow combustion reaction. During respiration, oxygen gas is inhaled which combines with haemoglobin of blood to form oxyhaemoglobin. This oxygen oxidises the digested food (mostly present as glucose) to form carbon dioxide and water. During this process of combustion, energy is released. By this process, oxygen supports life on earth.

$$C_6H_{12}O_6 + 6O_2 \longrightarrow 6CO_2 + 6H_2O + \text{Energy}$$

Though respiration is similar to the combustion of organic compounds, these two processes differ in some respects.

TABLE 4.2 Differences between combustion and respiration

Combustion	Respiration
Fast process	Slow process
Takes place at high temperatures	Takes place at body temperature
Catalysts are not essential	Enzymes are essential
Energy is released in the form of heat and light	Energy is released in the form of heat only

2. **Reaction with metals:** Oxygen reacts with metals to form metal oxides which are generally basic in nature. Though most of the metals form metal oxides, the metals differ in their reactivities with oxygen.

(a) **Sodium and potassium**: Both react with oxygen vigorously and form oxides at room temperature.

$$4Na + O_2 \rightarrow 2Na_2O$$

$$4K + O_2 \rightarrow 2K_2O$$

(b) **Magnesium and calcium**: Both react with oxygen on heating slightly to form corresponding oxides.

$$2Mg + O2 \longrightarrow 2MgO$$

$$2Ca + O_2 \longrightarrow 2CaO$$

(c) **Aluminium and iron**: They react with oxygen at room temperature forming an oxide coating over the metal surface. In the case of aluminium, it prevents further oxidation of the metal.

$$4Al + 3O_2 \longrightarrow 2Al_2O_3$$

$$4Fe + 3O_2 \longrightarrow 2Fe_2O_3$$

(d) At higher temperature, iron gives reddish brown powder with crackling noise due to the formation of ferric tetraoxide or ferroso ferric oxide.

$$4Fe + 2O_2 \longrightarrow Fe_3O_4$$

(e) Copper and silver: On heating, copper reacts with oxygen to form black, powdery cupric oxide. Green sparks with crackling noise are also observed.

$$2Cu + O_2 \rightarrow 2CuO$$

$$2Ag + O_2 \rightarrow Ag_2O$$

(f) Gold and platinum: These metals do not react with oxygen even at a high temperature.

3. Reactions with non-metals: Oxygen also reacts with various non-metals to give corresponding oxides.

(a) Reaction with hydrogen: Under normal conditions, oxygen does not react with hydrogen. Only when an electric spark is generated in a mixture of oxygen and hydrogen in 1 : 2 ratio, they react with a flash and an explosion to form water. Oxygen and hydrogen are also made to react by applying high pressure and passing through a pipe having a small hole. The mixture gets ignited and burns with hot blue flame. This flame is known as oxyhydrogen flame. This is used for welding purpose.

$$2H_2 + O_2 \longrightarrow 2H_2O_{(l)}$$

(b) Reaction with nitrogen: Nitrogen being chemically less reactive does not react with oxygen under normal conditions. But when an electric spark is produced in a 1 : 1 mixture of nitrogen and oxygen, they react to form nitric oxide.

$$N_2 + O_2 \underset{300}{\overset{\text{Electric spark}}{\rightleftharpoons}} 2NO$$

(c) Reaction with carbon: Red hot charcoal when burnt with oxygen produces CO_2 gas with the evolution of a large amount of heat.

$$C + O_2 \rightarrow CO_2 + \text{Heat}$$

Due to the evolution of large amount of heat in this reaction, charcoal, coal, coke, etc., are used as fuels.

(d) Reaction with sulphur: Sulphur burns with oxygen to form sulphur dioxide gas. Along with SO_2 gas, trace amounts of sulphur trioxide are also produced. This mixture of oxides imparts brilliant blue colour to the flame.

$$S + O_2 \longrightarrow SO_2$$

$$2S + 3O_2 \longrightarrow 2SO_3 \text{ (only in traces)}$$

(e) Reaction with phosphorous: Phosphorous on burning with oxygen produces dense white fumes of phosphorous pentoxide.

$$4P + 5O_2 \longrightarrow 2P_2O_5$$

4. Reaction with hydrocarbons: Hydrocarbons react with oxygen to form carbon dioxide and water. Different hydrocarbons react with oxygen at different temperatures. A large amount of heat is evolved during this reaction.

Due to the highly exothermic nature of the reaction, a mixture of hydrocarbons acts as a very good fuel, e.g., wood, petrol, diesel and LPG.

A candle made up of a mixture of lower hydrocarbons also burns in oxygen producing heat and light.

$$C_xH_y + O_2 \longrightarrow xCO_2 + \frac{y}{2}H_2O + \text{Energy}$$

The addition of oxygen to a metal or a non-metal is termed as oxidation. Some non-metal oxides also undergo oxidation to their higher oxides. As oxygen oxidises most of the substances, it is a good oxidising agent.

5. Oxidation of non-metal oxides

(a) Sulphur dioxide

$$2SO_2 + O_2 \xrightarrow[\text{Or Pt}]{V_2O_5} 2SO_3$$

SO_2 on oxidation with V_2O_5 (vanadium pentoxide) or platinum gives SO_3. This reaction is made use of in the manufacturing of H_2SO_4. This reaction also takes place in the catalytic convertors of automobiles.

(b) Carbon monoxide: $2CO + O_2 \longrightarrow 2CO_2$

Carbon monoxide which is a major constituent of automobile exhaust gets converted to CO_2 which is less polluting in the catalytic convertors of automobile engines.

(c) Nitric oxide: $2NO + O_2 \longrightarrow 2NO_2$

Nitric oxide reacts with oxygen to form nitrogen dioxide which is reddish brown in colour.

6. Oxidation of other compounds

(a) Oxidation of ammonia: When a mixture of ammonia and oxygen in 4 : 5 ratio is passed over platinum gauze at 800°C, they react to form nitric oxide and steam.

$$4NH_3 + 5O_2 \xrightarrow[800\ C]{Pt} 4NO + 6H_2O$$

When ammonia is burnt with limited amount of oxygen, it burns with a blue flame with the evolution of nitrogen gas.

$$4NH_3 + 3O_2 \xrightarrow{\Delta} 2N_2 + 6H_2O$$

(b) Oxidation of metallic sulphides: Sulphides of some metals react with oxygen at higher temperature to form the corresponding metal oxides with the evolution of SO_2 gas.

$$2ZnS + 3O_2 \longrightarrow 2ZnO + 2SO_2$$

$$2FeS + 3O_2 \longrightarrow 2FeO + 2SO_2$$

$$2FeS_2 + 11O_2 \longrightarrow 2Fe_2O_3 + 8SO_2$$

$$2PbS + 3O_2 \longrightarrow 2PbO + 2SO_2$$

(c) Oxidation of non-metallic sulphides: Both hydrogen sulphide and carbon disulphide react with oxygen liberating SO_2 gas.

$$2H_2S + 3O_2 \longrightarrow 2H_2O + 2SO_2$$

$$CS_2 + 3O_2 \longrightarrow CO_2 + 2SO_2$$

Rusting of Iron

Corrosion of iron is generally termed as rusting of iron. It is a process in which iron is converted into the hydrated form of oxide in the presence of air and moisture.

Process

Atmospheric air contains oxygen and water vapour. When iron comes into contact with this atmospheric air, it slowly reacts with oxygen to form ferric oxide. This ferric oxide on further reaction with water vapour forms hydrated ferric oxide. This is called **rust**.

$$4Fe_{(s)} + 3O_2 \longrightarrow 2Fe_2O_{3(s)}$$

$$Fe_2O_{3(s)} + H_2O_{(l)} \longrightarrow Fe_2O_3.xH_2O_{(s)}$$

(x = number of water molecules which is variable)

Effects

Rust formed is in the form of flakes which crumbles from the surface of the metal. In addition to corroding the metal, rusting also weakens the iron structures.

Prevention

1. The metal surface when coated with some other material prevents the exposure of the metal to the moist air. Thus, rusting is prevented. Since iron is used for making different structures used for different purposes, it is also necessary to coat the surfaces with different materials depending on their nature.

   (a) Doors, windows, cars, buses, vehicles, etc., are coated with red lead oxide paint. This coating prevents iron from rusting. In addition to protecting the metal from rusting, coating in these cases should also enhance the appearance of the structure. For this purpose, the enamel paint is coated on the surface of the red lead oxide paint.

   (b) Ships, bridges, electric poles, etc., are coated with tar or red lead oxide paint. Though this is a costly process, this effectively prevents rusting. As these structures are in contact with water always, an effective method of protecting the metal from corrosion is absolutely essential.

   (c) Cooking stoves, ovens, refrigerators, washbasins, utensils, etc., coated on the metal surface at a high temperature. This process is called **enamelling**. This coating is resistant to high temperature. It also gives good appearance to the articles.

   (d) Machine parts/engine parts: A protective layer on these parts is of no use since these parts keep moving which results in the weathering of the coating. Hence, these parts are coated with a layer of oil or grease. In addition to preventing rusting, this also acts as a lubricant for machines.

   (e) Furniture and fixtures coated with a thin layer of plastic.

2. **Galvanization**: Iron sheets are dipped in molten zinc and passed through heavy rollers. This iron coated with zinc metal is called **galvanized iron** and the process as galvanisation. e.g., tin roofs, buckets, tubs, iron trunks and suitcases.

3. **Tinning**: Forming a layer of tin over the iron surface is called **tinning**. This process is similar to galvanization.

Example: containers for edible materials, like, oils, fruit juices, vegetables, meat, etc.

4. **Electroplating**: The process of coating the iron metal by another metal by means of electrolysis is called **electroplating**. The metals used for this purpose are nickel and chromium. Though it is an expensive process, coating is long lasting and effective. For example, bicycle handles, rims, car bumpers, etc.
5. **Alloying**: The process of mixing of other metals with iron to make a homogeneous mixture is called **alloying**.

The most commonly used alloy of iron is stainless steel, which contains 12%–20% chromium and 0.07%–0.1% carbon. By making this stainless steel alloy, iron metal is protected from corrosion.

Example: surgical instruments, utensils, tools and cutlery.

Detection of Oxygen (Tests)

The following tests can be performed to detect the evolution of oxygen gas:

1. Rekindles a glowing splinter
2. Neutral to litmus
3. Colourless nitric oxide changes to reddish brown NO_2 gas
5. Turns alkaline pyrogallol to dark brown

Uses of Oxygen

1. Respiration of living organisms
2. Combustion or burning of fuels
3. Manufacture of H_2SO_4 and HNO_3 in industry
4. **Explosive:** For blasting big rocks in mines, a mixture of coal, petroleum jelly and liquid oxygen is used in the form of a cartridge.
5. **Metal extraction:** Used in a blast furnace for the extraction of iron.
6. **Welding:** A mixture of oxygen and hydrogen on burning gives an oxyhydrogen flame which is at a temperature of 2800°C. In place of hydrogen, when acetylene is used, it becomes oxyacetylene flame which gives a still higher temperature of 3300°C. Both are used for welding purposes.
7. **Stimulant for breathing:** A mixture of 95% oxygen and 5% CO_2 is called **carbogen**. It is used for aiding breathing in patients with breathing problems.
8. **As an anaesthetic:** A mixture of N_2O and oxygen is used as an anaesthetic during surgical operations.
9. **Rocket fuel:** Liquid oxygen is used as a rocket fule.
10. **Artificial respiration:** Oxygen cylinders are carried by mountaineers, astronauts, miners, divers, submariners, aviators, firemen, etc.

EXAMPLE

CO_2 is collected by upward displacement of air and O_2 is collected by downward displacement of water. Justify.

SOLUTION

Oxygen is collected by downward displacement of water and CO_2 is collected by upward displacement of air. This is due to more soluble nature of CO_2 in water forming carbonic acid whereas O_2 is slightly soluble in water. Since the difference in densities of O_2 and air is very less, O_2 cannot be effectively collected by upward or downward displacement of air.

EXAMPLE

State two reactions between non-metallic oxides and oxygen which take place in catalytic converter.

SOLUTION

SO_2 on oxidation in presence of V_2O_5 or platinum gives SO_3. This reaction takes place in the catalytic converter of automobiles.

$$2SO_2 + O_2 \xrightarrow[\text{or Pt}]{V_2O_2} 2SO_3$$

Carbon monoxide which is a major constituent of automobile exhaust gets converted to CO_2 in the catalytic converter of automobile engines.

$$2CO + O_2 \longrightarrow 2CO_2$$

EXAMPLE

A cotton plug is kept at the mouth of test tube during the preparation of oxygen by $KMnO_4$. Why?

SOLUTION

In the preparation of oxygen from $KMnO_4$ a cotton plug is kept near the mouth of test tube. It is to prevent the spillage of $KMnO_4$ into the gas jar in which the oxygen gas is being collected.

EXAMPLE

What is the advantage of preparation of O_2 by H_2O_2 over its preparation by $KClO_3$ and $KMnO_4$?

SOLUTION

The advantage of preparation of oxygen from H_2O_2 over its preparation from $KClO_3$ and $KMnO_4$ is that no heating is required and the reaction takes place at room temperature only.

EXAMPLE

What are the advantages of preparation of O_2 by electrolysis over fractional distillation of air?

SOLUTION

The advantage of preparation of oxygen by electrolysis of water over its preparation by fractional distillation of air is that industrially the process of electrolysis gives pure oxygen. Also, hydrogen gas is obtained as a by-product in this process.

Air Pollution

In addition to the various components (both major and minor) present in it air also contains some other gases produced by the human activity. These gases are not only useless but also cause damage to the environment. Due to the presence of these gases, the composition of air in the atmosphere changes. The variation in the composition of air in the atmosphere due to the release of these gases is called **air pollution**.

Major Factors Affecting the Composition of Air

1. The area of forests in the region,
2. The industries present in the area,
3. Density of population and
4. Urbanisation.

Pollutants	Sources	Processes	Effects on environment
Carbon monoxide	Automobiles	Incomplete combustion of fuels	Respiratory problems (reduction in intake of oxygen)
Sulphur dioxide	(i) Automobiles (ii) Industries (iii) Thermal power plants	(i) Incomplete combustion of fuels (ii) Metals' extraction (iii) Paper making	(i) Main cause of acid rain (ii) Respiratory disorders
Nitrogen oxides	(i) Automobiles (ii) Industries	Incomplete combustion of fuels	(i) Formation of smog (ii) Causes acid rain
Carbon dioxide	(i) Automobiles (ii) High density of population (iii) Decrease in forest area	Combustion of fuels and deforestation	Global warming
Ozone	(i) Industries		Global warming
CFCs (chlorofluorocarbons)	(i) In air conditioners as organic chemicals (ii) Refrigeration systems		Depletion of ozone layer
Metals	(i) Automobiles (Pb) (ii) Thermal power plants (Pb, Hg, As, Co, Cu)	(i) Present in petrol as anti-knock (ii) Chemical reactions	(i) Nervous disorders (ii) Problems of digestion (iii) Cancer
Hydrocarbons	(i) Automobiles (ii) Degradation of organic wastes	Exhaust gas	(i) Carcinogenic
Fly ash	(i) Thermal power plants	Combustion of coal	(i) Metal oxides and toxic metals of fly ash cause health problems. (ii) Silica causes bronchitis and lung cancer. (iii) Contamination of ground water and clogging of drainage

Pollutants	Sources	Processes	Effects on environment
Suspended particulate matter (SPM)	(i) Automobiles (ii) Industries	Exhaust gas	(i) Lung and respiratory disorders (ii) Formation of smog

HAZARDS OF AIR POLLUTION AND THEIR PREVENTION

1. **Acid rain:** Rain water is actually the purest form of water. However, the presence of pollutants, such as, oxides of nitrogen and sulphur in the air imparts acidity to the rain water. The sources of these gases are the eruption of volcanoes and the burning of fossil fuels, factory chimneys, etc. These gases dissolve in rain water forming nitric acid and sulphuric acid.

$$SO_3 + H_2O \longrightarrow H_2SO_4$$

$$2NO_2 + H_2O \longrightarrow HNO_3 + HNO_2$$

Acid rain reduces the fertility of soil, and thus, damages vegetation. It also pollutes water bodies, thus, affecting animal and aquatic life. Acid rain also results in the corrosion of buildings, statues and archaeological monuments.

Acid rains are not confined only to industrial areas. The regions free of industrial pollution may also be affected by acid rains due to the movement of the rain clouds from one region to the other region.

Prevention: The casual agents for acid rain being the oxides of sulphur and nitrogen are difficult to be controlled. But, avoiding the usage of fossil fuels, the use of the non-conventional sources of energy and safe disposal of industrial wastes to some extent can reduce the levels of these pollutants, thus, preventing the ill-effects of acid rains.

2. **Greenhouse effect and global warming:** Land and ocean absorb solar energy to warm the earth's atmosphere. In turn, they release infrared radiation or heat into the atmosphere. The blanket of gases covering the earth's surface traps this radiation. Thus, the absorption of heat maintains the temperature of the earth's surface which is absolutely essential to support life on earth. This natural process is called **greenhouse effect**.

This natural phenomenon of greenhouse effect is caused mostly by CO_2 and water vapour in the atmosphere. Hence, these gases are called **greenhouse gases**.

However, increase in the levels of CO_2 and the presence of some other gases, such as, CH_4, ozone, etc., in the atmosphere result in a gradual rise in the temperature of earth's surface. This increasing greenhouse effect occurring due to the polluted gases in the atmosphere is called **global warming**. These gases which cause global warming are called **greenhouse gases**.

Melting of ice caps and glaciers, excessive evaporation of sea and ocean waters, increase in frequency of floods, soil erosion, unseasonal rains, health hazards for human beings and animals as a consequence of increased temperature on the earth are some harmful effects of global warming.

Reduction of global warming: Reduction in the use of fossil fuels, controlling deforestation and restricting the use of (CFCs) chlorofluorocarbons are some measures to be taken against increasing greenhouse effect. Growing more and more plants is obviously the most essential requirement for controlling global warming.

3. **Ozone depletion:** Ozone when present in the troposphere causes greenhouse effect and contributes to pollution. But, in stratosphere, ozone has a very useful role to play. It absorbs ultraviolet radiations coming from the sun and prevents them, from reaching the earth's atmosphere. Ultraviolet radiations are biologically harmful. The ozone layer acts as a screen for these radiations.

   Some pollutants, such as, chlorofluorocarbons are chemically inactive and do not dissolve in rain water. Hence, they reach the stratosphere over a period of time. There they react with ozone and cause depletion of ozone in that region. Therefore, it cannot perfectly screen the UV radiations. Once this radiation reaches the earth's surface it causes many undesirable effects, like, skin cancer, cataract, damage of plants and crops, etc.

   Prevention: The most effective way of protecting the ozone layer is developing alternatives for chlorofluorocarbons in the refrigerating systems and aerosols.

   Acid rains, global warming and ozone depletion are the major hazards to environment. In addition to these, the other pollutants, like, carbon monoxide, fly ash, suspended particulate matter and toxic metals also cause considerable damage to man and environment. Some general methods have to be followed for curbing the air pollution in all respects.

   Instead of finding out ways and means for the safe disposal of waste products, now focus has been shifted to designing of industrial equipment, like, scrubbers and precipitators and synthesis of chemicals which are environment friendly. This involves the usage of raw materials and solvents which do not cause release of any harmful products. Researches are going on for the development of alternative chemical reactions which do not give an undesirable product. This is in fact a new area of chemistry known as green chemistry which has come to the forefront in the recent years.

   Arresting the growth of population, judicious use of natural resources, recycling of products, such as, paper and restricting the usage of plastic bags are some easier control measures which can be of great help in controlling air pollution.

   Above all, arresting deforestation and increase in greenery in our surroundings can go a long way in curbing the pollution. Following stringent norms and the maintenance of industrial units and avoiding accidents in industries also can contribute to a large extent for the control of air pollution.

EXAMPLE

Explain the working principle of scrubber.

SOLUTION

Scrubbers are used to remove acidic oxides, like oxides of sulphur and nitrogen. Lime water is spread in scrubber through which acidic oxides of sulphur and nitrogen are precipitated.

EXAMPLE

What is meant by fly ash? Give the sources of fly ash and its effect on the environment and human beings.

SOLUTION

Fly ash is the residue produced during the combustion of coal. Thermal power plants are the major sources of fly ash.

Effects of fly ash on environment and on human beings are given below.

(i) Metal oxides and toxic metals present in fly ash cause health problems.

(ii) Silica causes bronchitis and lung cancer.

(iii) Fly ash is also responsible for contamination of ground water and clogging of drainage.

TEST YOUR CONCEPTS

Very Short Answer Type Questions

1. What is meant by atmospheric pressure?
2. Name the different types of instruments used to measure atmospheric pressure.
3. Give the functions of nitrogen in the atmosphere.
4. S I unit of atmospheric pressure is ________.
5. What are the products of combustion of carbon compounds?
6. Under what conditions, oxygen and hydrogen react with each other?
7. How does oxygen exist in the combined state in nature?
8. What happens when mercuric oxide is subjected to heating?
9. Name the layers of the atmosphere.
10. Give a balanced chemical equation for the combustion of glucose.
11. The minimum temperature at which a substance burns in air is called ________.
12. What is meant by an oxyhydrogen flame? For what purpose is it used?
13. Give the electronic configuration of oxygen. Also mention the period and the group to which the element belongs.
14. What are the uses of neon and argon?
15. A mixture of 95% oxygen and 5% CO_2 is called ________.
16. What is the layer of the atmosphere present just above the earth's surface?
17. Why is mercury taken in a barometer?
18. What is the SI unit for atmospheric pressure? Define it.
19. What are the major components of air? Among these, which is the active component and which is the inactive component?
20. How is oxygen gas collected?
21. What happens when iron is subjected to strong heating with oxygen?
22. Name the metals which react with oxygen at room temperature.
23. Coating of tin over iron is called ________.
24. Why is the atmospheric pressure measured at sea level?
25. Give the composition of nitrogen and oxygen by volume in air.
26. What is the main advantage of the manufacturing of oxygen gas by the electrolysis of water?
27. Among all the layers of the atmosphere the layer with the highest temperature is ______.
28. Define ignition temperature.
29. Define atmosphere.

Short Answer Type Questions

30. What is meant by greenhouse effect? Name some greenhouse gases.
31. How can the growing of plants control pollution?
32. Explain why the atmospheric pressure changes with altitude?
33. Give the differences between combustion and respiration.
34. Name some measures to control air pollution.
35. Why are acid rains not confined to only industrial areas?
36. Give some uses of oxygen.
37. Give any four characteristics of air as a mixture.
38. Which metals react with oxygen at room temperature? Give equations.
39. What is meant by fly ash? Give the sources of fly ash and its effect on the environment.
40. What is the role of atmosphere in nature?
41. How do chlorofluorocarbons cause air pollution?

42. Give the effect of acid rains.

43. How can you detect oxygen gas?

44. What are the sources of carbon monoxide and sulphur dioxide in air?

Essay Type Questions

45. Explain the construction and working of the
    (i) Mercury barometer
    (ii) Aneroid barometer

46. Give equations for the decomposition of potassium permanganate and hydrogen peroxide. In what way do the two processes differ from each other?

47. What is meant by rusting? What are its effects? Explain different methods adopted for the prevention of rusting?

48. What are the effects of oxides of sulphur and nitrogen on the atmosphere?

49. How is oxygen gas prepared from potassium chlorate? What is the role of MnO_2 in this process?

For Answer key, Hints and Explanations, please visit: www.pearsoned.co.in/IITFoundationSeries

CONCEPT APPLICATION

Level 1

Directions for questions from 1 to 7

State whether the following statements are true or false.

1. Air is a mixture.
2. An increase in the levels of CO_2 in the atmosphere increases the temperature of the earth.
3. Nitrates on thermal decomposition give oxygen.
4. With increase in altitude the atmospheric pressure increases.
5. Gold and platinum do not react with oxygen even at high temperatures.
6. The atomicity of the allotropic form of oxygen is three.
7. Oxygen gas is collected by the downward displacement of air.

Directions for questions from 8 to 14

Fill in the blanks.

8. The minimum temperature at which a substance burns in air is called ________.
9. The catalyst in the decomposition of hydrogen peroxide is ________.
10. Dust particles from air are removed by passing air through ________ or ________.
11. When ammonia gas is burnt in excess of oxygen at high temperature, the products formed are ________.
12. The vacuum present above the column in mercury barometer is called ________.
13. FeS_2 on burning in oxygen gives ________.
14. Thermosphere is associated with high temperature due to the absorption of ________.

Direction for question 15

Match the entries in Column A with the appropriate ones in Column B.

15.

Column A		Column B
A. SO_3	( )	a. Greenhouse effect
B. O_3	( )	b. Carbonic acid
C. CO_2	( )	c. Artificial breathing
D. $N_2O + O_2$	( )	d. Acid rain
E. 95% + 5% CO_2	( )	e. Anaesthetic
F. $O_2 + H_2$	( )	f. Stratosphere
G. $H_2O + CO_2$	( )	g. Welding

Directions for questions from 16 to 45

For each of the questions, four choices have been provided. Select the correct alternative.

16. Which among the following processes does not add suspended particulate matter (SPM) to air?
    (a) usage of air conditioners
    (b) burning of fuels
    (c) paper industry
    (d) combustion of coal

17. Hydrogen sulphide from air is removed by passing air through
    (a) caustic potash
    (b) concentrated H_2SO_4
    (c) anhydrous $CaCl_2$
    (d) filters

18. Which of the following substance is used in refrigerators?
(a) hydrocarbon (b) CFC
(c) ozone (d) metal oxide

19. Which of the following distinguishes respiration from combustion?
(a) requirement of oxygen
(b) exothermic nature of reactions
(c) energy can be released only in the form of heat and not light
(d) can take place at any temperature

20. Global warming is mainly due to
(a) reradiation of UV rays by CO_2 and H_2O
(b) reradiation of IR rays by CO_2 and H_2O
(c) reradiation of IR rays by O_2 and N_2
(d) reradiation of UV rays by O_2 and N_2

21. Which of the following minerals does not contain oxygen?
(a) silicates (b) carbonates
(c) pyrites (d) none of these

22. $X + O_2 \longrightarrow Y$, $Y + H_2O \longrightarrow Z$, Z turns red litmus to blue then X may be
(a) Ca (b) S
(c) C (d) P

23. Tropospheric atmosphere is turbulent. Which of the following reasons can be attributed to this?
(a) convectional current of air rises up due to high temperature in lower layers of the earth
(b) temperature changes result in change in air pressure
(c) more effect of centrifugal force is more in this layer
(d) none of these

24. The layer of atmosphere that is just above the earth's surface is called ________.
(a) thermosphere (b) troposphere
(c) stratosphere (d) mesosphere

25. Which of the following pairs of oxides can give out oxygen on heating?
(a) MgO, PbO_2 (b) Na_2O, CaO
(c) K_2O, HgO (d) Ag_2O, Pb_3O_4

26. Which of the following are used in air conditioning and refrigeration systems?
(a) CO (b) CO_2
(c) CFCs (d) O_3

27. If a balloon filled with air is sent to moon, what would happen?
(a) The balloon expands because the atmospheric pressure of the moon is slightly lower than that of the earth.
(b) The balloon bursts because the atmospheric pressure of the moon is much lower than that of the earth.
(c) The balloon contracts because the atmospheric pressure of the moon is much lower than that of the earth.
(d) No change is observed because change of atmospheric pressure has no effect on the balloon.

28. A gas which is combustible and can support combustion is
(a) oxygen. (b) nitrous oxide
(c) nitric oxide (d) carbon monoxide

29. Which among the following has the lowest boiling point?
(a) O_2 (b) N_2
(c) F_2 (d) Ne

30. Passengers travelling in an aeroplane are advised not to carry fountain pens because at higher altitudes
(a) ink vaporises due to high external pressure
(b) solidification of ink takes places due to very low external pressure
(c) pressure within the tube is more than the external pressure and causes leakage of ink
(d) pressure within the tube is lesser than the external pressure and causes leakage of ink

31. With increase in altitude the temperature in the stratosphere
(a) first remains almost constant and then increases
(b) decreases
(c) remains same
(d) first decreases and then increases

PRACTICE QUESTIONS

32. Which of the following can be considered as spontaneous combustion?
(a) Burning of LPG
(b) Burning of magnesium ribbon
(c) Burning of camphor
(d) Burning of white phosphorus

33. Which of the following metals gives reddish powder on reaction with O_2 at higher temperature?
(a) Fe (b) Pb
(c) Zn (d) Sn

34. Which of the following reactions is associated with the formation of shining white globules?
(a) $2HgO \xrightarrow{\Delta} 2Hg + O_2$
(b) $2Ag_2O \xrightarrow{\Delta} 4Ag + O_2$
(c) $2Pb_3O_4 \xrightarrow{\Delta} 6PbO + 4O_2$
(d) $2NaNO_3 \xrightarrow{\Delta} 2NaNO_2 + O_2$

35. The ratio of $KClO_3$ and MnO_2 taken for the preparation of oxygen is
(a) 4 : 1 (b) 3 : 1
(c) 2 : 1 (d) 2 : 5

36. When ammonia is burnt in a limited supply of oxygen, which gas is evolved?
(a) NO (b) N_2O
(c) N_2 (d) NO_2

37. Which of the following compounds produces oxide on heating?
(a) PbO_2 (b) KNO_3
(c) Ag_2O (d) $NaNO_3$

38. Which of the following metals does not react with O_2 even at high temperatures?
(a) magnesium (b) iron
(c) aluminium (d) gold

39. Carbon dioxide from air is removed by passing air through ______.
(a) caustic potash
(b) concentrated H_2SO_4
(c) anhydrous $CaCl_2$
(d) filters

40. Which of the following reactions is associated with the formation of a mirror-like surface near the cooler part of the test tube?
(a) heating of mercuric oxide
(b) heating of silver oxide
(c) heating of trilead tetroxide
(d) heating of lead dioxide

41. You are asked to prepare oxygen from air after eliminating the impurities in the order, i.e., at first dust particles, then water vapour and CO_2 at the end. Based on the given instruction arrange the processes given below in a sequence:
(1) passing the sample of air through concentrated NaOH
(2) repeated compression followed by sudden expansion
(3) fractional distillation of liquefied air
(4) passing the air through electrostatic precipitator
(5) passing the air through anhydrous $CaCl_2$
(a) 1 4 5 2 3 (b) 1 3 5 2 4
(c) 4 5 1 2 3 (d) 2 1 5 4 3

42. Arrange the following products (oxides) in the ascending order of the ratio of metal atoms to oxygen atom(s) present in one molecule of the respective oxide.
(1) magnesium is heated in the presence of oxygen
(2) iron produces a reddish brown powder with a crackling sound when it is heated at higher temperature
(3) sodium undergoes oxidation in moist air
(4) formation of a coating of aluminium oxide on aluminium at normal temperature
(a) 1 4 3 2 (b) 4 2 1 3
(c) 1 3 2 4 (d) 3 1 2 4

43. The description of the different layers of the atmosphere is given below. Arrange them in the increasing order of their altitude.
(1) the layer of atmosphere in which the number of molecules is less but they are sufficient to burn the meteorites
(2) the layer in which the temperature increases with attitude
(3) the layer with the least number of particles
(4) the convection current of air plays a significant role in this layer
(a) 2 4 1 3 (b) 2 3 1 4
(c) 4 2 3 1 (d) 4 2 1 3

44. Arrange the products of the following reactions in the increasing order of the number of oxygen atoms associated with one non-metallic atom.
   (a) burning of phosphorus in an adequate supply of oxygen to produce an oxide of phosphorus
   (b) the complete combustion of coke with the supply of sufficient oxygen
   (c) an electric spark is provided to a 1 : 1 mixture of nitrogen and oxygen
   (d) burning of sulphur dioxide gas in oxygen
   (a) 3 4 1 2 (b) 3 2 1 4
   (c) 2 3 1 4 (d) 3 2 4 1

45. Arrange the following steps involved in the preparation of oxygen from $KClO_3$ in a proper order.
   (1) content of the test tube is heated
   (2) A mixture of finely ground KClO3 and MnO_2 is taken in a test tube.
   (3) The open end of the test tube is plugged with cotton.
   (4) delivery tube is taken out
   (5) The test tube is fixed in a slanting position.
   (6) Bunsen burner is put off.
   (7) Oxygen is collected by downward displacement of water.
   (a) 2 3 4 1 5 6 7 (b) 5 6 3 2 4 1 7
   (c) 1 2 3 4 6 7 5 (d) 2 3 5 1 7 4 6

Level 2

1. What are the advantages of an aneroid barometer over a mercury barometer? Give the applications of the aneroid barometer.

2. Why are tin coated iron cans used for cool drinks but not galvanised iron cans? Explain.

3. LPG stove can be lighted by using an automatic gas lighter. Is it possible to light kerosene stove by using the same?

4. The combustion of sulphur and phosphorous is possible even in the presence of nitrous oxide and nitric oxide at high temperatures. Justify

5. Is it possible to drink a soft drink by using a straw on the moon? Give reasons in support of your answer.

6. How do catalytic converters reduce air pollution?

7. A student was asked to prepare oxygen from $KClO_3$ in a laboratory. After the experiment was over, he put the burner off immediately. What do you think happened then?

8. Water is not suitable to extinguish fire caused by petrol. Explain.

9. Fishes and many other aquatic species live in river water. When they are kept in aquarium, we need to change the water very often. Give reasons.

10. Why don't we use soda acid fire extinguishers to extinguish metal fires?

11. Explain the principle of the working of smoke precipitators.

12. Explain the principle involved in the liquefaction of air.

13. Though the dust particles cause air pollution, the presence of dust particles help in sustenance of life. Explain.

14. In a chemistry laboratory, a laboratory assistant by mistake placed one currency note with a denomination of 100 on the desk and some amount of alcohol fell on it. The currency note was completely wet with alcohol. In order to dry it he immediately brought a burning match stick and exposed the currency note to its flame. Immediately the currency caught fire. But after few seconds, fire was put off by him and the note remained intact. Explain.

15. Two students A and B were asked to carry out one experiment. The smoke released due to the burning of a candle should be passed through lime water and anhydrous copper sulphate to prove the release of CO_2 and H_2O, respectively, due to the burning of the candle. A first passed the gases through lime water and then through copper sulphate, whereas B did it the other way round. The teacher commented

that the set up used by A was wrong. What could be the reason for it?

16. When lime water is exposed to air for a long time, very thin white coating is found floating on the surface. Give reasons.

17. MnO_2 used as a catalyst in the preparation of oxygen from $KClO_3$ should be completely free of carbon. Justify.

18. Is it possible to prepare oxygen and hydrogen by the electrolysis of pure water? Give reasons in support of your answer. How are hydrogen and oxygen prepared in industry by the electrolysis of water?

19. Rain water is found to contain more percentage of oxygen than ordinary water. Explain.

20. Why is the carbon monoxide of automobile exhaust converted to carbon dioxide in the catalytic converters though both carbon monoxide and carbon dioxide add to air pollution?

21. Why is LPG a better fuel than coal?

22. Rimjhim was dreaming in the morning that she went to a planet Pandora and in the atmosphere of Pandora there is no water vapour. Suddenly she woke up and started thinking what would happen if earth's atmosphere loses water vapour completely. Rimjhim was really worried. Can you find out the reason for Rimjhim's worry?

23. Why is the atmospheric pressure measured at sea level? Why is the atmospheric pressure not felt by us?

Level 3

1. 'Though oxygen is the supporter of life on earth, the presence of nitrogen in the atmosphere also contributes equally to the life processes on earth.' Justify the statement.

2. Why the position of freezer in the refrigerator is generally at the top? Explain.

3. How does sky appear from the moon?

4. Two liquids A and B were taken in two different barometers, and the density of A is greater than that of B. Which liquid is preferable to be used as barometric liquid if the variation in pressure is every minute and why?

5. What would happen if people travel in a non-pressurised aeroplane?

6. Electric bulbs are filled with argon gas but not air. Explain.

7. The body temperature of a healthy person is around 98.4°F. Justify.

8. UV rays find application in the purification of water, although it is harmful to human beings. Explain.

9. Deep sea divers carry oxygen diluted by helium in cylinders instead of air. Give reasons.

10. The temperature of the troposphere decreases with increase in altitude. Is the same true for the stratosphere? Justify.

CONCEPT APPLICATION

Level 1

True or false

1. True 2. True 3. False 4. False 5. True
6. True 7. False

Fill in the blanks

8. Ignition temperature 9. MnO_2 10. precipitators, filters
11. NO, H_2O 12. toricellian vacuum 13. FeO, SO_2
14. Intense solar radiation

Match the following

15. A →d C →a E →c G →b
B →f D →e F →g

16. a 17. a 18. b
19. c 20. b 21. c
22. a 23. a 24. b
25. d 26. c 27. b
28. b 29. d 30. c

31. With the increase in altitude the temperature in the stratosphere first remains constant and then increases.

32. Spontaneous combustion is the burning of a substance at room temperature. White phosphorus burns at the room temperature.

33. At higher temperature oxygen on reaction with iron gives a reddish brown powder with crackling noise due to the formation of ferric tetroxide or ferroso ferric oxide.

$$3Fe + 2O_2 \rightarrow Fe_3O_4$$

reddish brown powder

34. Silver (i) oxide on heating forms silvery white globules:

$$2Ag_2O \rightarrow 4Ag + O_2$$

35. 4 parts of $KClO_3$ and 1 part of MnO_2 on heating gives oxygen gas.

36. When ammonia is burnt with limited amount of oxygen, it burns with a blue flame with the evolution of nitrogen gas.

$$4NH_3 + 3O_2 \xrightarrow{\Delta} 2N_2 + 6H_2O$$

37. $2PbO_2 \rightarrow 2PbO + O_2$

$2KNO_3 \rightarrow 2KNO_2 + O_2$

$2Ag_2O \rightarrow 4Ag + O_2$

$2NaNO_3 \rightarrow 2NaNO_2 + O_2$

38. Gold and platinum are the two metals which do not react with oxygen even at a higher temperature.

39. Carbon dioxide from air is removed by passing air through caustic potash.

40. Heating of mercuric oxide is associated with the formation of a mirror-like surface near the cooler part of the test tube.

HINTS AND EXPLANATION

41. (i) passing the air through electrostatic precipitator
(ii) passing the air through anhydrous $CaCl_2$
(iii) passing the air through concentrated NaOH solution
(iv) repeated compression followed by sudden expansion
(v) fractional distillation of liquefied air

42. (i) Formation of coating of aluminium oxide (Al_2O_3) on aluminium at normal temperature. Here the ratio of metal atom(s) to oxygen atoms in one molecule of oxide is 2/3, i.e., 0.67.
(ii) Iron gives a reddish brown powder with crackling sound when it is heated at a higher temperature. Here the ratio of metal atoms to oxygen atoms in one molecule of oxide is ¾, i.e., 0.75.
(iii) Magnesium oxide (MgO) is formed when magnesium is slightly heated with oxygen. Here, the ratio of metal atom to oxygen atom is 1.
(iv) Sodium oxide (Na2O) is formed when sodium undergoes oxidation in moist air. Here the reaction of metal atoms to oxygen atom is 2.

43. d b a c
(i) Convection current of air plays a significant role in this layer.
(ii) The layer at which the temperature increases with altitude.
(iii) The layer of atmosphere in which the number of molecules i less but they are sufficient to burn the meteorites.
(iv) The layer with the least number of particles.

44. (a) Burning of phosphorus gives P_2O_5.
(b) Complete combustion gives CO_2
(c) When an electric spark is provided to a 1 : 1 mixture of N2 and O2, NO is produced.
(d) Burning of SO_2 gives SO_3.
∴ The correct sequence is c b a d. Arrange the statements in this order—(i), (ii), (iii), (iv).

45. (i) A mixture of finely ground $KClO_3$ and MnO_2 is taken in a test tube.
(ii) The open end of the test tube is plugged with cotton.
(iii) The test tube is fixed in a slanting position.
(iv) Content of the test tube is heated.
(v) Oxygen is collected by downward displacement of water.
(vi) Delivery tube is taken out.
(vii) Bunsen burner is put off.

Level 2

1. (i) comparison of components of both the types of barometers
(ii) comparison of ease of usage and construction
(iii) comparison of sensitivity

2. (i) comparison of reactivities of iron, tin with the component (metal) used for galvanisation
(ii) changes that take place in the food kept in the galvanised container
(iii) effect of the reactivity of tin on the food content

3. (i) ignition temperature
(ii) conditions at which a fuel can be burnt
(iii) comparison of these conditions to LPG and kerosene
(iv) Temperature produced by automatic gas lighter and the substance used to light kerosene stove

4. (i) changes that take place in N_2O and NO at high temperatures
(ii) products obtained from the oxides of nitrogen at high temperature
(iii) requisite for combustion

5. (i) conditions for fluid to rise up in straw
(ii) principle used in sucking a liquid through a straw
(iii) conditions existing on moon
(iv) effect of these conditions

6. (i) Metal used in catalytic converter
(ii) property of the metal used in catalytic converter
(iii) places where catalytic converter finds application
(iv) composition of petroleum products used in automobiles
(v) pollutants present in the automobile exhaust gases
(vi) influence of the metal present in the catalytic converter on the exhaust gases

7. (i) collection of oxygen
(ii) experimental set up

(iii) changes that take place after the burner is put off

(iv) effect of these changes

8. (i) difference in the physical property of water and petrol

(ii) role of water for extinguishing fire

9. (i) respiration of fishes in water

(ii) components required for the survival of fishes and aquatic species

(iii) comparison of these amounts in river water and aquarium

10. (i) material used in soda and fire extinguisher

(ii) reaction that takes place in soda acid fire extinguisher

(iii) products obtained

(iv) reaction between one of the products with metal that causes fire

(v) products obtained in the above reaction

(vi) effect of one of the products on the atmosphere

11. (i) reactivity of gaseous species at electrodes

(ii) components present in smoke

(iii) voltage in smoke precipitators

(iv) change in components of smoke

12. (i) result of sudden expansion of gases

(ii) temperature required for air to liquefy

(iii) conditions to attain the liquefaction

(iv) forces between molecules

(v) effect of temperature on movement of molecules

13. (i) role of dust particles in formation of cloud

(ii) role of cloud formation in water cycle

(iii) role of water cycle in sustenance of life

14. Currency notes are made up of thick papers and the ignition temperature of this type of paper is higher than the ordinary paper. When the currency note is soaked in alcohol, which has low ignition temperature and high volatility, it vaporises and burns before the ignition temperature of the paper is reached. Hence, the currency note does not burn.

15. The products of the combustion of a candle (mixture of hydrocarbons) are CO_2 and water vapour. CO_2 can be detected by passing it through lime water which turns milky. H_2O can be detected by passing it through anhydrous $CuSO_4$ which turns blue. After passing it through anhydrous $CuSO_4$ first, H_2O is removed and only CO_2 will be passed through lime water. If the process is reversed, then CO_2 will be absorbed in lime water and water vapour gets condensed. Hence, colour of anhydrous $CuSO_4$ remains unchanged.

16. Air contains a low percentage of CO_2. Though CO_2 turns lime water milky, since the amount of CO_2 is less in the atmospheric air, it does not turn lime water milky. Only over a long period of exposure, a thin white film of $CaCO_3$ is formed due to the minor amounts of CO_2 in the atmospheric air.

17. MnO_2 usually contains coal as impurity. If such MnO_2 is used, carbon when heated with potassium chlorate leads to an explosion with the release of enormous amount of heat since it is a highly exothermic reaction.

18. Electrolysis of pure water cannot give oxygen and hydrogen since water is a poor conductor. To make it an electrolytic conductor, some amount of acid should be added to water which is called **acidulated water**. Electrolysis of acidulated water gives hydrogen and oxygen at the respective electrodes.

19. Rain is due to condensation of water droplets in the atmosphere. It does not contain any dissolved salts like ordinary water. Therefore, rain water can dissolve more amount of oxygen than ordinary water. Moreover, rain water is in contact with atmospheric air. Hence, it contains more percentage of oxygen.

20. Carbon monoxide is formed by the incomplete combustion of fuels. It is not a constituent of normal atmospheric air. It is a pollutant. When it is released, the inhalation of the air with carbon monoxide results in reduction in the oxygen intake. Hence, it is converted to CO_2 in the catalytic converters. Though CO_2 is released into the atmosphere, it does not cause much damage immediately. Only in the long run, an increase in the levels of CO_2 in the atmospheric air results in global warming. This can be prevented by growing more trees and decreasing the density of the population. Such measures are not possible for carbon monoxide pollution. Hence, CO_2 is a less harmful pollutant than CO.

21. LPG is a mixture of lower hydrocarbons. It has very low ignition temperature and the heat evolved per unit mass of LPG called calorific value of the fuel is very high. Coal is an allotropic form of carbon and has very high ignition temperature. Its calorific value is very low. Apart from these two reasons, LPG undergoes complete combustion and does not produce any ash. Burning coal produces ash and causes acid rain due to the presence of nitrogen and sulphur in it.

22. Water vapour present in the atmosphere forms clouds that result in rains. Rain water is the main source of drinking water and is used for irrigation. If there are no rains, drought prevails. Life in the desert regions is very difficult as water vapour in the atmosphere here is very low. Water vapour also controls the excessive evaporation of water from living cells.

23. Since the composition and the density of air varies with the altitude, the pressure exerted by air also varies. The atmospheric pressure decreases with an increase in the altitude. It is due to this reason that the atmospheric pressure is measured at sea level where it is maximum. At sea level, atmospheric pressure is almost equal to the weight of a 1 kg mass acting on every square centimetre. We do not feel the atmospheric pressure because the pressure inside the body is equal to the atmospheric pressure.

Level 3

1. (i) consequences of breathing air with 100% oxygen
   (ii) effect on body on breathing 100% O_2
   (iii) components of the air we breathe in (under normal conditions)
   (iv) role of nitrogen

2. (i) movement of air due to the change of temperature
   (ii) change in temperature of air near the freezer
   (iii) effect of change in temperature on the density of air
   (iv) cause for movement of air inside the refrigerator
   (v) requirement of movement of air inside the refrigerator
   (vi) influence of the position of the freezer on the movement of air

3. (i) particles present in the earth's atmosphere which are responsible for scattering of light
   (ii) atmosphere in moon
   (iii) reason for the specific colour (blue) of the sky when observed from the earth
   (iv) influence of the atmosphere on the colour of the sky

4. (i) relation between density of liquid, pressure variation and height of the column
   (ii) relation between the density of the barometric liquid and height of the column of the liquid
   (iii) Effect on the height of the column of the liquid due to the change in external pressure
   (iv) Comparison of the change in the heights of column of liquid A and that of B with a minute change in external pressure.

5. (i) pressure inside non-pressurised aeroplanes at higher altitudes
   (ii) comparison of pressure inside and outside a human body at sea level
   (iii) comparison of pressure in a human body and non-pressurised aeroplane.
   (iv) effect of difference in pressure

6. Argon is used in filling the ordinary electric bulbs because it is inert. Air containing oxygen cannot be used because it causes oxidation of tungsten. Moreover nitrogen and oxygen present in air can react at the high voltage to give nitric oxide.

7. Oxygen in the air is used for burning the fuel which gives energy in the form of heat. In the same way oxygen inhaled by us is used inside the tissues to break down the glucose and liberate energy in the form of heat. This liberated heat maintains the body temperature at 98.4°F.

8. UV rays convert O_2 to O_3. Ozone is used to purify drinking water as it produces nascent oxygen which kills the bacteria present in water.

9. In deep sea the pressure is more than the normal atmospheric pressure. Solubility of a gas increases with the increase in pressure. Normal air contains 20% oxygen. Due to increase in solubility in deep sea, only 4% oxygen is required. If N_2 is used to dilute O_2, it also dissolves in blood due to high pressure. When the diver comes up, the dissolved nitrogen escapes out in the form of bubbles which hinders the flow of blood. This causes painful sensation called **blend**. The solubility of helium is the least among all the gases. Hence, He is used for diluting O_2.

10. The layer of atmosphere which is close to the earth's surface is called troposphere. Hence, the temperature of troposphere is inversely proportional to the distance between surface of the earth and the different regions of the troposphere. Hence, temperature in this layer decreases with an increase in altitude. Interconversion of ozone and oxygen is more in the upper layer of stratosphere. During this process lot of heat energy is released, and hence, with increasing altitude temperature also increases in the stratosphere.

Chapter 5

Water, Solution, Solubility and Hydrogen

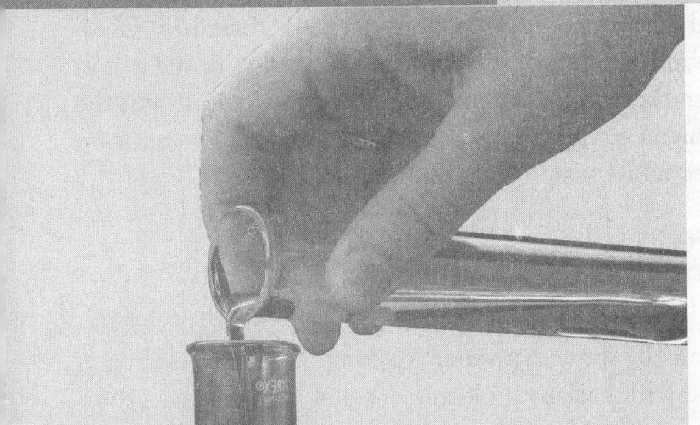

Remember

Before beginning this chapter, you should be able to:

- know the importance, different sources and forms of water.
- physical properties and uses of water.

Key Ideas

After completing this chapter, you should be able to:

- understand the physical properties of water and its role in day to day life and for industrial uses.
- study about the causes and consequences of water pollution.
- expalin the concept of solubility and the factors affecting it with special emphasis on solubility curves.
- learn the types of crystals and the process of crystallisation.
- understand various phenomena associated with different salts.
- study the various methods of preparation and properties of hydrogen and applications and uses of hydrogen in various fields.

INTRODUCTION

In the entire universe, only planet Earth has the unique gift of being endowed with a wide variety of flora and fauna. This existence of life on the Earth's surface can be attributed to various factors among which the abundant availability of water on the Earth is the most important one. The most common occurrence of water in liquid state, the easy interconversion of this substance into different physical states and its characteristic as a universal solvent and many other special features of this chemical substances make it play the most vital role in the biosphere. Therefore, water—being a crucial compound for man's survival—has become the most studied chemical substance.

Historical Aspects

Water in liquid form came into existence on the Earth about 43 billion years ago. Origin of life in this part of the universe also dates back to the same time since it is intimately linked with the origin of water. Water was believed to be an element in the ancient age. In 1781, Henry Cavendish was the first scientist to synthesise water from hydrogen and oxygen. This process of synthesis of water from its constituent elements led later scientists to recognise water as a compound.

WATER

Composition

A. I. Lavoisier was the first scientist to experimentally show that water is a compound with hydrogen and oxygen as its constituents. It has been established that one molecule of water contains two atoms of hydrogen and one atom of oxygen.

Occurrence

The distribution of water over the Earth's surface is not uniform throughout. Water is available in nature mostly in a free state and to a somewhat lesser extent in a combined state. Water exists in the free state in all the three physical states, namely, solid, liquid and gaseous states.

1. **Solid state**: Certain regions on the Earth, like, high peaks of mountains, polar regions in Antarctica and the arctic circle contain water as snow or ice. In these places, water exists in a solid state due to the very low temperatures prevailing in these regions.
2. **Liquid state**: It is the most common state in which water exists. Most of the liquid water is found in oceans and seas. Apart from this, liquid water is also found in rivers, lakes, streams and other water bodies. Water available in the above sources is called **surface water**. Water present in oceans and seas contain appreciable proportions of dissolved salts, predominantly sodium chloride. The presence of these salts imparts salty taste to water and this water is, hence, called **saline water**.

   In addition to surface water, water is also available under the Earth's surface. This is called **underground water**. This water is stored due to the seepage of rain water through the soil. The underground water may come out in the form of springs. This can be drawn out artificially by digging wells or with the help of tube wells.
3. **Gaseous state**: In gaseous state, water exists as water vapour in the atmospheric air. Clouds, fog, mist, etc., contain water vapour in condensed form.

   Water exists in a combined state in the form of body fluids in the body of living beings. Water is also present in the combined state in hydrated crystals, like, $CuSO_4.5H_2O$, $FeSO_4.7H_2O$, etc. Saline water of oceans and seas can also be considered as one form of combined state of water.

Distribution of Water on Earth's Surface

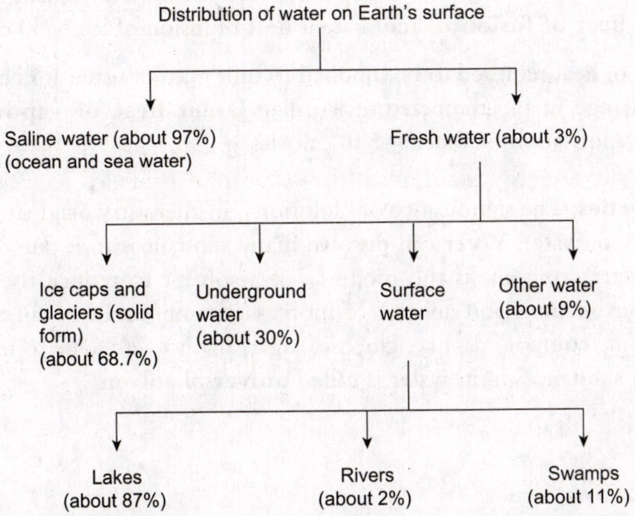

FIGURE 5.1 Distribution of water on earth's surface

Physical Properties of Water

The significance of water as the most important liquid is mainly due to its physical properties. Some important physical properties of water are discussed in detail in the following section:

1. **Nature**: Water is an odourless, tasteless and transparent liquid. However, the taste of water is attributed to the presence of dissolved salts in it. Volatile impurities also impart some odour to water. Water is colourless in thin layers but it appears bluish in thick layers.

2. **Freezing point**: The freezing point of water is 0°C under normal atmospheric pressure. The freezing point of water decreases with an increase in external pressure. Presence of soluble impurities decreases the freezing point of water.

3. **Boiling point**: The boiling point of pure water is 100°C under normal atmospheric pressure. The boiling point of water gets elevated due to the presence of soluble impurities. Increase in external pressure increases the boiling point of water.

4. **Density**: The maximum density of water is 1 g/cc and is obtained at 4°C.The density of water increases with increase in temperature up to 4°C. Later, density of water decreases with increase in temperature beyond 4°C.

   Water shows an unusual behaviour between 0°C and 4°C. In this range of temperature, water expands on cooling instead of contracting. This phenomenon of unusual expansion of water between 0°C and 4°C is called **anomalous expansion**.

5. **Conductivity**: Pure water is a bad conductor of heat and electricity. The electrical conductivity of water is due to the presence of dissolved salts in water.

6. **Specific heat**: The amount of heat energy required to raise the temperature of unit mass of a substance through 1°C or 1 K is called **specific heat capacity of that substance**. Specific heat capacity of pure water is 1 calorie $g^{-1}°C^{-1}$ = 42 joule $g^{-1}°C^{-1}$. Water has the highest specific heat capacity among all the substances.

7. **Latent heat of fusion and latent heat of vaporisation**: The amount of heat required to be supplied to unit mass of ice for converting it to water without any change in the temperature is called **latent heat of fusion of ice**. Latent heat of fusion of ice = 80 calories/g.

   The amount of heat required to be supplied to unit mass of water for converting it to steam without any change in the temperature is called **latent heat of vaporisation of water**. Latent heat of vaporisation of water = 540 calories/g.

8. **Solvent properties**: The significance of "solutions" in chemistry originates from the universal solvent property of water. Water can dissolve many substances in it due to its high dielectric constant. Dielectric constant is the property of a solvent to reduce the force of attraction between the ions (cations and anions) of inorganic compounds. It can also dissolve a large number of organic compounds, like, glucose, sugar, alcohol, etc. Due to the ability to dissolve a wide range of substances in it, water is called **universal solvent**.

EXAMPLE

Two containers A and B contain 30 g and 20 g of water, respectively. If the rate of supply of heat is same and their initial temperature is also same, then water in which container starts boiling first?

SOLUTION

Amount of water present in container A = m_A = 30 g

Amount of water present in container B = m_B = 20 g

Specific heat of water in A = Specific heat of water in B.

Heat required to be supplied to make the water boil = mass of water × specific heat × difference in boiling point of water and initial temperature of water.

∴ Mass of water in B is less, heat required to boil it is less.

∴ Water in container B will boil first.

Day to day human activities, like, washing, cooking, cleaning, etc., and all life processes occurring in nature involve the formation of solutions with water. Therefore, the ability of water to form solutions is responsible for sustenance of life. On the other hand, the same characteristic forms the basic cause for adding pollutants to water. In whichever way it is considered, the ability of water to form solutions influences the survival of man on the Earth.

Chemical Properties of Water

1. **Nature**: Water, being a compound of hydrogen and oxygen, is considered an oxide of hydrogen. Since it does not respond to litmus test, it is a neutral oxide.
2. **Catalytic property**: Water catalyses some chemical reactions.

   Examples:

   (a) The reaction between perfectly dry hydrogen and chlorine does not take place even in the presence of direct sunlight.

   The reaction is catalysed by a few drops of water.

(b) Some other reactions like the reaction between hydrogen and oxygen and the combustion of phosphorous also occur only in the presence of trace amounts of moisture.

$$2H_2 + O_2 \xrightarrow{\text{moisture}} 2H_2O$$

$$4P + O_2 \xrightarrow{\text{moisture}} 2P_2O_5$$

3. Action of water on metals

Reactions	Observations
(a) **Potassium** Potassium reacts with cold water. It even reacts with moisture (water vapour) $2K + 2H_2O \longrightarrow 2KOH + H_2$	(i) Potassium floats on water in the form of silvery grey globules (ii) Reaction is vigorous and exothermic (iii) It catches fire and burns with lilac flame (iv) Effervescence of hydrogen is observed and water becomes alkaline
(b) **Sodium** The reaction takes place in cold water $2Na + 2H_2O \longrightarrow 2NaOH + H_2$ It even reacts with moisture (water vapour)	(i) Sodium floats on water in the form of silvery globules (ii) Reaction is less exothermic and vigorous than that with potassium (iii) It catches fire and burns with a golden yellow flame (iv) Effervescence of hydrogen is observed and water becomes alkaline
(c) **Calcium** The reaction takes place in cold water $Ca + 2H_2O \longrightarrow Ca(OH)_2 + H_2$	(i) Calcium sinks in water and the water becomes milky and alkaline (ii) It does not catch fire (iii) Effervescence of hydrogen is observed
(d) **Magnesium** The reaction takes place with boiling water, but a moderate reaction takes place when burning magnesium reacts with steam $Mg + H_2O \longrightarrow MgO + H_2$	(i) It burns brilliantly with white light (ii) White ash of MgO is produced (iii) Liberation of hydrogen takes place
(e) **Zinc** The reaction takes place when steam is passed over red hot zinc $Zn + \underset{\text{(steam)}}{H_2O} \longrightarrow ZnO + H_2$	(i) Yellow-coloured ZnO is produced. On cooling, yellow-coloured ZnO becomes white in colour (ii) Liberation of hydrogen takes place
(f) **Aluminium** Aluminium also reacts with steam $2Al + \underset{\text{(steam)}}{3H_2O} \longrightarrow Al_2O_3 + 3H_2$	(i) A coating of Al_2O_3 is formed over the metal which protects the metal from further reaction (ii) Liberation of hydrogen is observed
(g) **Iron** When steam is passed over red hot iron, the reaction takes place $3Fe + 4H_2O \longrightarrow Fe_3O_4 + 4H_2$	(i) Brown coloured ferroso ferric oxide is formed and hydrogen is liberated (ii) Reaction is reversible when it takes place in a closed container

Action of Water on Non-metals

1. **Reaction with carbon**: When superheated steam is passed over red hot coke, a mixture of carbon monoxide and hydrogen, called **water gas**, is produced. It is a good fuel and a reducing agent.

$$C + H_2O \longrightarrow CO + H_2 \text{ (water gas)}$$

2. **Reaction with chlorine**: When chlorine gas is passed through water, hydrochloric acid and hypochlorous acid are produced.

$$Cl_2 + H_2O \longrightarrow HCl + HOCl$$

Reaction with Metallic Oxides

Metallic oxides react with water to form respective bases.

Examples: $K_2O + H_2O \longrightarrow 2KOH$

$$Na_2O + H_2O \longrightarrow 2NaOH$$

$$CaO + H_2O \longrightarrow Ca(OH)_2$$

Reaction with non-metallic oxides

Non-metallic oxides react with water to form respective acids.

$$SO_2 + H_2O \longrightarrow H_2SO_3$$

$$P_2O_5 + 3H_2O \longrightarrow 2H_2PO_4$$

$$CO_2 + H_2O \longrightarrow H_2CO_3$$

Tests for Water

1. Water turns white coloured anhydrous copper sulphate to blue coloured hydrated copper sulphate ($CuSO_4.5H_2O$).
2. Blue coloured anhydrous cobalt chloride turns pink on addition of water due to the formation of cobalt chloride hexahydrate ($CoCl_2.6H_2O$).

Uses of Water

Fresh water is widely used for our day to day domestic activities, for power generation, irrigation and many industrial activities.

1. About 8% of the water is used for domestic purposes, like, cooking, washing, cleaning, flushing, etc.
2. About 22% of fresh water is used in industries.
   - **(a)** Water is used in chemical laboratories because of its solvent property. Many reactions are carried out in the laboratory in aqueous solutions. Many organic compounds do not dissolve in water, hence, water is used for solvent extraction process to separate organic and inorganic compounds. It is also used in the manufacturing of hydrogen, oxygen, acids, alkalis, salts, water gas, etc.
   - **(b)** Pharmaceutical industries also use water extensively.
   - **(c)** Water in the form of steam is used for the generation of electricity.
   - **(d)** Water is used in cooling systems due to its high specific heat capacity.

3. About 70% of the fresh water is used for irrigation.
   (a) Water acts as a medium for the transportation of mineral nutrients through soil in plants.
   (b) Fertilisers and insecticides dissolve in water and they are sprayed on plants in the form of solutions in required concentrations.
4. Saline water is used as a major source for the production of common salt. It is also used for the production of magnesia (MgO) which is used in refractories.

All these uses make water as the most essential chemical substance. The constituent elements of water, namely, oxygen and hydrogen also have equal significance in various fields.

SOLUTION

A solution is a homogeneous mixture of two or more substances. The proportion of the constituents of the solution can be varied within certain limits. The solutions comprising of the two components are called **binary solutions**.

That component of a solution which is in the same physical state (i.e., solid, liquid or gas) as the solution is called **solvent**, and the other component is called **solute**.

If both the components are in the same state, the component which is present in larger proportions is called solvent and the one which is present in minor proportions is called solute.

Classification of Solutions

Depending on the physical states of the solute and the solvent, solutions can be classified into various types.

Solvents	Solutes	Examples
Solid	Solid	Alloys like brass,bronze, etc
	Liquid	Hydrated crystalline salts
	Gas	Hydrogen gas adsorbed on platinum or palladium
Liquid	Solid	Common salt in water
	Liquid	Petrol in kerosene
	Gas	Aerated water or soft drinks
Gas	Gas	Air

When the solvent is a gas and the solute is a solid or a liquid, the resultant mixture becomes heterogeneous. All other solutions being homogeneous are called **true solutions**. The other two types of mixtures being heterogeneous are called **suspensions**.

Examples: fog, mist and dust particles in air.

The study of solutions is generally confined to the solutions of a solid solute in a liquid solvent.

In most of the cases, water is taken as the solvent since it can dissolve a wide range of chemical compounds. Those solutions in which water is taken as the solvent are called **aqueous solutions**.

Apart from water, other liquids can also be taken as solvents. Examples of such solvents are alcohol, petrol, ether, benzene, etc. Those solutions in which a liquid other than water is taken as a solvent are called **non-aqueous solutions**.

Aqueous solutions can be further classified on the basis of relative proportions of a solute in the solution.

Dilute Solution

A solution in which there is a small amount of solute dissolved in a given mass of a solvent is called **dilute solution.**

Concentrated Solution

A solution containing a relatively large amount of a solute dissolved in a given mass of a solvent is called **concentrated solution.**

Solubility

The process of dissolving a substance in the given solvent is called **dissolution**. The amount of a solute dissolved in a definite quantity of a solvent depends upon the nature of the solute as well as nature of the solvent.

The maximum amount of a particular solute in grams, which can dissolve in 100 g of solvent at a given temperature is called **solubility**.

$$\text{Solubility} = \frac{\text{Mass of solute}}{\text{Mass of solvent}} \times 100$$

Example:

Solubility of copper sulphate in water at 20°C is 20.7 g and solubility of potassium chloride in water at 20°C is 34 g.

A given solution may or may not contain the maximum amount of a solute in it. The further dissolving capacity of a given solution depends on the amount of the solute already present in the solution. On the basis of the capacity of the solution to dissolve certain amount of solute further, the solutions are classified into three types as discussed hereunder.

Saturated Solution

A solution which contains the maximum amount of the solute that can be dissolved in the solvent at a given temperature is called **saturated solution** at that particular temperature. This solution can no longer dissolve any more solute under the given conditions.

Unsaturated Solution

The solution containing lesser amount of the solute than the saturated solution at a given temperature is called an **unsaturated solution**. In an unsaturated solution the solvent has the capacity of dissolving more amount of the solute at that particular temperature.

Supersaturated Solution

If a solution holds more solute than the saturated solution at a given temperature, it is called **supersaturated solution**.

When more solute is made to dissolve in a saturated solution by raising its temperature and then cooling it slowly without causing any disturbances (like shaking), then the resultant solution holds more solute than the saturated solution.

Supersaturated solution is metastable and slight disturbances, like, shaking, stirring and scratching the wall of the container or adding a solute crystal to the solution make the additional amount of the solute to precipitate out, thereby resulting in the formation of the saturated solution again.

Factors Affecting Solubility

1. **Nature of the solute**: Ionic compounds or polar compounds are more soluble in polar solvents like water. Non-polar compounds are more soluble in non-polar solvents like benzene.
2. **Nature of the solvent**: The solvents which have high dielectric constants can dissolve polar and ionic compounds to a greater extent than the solvents with low dielectric constants.

   Example:

   NaCl is highly soluble in water.

   NaCl is sparingly soluble in benzene.
3. **Temperature**: For most of the substances, solubility increases with the increase in temperature. However, the solubility of some substances decreases with increase in temperature. In case of some substances the temperature has no or little effect on the solubility.

   Solubility curves: The graphs which show variation of solubility with temperature are called solubility curves.

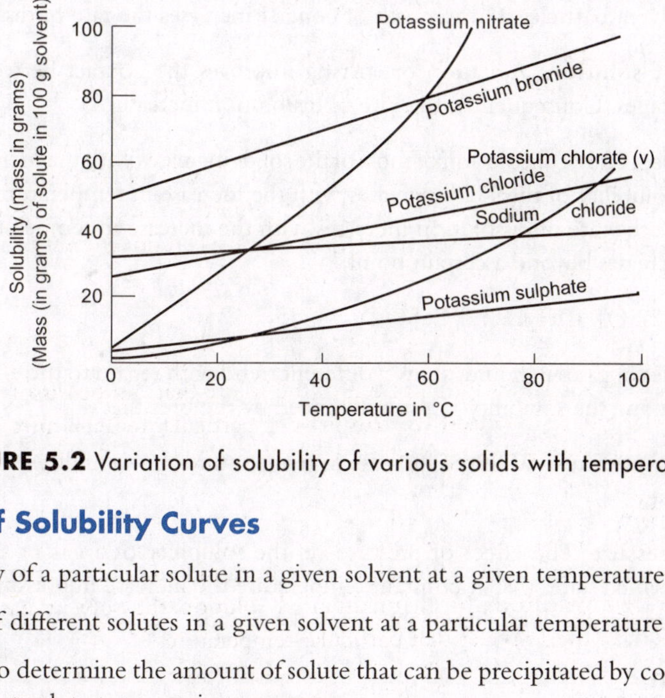

FIGURE 5.2 Variation of solubility of various solids with temperatures

Importance of Solubility Curves

1. The solubility of a particular solute in a given solvent at a given temperature can be found out.
2. Solubilities of different solutes in a given solvent at a particular temperature can be compared.
3. It is possible to determine the amount of solute that can be precipitated by cooling the saturated solution of that solute to a certain temperature.
4. From the solubility curves, it is possible to know the preferential precipitation of different salts during the fractional crystallisation process since the solution contains more than one salt dissolved in it.

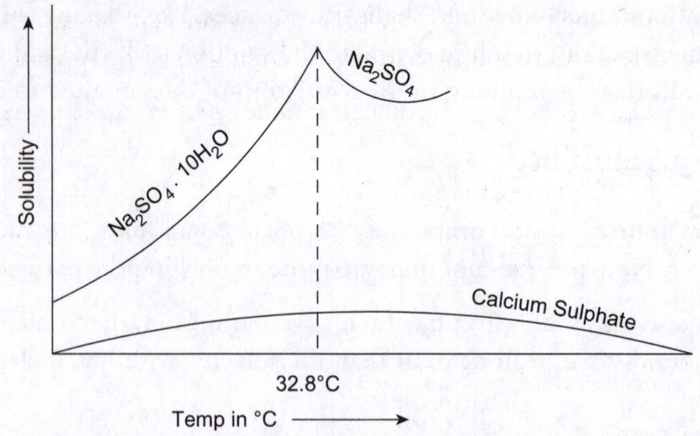

FIGURE 5.3 Solubility curve of $Na_2SO_4 . 10H_2O$ and $CaSO_4$

Rate of Dissolution of a Solid in a Liquid

Though each solute has a certain fixed value of solubility, the rate at which a solute dissolves in a particular solvent depends on certain factors.

1. **Size of the solute particles**: The smaller the solute particles, the faster the rate of dissolution. This is because division into smaller particles increases the surface area of contact between the solute and solvent particles. Greater area of contact increases the rate of dissolution.

2. **Agitation of solution**: Agitation or stirring improves the contact between the solute and solvent molecules. Consequently, the rate of dissolution increases.

3. **Temperature**: Rate of dissolution of most of the solids increases with the increase in temperature because the solubility of the solid increases with the increase in temperature. However, in case of some solids the rate of dissolution increases with the increase in temperature up to a certain point and decreases beyond a certain point.

   Examples: $Na_2SO_4 . 10H_2O$ and $CaSO_4$

   The solubilities of gases in liquids show a different trend with regard to the effect of temperature. In these solutions, the solubility is also influenced by the pressure.

   Effect of temperature: With the increase in temperature, the solubility of a gas in a particular liquid decreases.

   Effect of pressure: The effect of pressure on the solubility of a gas in a liquid is given by Henry's law, which states that at constant temperature the increase in pressure on the surface of the liquid increases the solubility of the gas in the liquid.

Crystallisation

When a saturated solid–liquid solution is cooled slowly, solid solute settles down with a highly regular arrangement of its constituent particles (atoms, molecules or ions). This regular arrangement of component particles in a three-dimensional system is uniform throughout the entire solid. This type of solid is called **crystalline solid**. The smallest unit of this arrangement of particles which gets repeated throughout the crystalline solid is called **unit cell**. Unit cell of each substance has a definite geometric shape.

Hence, crystals can be defined as solids in which the constituent atoms, molecules or ions are packed in a regularly ordered and repeating pattern extending in all three spatial dimensions.

Crystallisation is the process of formation of a crystalline solid from the corresponding solution.

Different Processes of Crystallisation

1. Slow cooling of a hot saturated solution of a solid solute from a higher temperature to a lower temperature.
2. Evaporation of an unsaturated solution at moderate temperature.
3. Slow cooling of a molten solid.
4. Sublimation of the solid followed by condensation of the resultant vapours.

Types of Crystals

Each crystal consists of a set of three axes in a particular geometrical arrangement. There are seven unique crystal systems depending on the orientation of the particles along the three axes.

Types of crystal systems	Examples
Cubic	NaCl, CsCl
Hexagonal	Graphite, ZnO
Tetragonal	SnO_2,TiO_2
Rhombohedral	$CaCO_3$, HgS
Orthorhombic	Rhombic sulphur
Monoclinic	Monoclinic sulphur, $PbCrO_2$
Triclinic	$K_2Cr_2O_7$, $CuSO_4.5H_2O$

Water of crystallisation: When a solid gets crystallised from its respective hot concentrated aqueous solution, a certain fixed number of water molecules also get attached to the solid crystals to form unit cells of the crystals.

The fixed number of water molecules which combine with a crystal and are necessary for the maintenance of crystalline properties, but capable of being lost either at normal temperature or at a higher temperature is called **water of crystallisation.**

Examples of such solids (salts) are green vitriol ($FeSO_47H_2O$), blue vitriol ($CuSO_45H_2O$), washing soda ($Na_2CO_3.10H_2O$), etc.

Hydrated salts and anhydrous salts: The salts which contain water of crystallisation are called **hydrated salts.**

When the hydrated salts completely lose their water molecules, then such salts are called **anhydrous salt**. When a hydrated salt gets dehydrated and forms anhydrous salt, the colour of the salt changes. For example, $CuSO_4.5H_2O$ is blue in colour. It changes to white colour due to the loss of water molecules on heating.

Efflorescence and deliquescence: There are some hydrated crystals which lose some of the water of crystallisation or all the water of crystallisation on exposure to air at normal temperature. This phenomenon is known as **efflorescence** and the hydrated crystals which lose water molecules are called **efflorescent substances.**

After the release of the water molecules, efflorescent substances lose their crystalline property and get transformed into a powdery mass.

Example:

Glauber salt, $Na_2SO_4.10H_2O$ loses all of its water molecules on exposure to air at ordinary temperature.

Some crystalline salts absorb moisture on exposure to air and ultimately dissolve in it to form an aqueous solution. This phenomenon is called **deliquescence** and these crystalline salts are called deliquescent substances.

These salts may or may not contain water of crystallisation.

Examples of such salts are hydrated magnesium chloride ($MgCl_2.6H_2O$), hydrated calcium chloride ($CaCl_2$. $6H_2O$), etc.

Hygroscopic substances and desiccating agents: There are certain substances which absorb moisture from air without changing their physical state. These substances are called hygroscopic substances. They may exist in solid or liquid state under normal temperature and pressure.

Examples of such substances are calcium oxide (solid), concentrated sulphuric acid (liquid), etc.

After absorbing moisture, solid hygroscopic substances remain as solids and liquid substances remain as liquids.

Unlike deliquescent substances, these hygroscopic substances retain their physical states (solids or liquid) upon absorption of moisture.

Hygroscopic substances which are used to remove water from the surroundings are called desiccating agents. Examples of **desiccating agents** are calcium oxide and anhydrous calcium chloride.

Water has unique physical properties due to which existence of life on the earth is possible. However, chemical properties of water also play a vital role in the progress of human civilisation.

EXAMPLE

Hydrated copper sulphate is not considered as an efflorescent substance. Give reason.

SOLUTION

Hydrated copper sulphate does not lose its water molecules at normal temperature and pressure. Only on heating the water molecules can be released. Hence, it is not considered as an efflorescent substance.

HYDROGEN

Hydrogen is the lightest among all elements. Atmospheric air is found to contain only trace amounts of hydrogen. Hydrogen gas was first prepared by the action of H_2SO_4 on iron. In 1762, Henry Cavendish for the first time established the elemental nature of hydrogen. He prepared this gas by the action of H_2SO_4 on zinc. Lavoisier named it hydrogen which means water-former (Hydro—water, gen—producing).

Occurrence

Availability of hydrogen gas in a free state is very rare. Though it is present in trace amounts in the atmosphere, hydrogen is present in sun's atmosphere up to 1.1%. Very minute quantities of hydrogen are present in volcanic gases.

Most of the hydrogen is present in a combined state in nature. Hydrogen is present in various carbon compounds in the form of proteins, nucleic acids, vitamins, hormones, enzymes, etc., in plants and animals. Most of the naturally occurring substances, such as, wood, cotton, paper pulp, rubber, etc., contain hydrogen. Water is the most important source of hydrogen as hydrogen is present up to 11.1% by weight in water.

Preparation of Hydrogen

(i) General Methods of Preparation

Methods	Equations	Observations
Action of active metals with water	$2Na + 2H_2O \longrightarrow 2NaOH + H_2$	Na and K $\longrightarrow$ Reaction is violent. They float on the surface of water Ca $\longrightarrow$ Brisk reaction and metal sinks in water
Action of steam on hot metals	$Mg + H_2O \longrightarrow MgO + H_2$	Reaction is fast for Mg and slow for Al, Zn and Fe
Action of dil acids on metals	$Zn + 2HCl \longrightarrow ZnCl_2 + H_2$	—
Action of concentrated alkali on metals	$2NaOH + 2Al + 2H_2O \longrightarrow 2NaAlO_2 + 3H_2$	Reaction takes place only on boiling

Laboratory Method of Preparation

Principle: All the metals present above hydrogen in the reactivity series on reaction with dil HCl or dil H_2SO_4 liberate hydrogen gas. Zinc metal is preferred for this reaction.

$$Zn + 2HCl \longrightarrow ZnCl_2 + H_2\uparrow$$

$$Zn + H_2SO_4 \longrightarrow ZnSO_4 + H_2\uparrow$$

Experiment I

Some granulated zinc pieces are taken in a flat-bottomed flask fitted with a two holed air-tight cork. In the one hole, a thistle funnel is inserted and in the other hole, a long delivery tube is inserted. Dilute H_2SO_4 is allowed to fall into the flask dropwise through the thistle funnel.

Observation: Effervescence is observed in the initial stages of the reaction. Then a colourless and odourless gas evolves.

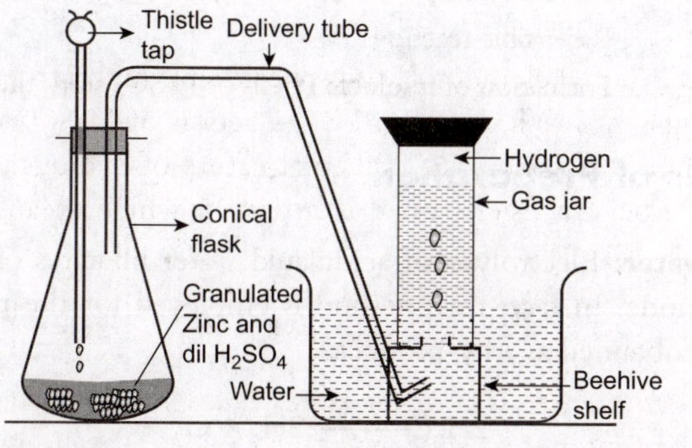

FIGURE 5.4 Laboratory preparation of Hydrogen

Collection of gas: Hydrogen is collected by the downward displacement of water.

Purification of hydrogen gas: Since impure zinc is used for hydrogen gas preparation, the hydrogen gas collected is found to contain some impurities, such as, H_2S, SO_2, PH_3, AsH_3 and CO_2. These impurities are removed in stages.

Impurities	Processes of removal
(a) AsH_3, PH_3	Silver nitrate solution
(b) H_2S	Lead nitrate solution
(c) CO_2, SO_2, NO_2	Caustic potash
(d) H_2O (water vapour)	$CaCl_2$ or P_2O_5 (drying agent)

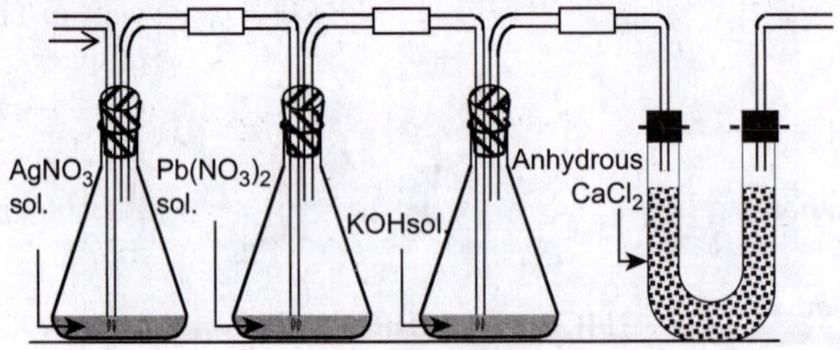

FIGURE 5.5 Purification of hydrogen gas

Collection of purified hydrogen gas: To obtain pure and dry hydrogen, pure hydrogen gas is collected over mercury.

Precautions

1. Entire apparatus should be kept air-tight.
2. Contact with flame should be avoided.
3. Collection of the gas should be done only after the expulsion of air.
4. The end of the thistle funnel should almost touch the bottom.

Though all active metals liberate hydrogen gas, zinc is the preferred metal and the other metals are not used for this preparation method.

Metals	Reasons for not using
Sodium and potassium	Violent reaction with explosion
Calcium and magnesium	Expensive metals
Aluminium	Formation of protective coating of Al_2O_3 renders the metal passive
Iron	Reversible reaction
Lead	Formation of insoluble $PbCl_2$ or $PbSO_4$ stops the further reaction

Industrial Methods of Preparation

1. **Electrolysis of water**: Electrolysis of acidulated water liberates oxygen at the cathode and hydrogen at the anode. In fact, this method is employed for the preparation of oxygen gas where hydrogen is obtained as a by-product.

$$2H_2O \longrightarrow 2H_2 + O_2$$

2. Bosch Process

Principle: Water gas is a mixture of carbon monoxide and hydrogen. Catalytic oxidation of carbon monoxide gives hydrogen gas. Water gas can be prepared by passing steam over red hot coke.

$$\underset{\text{Steam}}{C + H_2O} \longrightarrow \underset{\text{Water gas}}{CO + H_2}$$

$$CO + H_2 + H_2O \xrightarrow[450°C - 500°C]{Fe_2O_3} CO_2 + 2H_2$$

Process

(a) Superheated steam at 170°C when passed through white hot coke or charcoal gives a mixture of CO gas and hydrogen known as water gas.

(b) Water gas obtained is made to pass over Fe_2O_3 or Cr_2O_3 along with superheated steam at 500°C. Carbon monoxide gets oxidised to CO_2 leaving hydrogen gas.

3. The CO_2 gas is removed by compressing the gas at 30 atm pressure and passing it through water. Hydrogen being insoluble remains as such.

$$H_2O_{(1)} + CO_{2(g)} \xrightarrow{300\ atm} H_2CO_3$$

4. The water vapour present in the gas can be removed by cooling the gas to –20°C.

5. The traces of carbon monoxide remaining unoxidised can be removed by passing the gas through ammonical cuprous chloride solution.

$$CuCl + CO + 2H_2O \longrightarrow \underset{\text{addition compound}}{CuCl.CO.2H_2O}$$

Bosch process can also be carried out for the preparation of hydrogen from natural gas. Natural gas contains methane as a major constituent. Methane on mixing with superheated steam at high temperature followed by compression to 30 atm pressure also gives water gas. This is subjected to Bosch process for getting pure hydrogen gas.

Properties of Hydrogen

Physical Properties

Properties	Description
Colour	Colourless
Odour	No characteristic odour for pure hydrogen. But fishy odour of hydrogen gas is attributed to the presence of impurities
Solubility	Negligible
Density	Least density
Action on litmus	Neutral
Liquefaction	Difficult due to very low critical temperature and not possible at room temperature
Diffusion	Fast rate of diffusion

Adsorption or occlusion: In addition to the normal physical properties, hydrogen shows a specific property called **adsorption** or **occlusion**. The accumulation of molecules of one compound over the surface of another substance is called **adsorption**. Hydrogen gas gets adsorbed on the surface of some metals, like, palladium, platinum, nickel, etc.

Chemical Properties

1. **Reaction with air**: Hydrogen burns in air and reacts with oxygen forming water. A blue flame is also observed.

$$2H_2 + O_2 \longrightarrow 2H_2O$$

2. **Reaction with non-metals**: Hydrogen reacts with most of the non-metals forming corresponding hydrides.

   (a) **Reaction with chlorine**: Hydrogen reacts with chlorine in the presence of sun light to give hydrogen chloride. This is a photochemical reaction as shown below:

$$H_2 + Cl_2 \xrightarrow{\text{light}} 2HCl$$

   (b) **Reaction with nitrogen**: Nitrogen and hydrogen react in 1 : 3 ratio at high temperature and high pressure to form ammonia.

$$N_2 + 3H_2 \longrightarrow 2NH_3$$

   (c) **Reaction with sulphur**: On reaction with molten sulphur, hydrogen gas gives hydrogen sulphide.

$$H_2 + S \longrightarrow H_2S$$

3. **Reactions with metals**: Hydrogen reacts with highly electropositive metals to form metallic hydrides.

Examples:

$$2K + H_2 \xrightarrow{\Delta} 2KH$$

$$2Na + H_2 \xrightarrow{\Delta} 2NaH$$

$$Ca + H_2 \longrightarrow CaH_2$$

4. **Reactions with metal oxides**: Oxides of less reactive metals react with hydrogen to form the corresponding metal and water. This is due to the reduction of metallic oxide.

Examples:

$$ZnO + H_2 \longrightarrow Zn + H_2O$$

White — Bluish white

$$2Fe_2O_3 + 6H_2 \longrightarrow 4Fe + 6H_2O$$

Brown — Grey

$$PbO + H_2 \longrightarrow Pb + H_2O$$

Yellow — Grey

$$CuO + H_2 \longrightarrow Cu + H_2O$$

Black — Red

5. **Hydrogenation**: Catalytic addition of hydrogen to some carbon compounds is called hydrogenation.

$$\underset{\text{Ethylene}}{H_2C = CH_2} + H_2 \longrightarrow \underset{\text{Ethane}}{H_3C - CH_3}$$

This principle is used in the process of hydrogenation of oils or hardening of oils.

Hydrogenation of oils: Vegetable oil which contains carbon and oxygen in greater percentage and contains less amount of hydrogen cannot be solidified easily due to less percentage of hydrogen.

Examples: Ground nut oil and sunflower oil.

Animal oils such as ghee which contain hydrogen in greater percentage get solidified easily under normal conditions. Vegetable oils also get solidified when hydrogen gas is passed through them at high pressure and high temperature in the presence of a nickel catalyst.

Examples: Palm oil, vanaspathi, soap, etc.

Uses of Hydrogen

1. In the synthesis of industrial chemicals.

   (a) Manufacture of ammonia (Haber's process)

$$N_2 + 3H_2 \xrightarrow{Fe} 2NH_3$$

   (b) Manufacture of HCl

$$H_2 + Cl_2 \xrightarrow{\text{sunlight}} 2HCl$$

   (c) Manufacture of methyl alcohol

$$CO + H_2 + H_2 \xrightarrow[\text{Catalyst}]{\Delta} CH_3OH$$

   (d) Manufacture of dalda/vanaspathi and soap by hydrogenation of oils.

   (e) Manufacture of petrol/gasoline from coal.

2. **(a)** **Fuel**: Many fuel gases contain hydrogen as a major constituent. This is because of high heat of combustion of hydrogen.

   Examples: Water gas, coal gas, semi-water gas, etc.

   (b) Electrical cells called **fuel cells** are also designed which use hydrogen gas.

   (c) **Oxyhydrogen blow torch**: A mixture of hydrogen and oxygen is burnt to give a high temperature of 2800°C. This is used for welding of metals and for melting platinum and quartz.

   (d) Liquid hydrogen is used as a rocket fuel.

   (e) **Atomic hydrogen torch**: When an electric arc is generated in a stream of hydrogen between tungsten electrodes the hydrogen molecules dissociate to give hydrogen atoms by absorbing large amount of energy. The atoms recombine to form hydrogen molecules by evolving the absorbed heat energy. As a result, high temperature is generated. This can be made use of in welding alloys.

f. **Metallurgy**: Hydrogen is used as a good reducing agent in the extraction of some metals from their oxides.

Examples: Tungsten, molybdenum, etc.

$$WO_3 + 3H_2 \longrightarrow W + 3H_2O$$

EXAMPLE

Explain the principle of atomic hydrogen torch.

SOLUTION

When an electric arc is generated in a stream of hydrogen between tungsten electrodes, the hydrogen molecules dissociate to give hydrogen atoms. The atoms recombine to form hydrogen molecules by releasing heat energy. As a result, high temperature can be obtained. This can be made use of in welding alloys.

EXAMPLE

What makes the use of hydrogen as a fuel difficult? Give reasons in support of your answer.

SOLUTION

Though there are many advantages of hydrogen as an automobile fuel, there are a few drawbacks in this process.

(i) Liquefaction of hydrogen gas is very difficult since its critical temperature is very less. This makes liquid hydrogen very expensive.

(ii) Since hydrogen is highly inflammable, its storage and transportation are difficult.

TEST YOUR CONCEPTS

Very Short Answer Type Questions

1. Why does ice float on water?
2. What do you mean by hydrated salt? Give an example.
3. What do you mean by solubility?
4. What is the difference between surface water and underground water?
5. In alloys, constituent metals retain their _____ properties.
6. Name some compounds where the presence of water molecules provides colour to those substances.
7. How is fractional crystallisation process related to solubility curve?
8. What do you mean by a desiccating agent?
9. Differentiate between dilute and concentrated solutions.
10. The number of water molecules present in hydrated copper sulphate is _____.
11. Solubility of copper sulphate in water is 20.7 g at 20°C. What do you mean by this statement?
12. How does freezing point get affected due to the presence of impurities?
13. Name two metals which react with moisture.
14. How is hydrogen gas used in metallurgy? Give an example.
15. What is the value of specific heat capacity of water? How much heat energy is required to increase the temperature of 5 g of water to 1°C?
16. When phosphorus pentoxide reacts with water, the product is _____.
17. What is meant by hardening of oils? How is it done?
18. How is water gas formed?
19. _____ can catalyse the reaction between dry chlorine and hydrogen.
20. What is the difference between latent heat of fusion and latent heat of vaporisation? Discuss the difference taking water as an example.
21. What is unit cell of a crystal?
22. Will there be any change in the boiling point of water if we go to the top of a hill? Give reasons.
23. Complete the following table:

Solution	Solvent	Solute
1. Sugar solution		
2. Solution of alcohol and water (5% alcohol and 95% water)		
3. Blue vitriol		
4. Brass		
5. Hydrogen adsorbed by platinum		

24. Name the acid formed by the reaction between SO_2 gas and water. Also write the reaction involved.
25. Why is granulated zinc used for the preparation of hydrogen gas?
26. Hydrated copper sulphate is not considered an efflorescent substance. Give a reason.
27. What happens when steam is passed over hot magnesium metal?
28. Differentiate between efflorescent and deliquescent substances.
29. What is meant by occlusion? Give one example.
30. State whether the solution is a mixture or a compound. Justify your answer.

Short Answer Type Questions

31. Define specific heat capacity of a substance.
32. A piece of red litmus paper is dipped into the water kept in beakers A and B.

    (a) In beaker "A" some amount of CaO was poured.

    (b) SO_2 gas was passed through beaker "B."

PRACTICE QUESTIONS

Write the observations made in both the cases.

33. What is the difference between a deliquescent substance and a hygroscopic substance?

34. How are fog and mist formed?

35. Water obtained from which source contains more minerals and why?

36. What are the different factors on which solubility of a solid in a liquid depend? Explain with a reason.

37. In which way is water useful for generating electricity?

38. Establish water as a compound.

39. How can hydrogen be prepared from natural gas?

40. Why is pure water a bad conductor of electricity?

41. How do temperature and pressure affect the solubility of gases in water?

42. Why is distilled water not useful for drinking purpose though it is the purest form of water?

43. Give some examples of reactions where metal oxides react with hydrogen.

44. Differentiate solvent and solute with an example each when

(a) both are in the same physical state and

(b) the physical state of the solute and the solvent is different.

Essay Type Questions

45. Discuss in detail Bosch process of preparation of hydrogen gas.

46. Discuss the different physical properties of water with respect to the various uses.

47. What are solubility curves? Explain different areas of applications of solubility curves.

48. Explain the general methods of preparation of hydrogen giving one example each. Among these, which method is preferred for laboratory preparation and why?

49. Write the effect of impurities and external pressure on the freezing and boiling points of water. Explain with examples.

For Answer key, Hints and Explanations, please visit:
www.pearsoned.co.in/IITFoundationSeries

CONCEPT APPLICATION

Level 1

Directions for questions from 1 to 7
State whether the following statements are true or false:

1. Aqueous solutions are good conductors in comparison to their corresponding pure solvent.
2. Soluble impurities present in water increase the freezing point of water.
3. Solubility curves can be used for comparing the solubility of different substances at a given temperature.
4. The freezing point of water decreases with a decrease in pressure.
5. The density of water is maximum at 4 K.
6. Blue-coloured $CuSO_4$ can act as a dehumidifying agent.
7. Alloys are homogeneous mixtures.

Directions for questions from 8 to 14
Fill in the blanks.

8. _____ substances when exposed to moisture dissolve in it.
9. Metallic oxides on reaction with water give _____.
10. ______ solution is more concentrated than a saturated solution.
11. Due to its high _____, water is called universal solvent.
12. The number of oxygen atoms present in five molecules of ferrosoferric oxide is _____.
13. The formula for Glauber's salt is ______.
14. Salts with water of crystallisation are called ______ salts.

Directions for question 15

Match the entries given in Column A with appropriate ones in Column B.

15.

Column A		Column B
A. Alloy	( )	a. Deliquescent
B. Copper sulphate	( )	b. Hygroscopic
C. Washing soda	( )	c. Particles settle down on long standing
D. Hydrated calcium chloride	( )	d. Efflorescent
E. Calcium oxide	( )	e. Solid–solid solution
F. Suspensions	( )	f. Water of crystallisation is 5

Directions for questions from 16 to 45

For each of the questions, four choices have been provided. Select the correct alternative.

16. The graph given below represents the interconversion of ice to water vapour. Identify the point in the curve which indicates the boiling point of water.

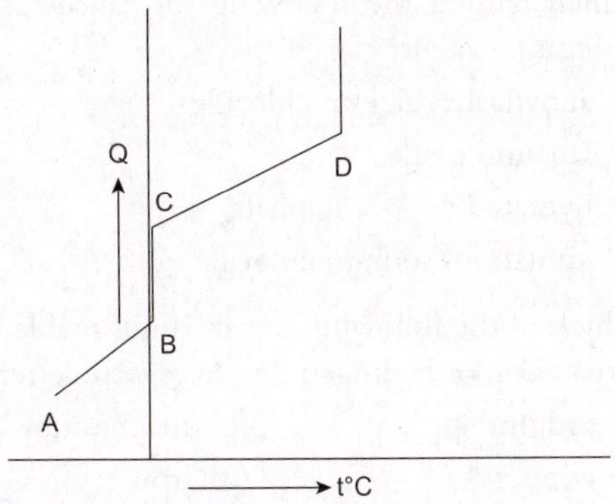

(a) B (b) C
(c) A (d) D

17. Which among the following is not a suspension?

(a) iodine in potassium iodide
(b) fog
(c) paints
(d) aerosol sprays

18. The solubility of $CaSO_4$

(a) increases with increase in temperature
(b) decreases with increase in temperature
(c) increases and then decreases with increase in temperature
(d) decreases and then increases with increase in temperature

19. If Glauber's salt, anhydrous calcium chloride, calcium oxide and concentrated H_2SO_4 are kept in air-tight containers A, B, C, D, respectively, in which container pressure becomes more?

(a) A (b) B
(c) C (d) D

20. Which among the following elements does not float on water?

(a) Na (b) K
(c) Ca (d) Ca, K

21. 50 g of oil "A" and 100 g of oil "B" are taken in separate containers at same temperature and specific heat of oil "B" is double that of oil "A." Both are heated in such a way that increase in temperature is also the same. Calculate the ratio of heat required to be supplied for increasing the temperature.

(a) 1 : 2 (b) 1 : 1
(c) 4 : 1 (d) 1 : 4

22. Anhydride of sulphurous acid is

(a) sulphur dioxide (b) sulphate ion
(c) sulphur trioxide (d) sulphite ion

23. Which of the following compounds is not associated with water molecules?

(a) blue vitriol (b) nitre
(c) washing soda (d) Epsom salt

24. When two substances A and B of same mass are heated under similar conditions, number of free surfaces has been found to reduce to zero from one. If A maintains constancy in the temperature for a longer time than B during heating, then

(a) latent heat of fusion of A is more than that of B
(b) latent heat of vaporisation of A is more than that of B
(c) latent heat of fusion of B is more than that of A
(d) latent heat of vaporisation of B is more than that of A

25. The specific heat capacity of water is

(a) more than petrol and kerosene
(b) less than oil and petrol
(c) less than kerosene
(d) less than honey and oil

26. In the given graph, identify the substance associated with the highest solubility at 10°C.

(a) A (b) B
(c) C (d) D

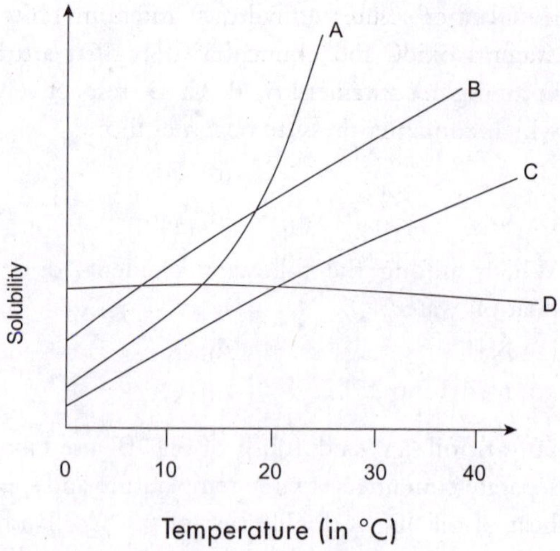

27. Reaction: Non-metal + H_2 A

$$A + PbO \longrightarrow Pb - \text{Non-metal}$$

If A formed in the above reaction has a rotten egg smell, identity the non-metal.

(a) N (b) P
(c) S (d) O

28. Identify the binary solution among the following:

(a) steel (b) bronze
(c) nichrome (d) gunmetal

29. Hydrogen acts as an oxidising agent when it

(a) reacts with highly electropositive metals
(b) burns in the presence of O_2
(c) forms ammonia when it reacts with nitrogen
(d) passes through boiling sulphur and forms H_2S gas

30. Tyndal effect cannot be shown by

(a) smoke
(b) dust particles present in air
(c) fog
(d) iron powder in hydrochloric acid

31. Sodium catches fire and burns with a

(a) lilac flame
(b) golden yellow flame
(c) blue flame
(d) green flame

32. Which of the following metals on reaction with steam provides a coating over the metal and prevents further reaction?

(a) Al (b) Ca
(c) Mg (d) K

33. The brown-coloured substance formed when steam is passed over red hot iron is

(a) ferric oxide (b) rust
(c) ferrosoferric oxide (d) ferrous oxide

34. Which among the following metals react only with steam?

(a) K (b) Ca
(c) Mg (d) Al

35. Crystals can be made

(a) by cooling hot saturated solution
(b) by evaporating unsaturated solution slowly
(c) by cooling a fused mass
(d) all of the above

36. Washing soda is an example of a/an ______ substance.

(a) efflorescent (b) deliquescent
(c) hygroscopic (d) both (1) and (2)

37. Which among the following substances acts as a desiccating agent?

(a) anhydrous calcium chloride
(b) calcium oxide
(c) hydrated copper sulphate
(d) anhydrous sodium chloride

38. Which of the following metals is unsuitable for the preparation of hydrogen due to reversible reaction?

(a) sodium (b) magnesium
(c) copper (d) iron

39. The reaction between perfectly dry hydrogen and chlorine takes place in the presence of direct sunlight only by the addition of a few drops of water. In this process water behaves as a/an

(a) catalyst
(b) solvent
(c) dehydrating agent
(d) efflorescent substance

40. Which of the following metals on treatment with concentrated alkali gives hydrogen gas?

(a) Na (b) Mg
(c) Cu (d) Al

41. Arrange the chemicals in sequence for the removal of impurities H_2S, SO_2, PH_3 and H_2O, respectively, in the purification of hydrogen gas.

PRACTICE QUESTIONS

(1) phosphorus pentoxide (2) lead nitrate solution
(3) silver nitrate solution (4) caustic potash
(a) 1 2 3 4 (b) 2 3 1 4
(c) 2 4 3 1 (d) 1 4 2 3

42. The specific heat capacity of water is
(a) 4.2 J kg^{-1}°C^{-1} (b) 4.2 J g^{-1}°C^{-1}
(c) 1 J g^{-1}°C^{-1} (d) 1 J kg^{-1}°C^{-1}

43. Colour changes observed during the reaction between metal oxides and hydrogen are given below:
(1) white → bluish white (2) brown → grey
(3) yellow → grey (4) black → red
Arrange the above colour changes as PbO to Pb, Fe_2O_3 to Fe, CuO to Cu and ZnO to Zn
(a) 3 2 4 1 (b) 3 4 1 2
(c) 3 2 1 4 (d) 2 3 4 1

44. Amount of solutes A, B, C, D and E in 1500 g of water at 25°C, 50°C and 75°C in their saturated solutions are given below:

	25°C	50°C	75°C
A	235 g	280 g	240 g
B	180 g	190 g	220 g
C	160 g	170 g	180 g
D	175 g	220 g	200 g

Arrange the solutes in the increasing order of the amount of solutes that crystallises out by cooling from 75°C to 25°C:
(a) ABDC (b) ACDB
(c) CABD (d) ACBD

45. Among the following oxides which one is converted to metal by treating with hydrogen?
(a) Al_2O_3 (b) ZnO
(c) CuO (d) BaO

Level 2

1. Two containers contain two different liquids A and B. The mass of liquid A is half the mass of liquid B. Both of them are heated to that extent so that the increase in the temperature of the liquids is the same. The heat supplied for this purpose in the case of liquid A is double that in the case of liquid B. Find out the ratio of the specific heat of liquid A and liquid B.

2. When sodium or potassium is dropped in water, we can observe a golden yellow or a lilac coloured flame, respectively, whereas when calcium is dropped, no flame is observed. Why is there a difference in observation in the above two cases?

3. When water, containing equal amounts of CO_2, O_2 NO_2, N_2O_3 gases, respectively, is subjected to heating, which gas is evolved out in maximum percentage? Give a reason.

4. Amount of solutes A, B and C in 500 g of water at 30°C, 60°C, 100°C in their saturated solutions are given below:

	30°C	60°C	100°C
A	140 g	135 g	131 g
B	160 g	175 g	182 g
C	152 g	170 g	161 g

When the hot saturated solutions of A, B and C are cooled slowly, identify the order in which they crystallise out of the solution. Give a reason in support of your answer.

5. "Steam at 100°C causes more burns when exposed to skin than water at 100°C." Justify.

6. Rain water and tap water are boiled in metallic containers A and B. The containers are emptied and then rain water samples are subjected to boiling in the same containers. In which case boiling gets delayed? Give a reason in support of your answer.

7. If a small crystal of a solute is added to unsaturated, saturated and supersaturated solutions, what observations do you find? Justify.

8. Why is pure water a bad conductor of electricity?

9. Why do the solubilities of most of the solids in water increase with an increase in temperature?

10. Explain why $CuSO_4.5H_2O$ can be dehydrated by reducing the external pressure at room temperature.

11. Explain why cobalt chloride acts as a humidity indicator.

12. The boiling point of a solution is more than that of the pure solvent. Justify.

13. With respect to the saturation of a solution, what type of solution is aerated water? Give reasons in support of answer.

14. What are the changes that take place in lead nitrate solution by passing impure hydrogen through it?

15. Why is water used widely in cooling systems?

16. $Na_2CO_3.10H_2O$ on exposure to air loses some water of crystallisation and the rest on heating. How do you account for the above phenomenon?

17. What do you observe when CaO and $CaCl_2$ are exposed to moisture separately?

18. A china dish weighs 25 g when empty. When saturated solution of potassium chloride is poured into it at 40°C, the weight of the dish is 63 g. When the solution is evaporated to dryness, the china dish along with crystals weighs 40 g. Find the solubility of potassium chloride at 40°C.

19. The reaction of sodium and potassium with humid air is violent and explosive. However, when these metals are kept in an air-tight container having silica gel, no reaction has been observed. Give a reason.

20. A deliquescent substance does not become sticky in an air-tight container. Justify.

21. Rain water does not leave any scales on boiling. Give a reason.

22. Potassium chloride has solubility of 32 g at room temperature in water. However, its solubility decreases to 2.4 g in alcohol at the same temperature. It becomes completely insoluble in benzene. How do you account for this variation?

23. Why does boiling of water expel the dissolved gases?

24. Two samples each of substances A and B are kept in an open container and air-tight container. Sample A in the first container became sticky and in the second container remained as such. Sample B in both the containers remained without any change. Comment on the above observations.

Level 3

1. How do we explain the survival of aquatic animals in the deep sea during winter in the cold region?

2. Water remains as drops on the polythene surface but it forms a thin layer on the surface of a properly cleaned glass plate. Explain.

3. Two containers A and B contain same kind of matter and kinetic energy of molecules in A is more than that of B. Explain in which container the specific heat of matter is more. Give a reason.

4. Why does water appear blue in deep waters, but transparent in shallow waters?

5. Impure granulated zinc is preferred to pure zinc for the preparation of hydrogen. How do you account for this?

6.

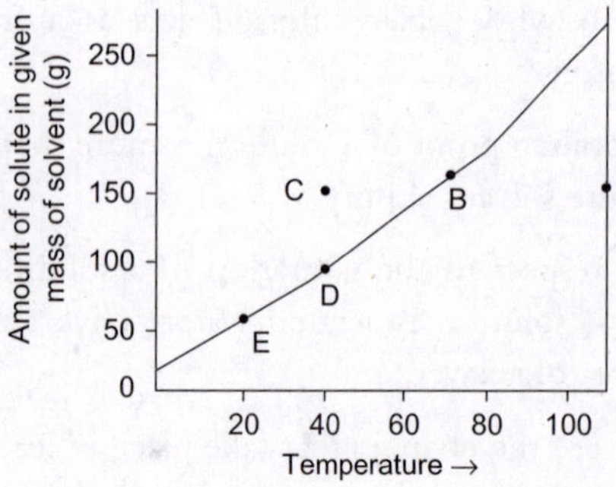

In the above graph, identify the states of solution at the various points A, B, C, D, E. If the solution is cooled from point A, at which temperature precipitation normally starts? Also find out the amount of solute precipitated at 40°C and the amount of solute in the solution at point E. What would be the maximum amount of solute that can be precipitated in the process?

7. A sample of common salt obtained from sea water contains 39 g of NaCl and 1 g of KCl. If it is dissolved in 100 g of water and then 90 g of water is evaporated, what observation do you find at 0°C? What is the maximum amount of pure NaCl that can be obtained by the above method? (solubilities of NaCl and KCl are 40 g, 55 g at 100°C and 35 g and 28 g at 0°C, respectively)

8. Explain why temperature in the coastal region is moderate throughout the year.

9. A desiccating material is used as a dehumidifying agent for absorbing moisture from highly humid air and again it is made reusable by low humid air. What is the principle involved in this process?

10. Some of the hydrated crystals are efflorescent. How do you account for this?

PRACTICE QUESTIONS

CONCEPT APPLICATION

Level 1

True or false

1. True 2. False 3. True 4. False 5. False
6. False 7. True

Fill in the blanks

8. deliquescent 9. bases 10. supersaturated
11. dielectric constant 12. 2O 13. $Na_2SO_4.10H_2O$
14. hydrated

Match the following

15. A →e B →f C →d
D →a E →b F →c

Multiple choice questions

16. d 17. a 18. c 19. a 20. c
21. d 22. a 23. b 24. b 25. a
26. b 27. c 28. c 29. a 30. d

31. Sodium catches fire and burns with a golden yellow flame.
32. Aluminium metal on reaction with steam provides a coating over the metal which prevents further reaction.
33. The brown-coloured substance formed when stream is passed over red hot iron is ferrosoferric oxide.
34. Aluminium metal reacts only with steam.
35. Crystals can be made by the following processes:
    (i) by cooling hot saturated solution,
    (ii) by evaporating unsaturated solution slowly and
    (iii) by cooling a fused mass.
36. Washing soda is an example of an efflorescent substance.
37. Calcium oxide acts as a desiccating agent
38. Iron is unsuitable for the preparation of hydrogen due to reversible reaction.
39. The reaction between perfectly dry hydrogen and chlorine takes place in the presence of direct sunlight only by the addition of a few drops of water. In this process, water behaves as a catalyst.
40. Al on treatment with concentrated alkali gives hydrogen gas.
41. (i) lead nitrate solution
    (ii) caustic potash
    (iii) silver nitrate solution
    (iv) phosphorus pentoxide
42. The specific heat capacity of water is 4.2 J $g^{-1}°C^{-1}$
43. $PbO + H_2 \rightarrow Pb + H_2O$
    yellow grey
    $Fe_2O_3 + H_2 \rightarrow Fe + H_2O$
    brown grey
    $CuO + H_2 \rightarrow Cu + H_2O$
    black red
    $ZnO + H_2 \rightarrow Zn + H_2O$
    white bluish white

HINTS AND EXPLANATION

44. Amount of solutes A, B, C and D that crystallises out are 5 g, 40 g, 20 g and 25 g, respectively.

45. In metals, which have lesser affinity towards oxygen, their oxides can be reduced by hydrogen. Among the given metals, copper has less affinity towards oxygen. Hence, its oxide can be reduced by hydrogen.

Level 2

1. (i) relation between specific heat and heat required to change the temperature of the substance
   (ii) relationship among heat energy, supplied specific heat, mass and change in temperature of a substance
2. (i) comparison of Na, Kand Ca with that of water
   (ii) comparison of physical properties of Na, K and Ca
   (iii) type of reaction that takes place when these metals react with water
   (iv) condition required for burning
3. (i) comparison of reactivity of gases with water
   (ii) conditions required for any gas to be present in maximum percentages in water
   (iii) relation between solubility of the gas and temperature
   (iv) effect of heating or rise in temperature on the gases present
4. (i) comparison of change in solubilities with change in temperature
   (ii) comparison of change in solubilities with decrease in temperature from 100°C to 30°C
   (iii) effect of cooling on nature of the solutions of A, B and C, respectively.
   (iv) relation between extent of solubility and crystallisation
5. (i) change of state of matter
   (ii) energy content of water molecules at 100°C
   (iii) energy content of steam molecules at 100°C
   (iv) comparison of energy
6. (i) components present in rain water and tap water
   (ii) effect of constituents on metallic containers due to boiling
   (iii) changes that take place in metallic containers due to boiling
   (iv) changes that are observed with respect to boiling when rain water is again taken in containers
7. (i) changes that takes place in particle size of solute in respective solutions
   (ii) comparison of amount of solutes present in respective solutions
   (iii) relation between changes with respect to crystal of solute and nature of the solution
8. (i) property of water
   (ii) condition required for a substance to conduct electricity
   (iii) composition of pure water
9. (i) principle of dissolution of solids in liquids
   (ii) process of dissolution
   (iii) movement of molecules during solubility
   (iv) effect of temperature on the movement of molecules
10. (i) vapour pressure of $CuSO_4.5H_2O$
    (ii) Comparison between atmospheric pressure and vapour pressure of hydrated copper sulphate
    (iii) Changes in hydrated $CuSO_4$ at lower pressure conditions
11. (i) change in physical property
    (ii) colour of cobalt chloride
    (iii) capour pressure of cobalt chloride
    (iv) changes in cobalt chloride in humid atmosphere
    (v) effect on colour of $CoCl_2$ due to these changes
12. (i) vapour pressure of solution
    (ii) comparison of composition of solution to pure solvent
    (iii) forces acting in solution and pure solvent
    (iv) relation between forces acting and vapour pressure
    (v) relation between vapour pressure and boiling point

13. (i) factors affecting the solubility of gases in water
 (ii) composition of aerated water
 (iii) pressure condition in aerated water can

14. (i) impurity present in hydrogen gas
 (ii) reactivity of lead nitrate with the impurity present in hydrogen

15. Water has high specific heat and it is available in the liquid state in temperature ranging between 0°C and 100°C.

 Hence, it can be conveniently used in cooling systems.

16. $Na_2CO_3.10H_2O$ on exposure to air loses 9 water molecules from its water of crystallisation because initially vapour pressure of the compound is more than vapour pressure of the moisture present in the atmospheric air. It is an example of an efflorescent substance. After the release of nine molecules of water of crystallisation its vapour pressure becomes equal to the pressure of the moisture present in the atmosphere. Hence, removal of the 10th water molecule requires heating.

17. Both calcium oxide and calcium chloride absorb moisture, and hence, act as hygroscopic substances. Calcium chloride absorbs moisture and dissolves in it and changes its physical state. So, it is called deliquescent substance. No change in physical state takes place when calcium oxide absorbs moisture.

18. Weight of saturated solution of KCl = 63 – 25 = 38 g

 Weight of crystal of KCl = 40 – 25 = 15 g

 Weight of water contained in saturated solution = 38 – 15 = 23 g

 Solubility of KCl

$$= \frac{\text{Weight of KCl crystals}}{\text{Weight of water}} \times 100$$

$$= \frac{15}{23} \times 100 = 65.2 \text{ at } 40°\text{C}.$$

19. Silica gel can absorb the moisture present in the air-tight container, and thus, air present in the container is free from the moisture. Metals Na and K can react with air only when the reaction is initiated with moisture. Therefore, when metals are kept in an air-tight container having silica gel, no reaction takes place since the air is absolutely dry.

20. The water vapour present inside the air-tight container is limited. After absorbing the water vapour, the deliquescent substances again release the water molecules to maintain the equilibrium of water vapour pressure. Hence, it cannot become sticky in the air-tight container.

21. Since the rain water is pure, it does not have any dissolved salts present in it. So, it does not leave any scales on boiling.

22. Water has a high dielectric constant. KCl being an ionic compound is highly soluble in water. Alcohol has a lower dielectric constant. Hence, solubility of KCl in alcohol is less. Benzene has still lower value of dielectric constant. Therefore, KCl becomes completely insoluble in benzene.

23. As temperature increases, the solubility of a gas in a liquid decreases. Hence, boiling of water expels the dissolved gases.

24. Substance A in an open container becomes sticky and that means it is a deliquescent substance and absorbs sufficient moisture in the open container. In an air-tight container, it absorbs little moisture but again loses some moisture for maintaining equilibrium of vapour pressure. Therefore, it does not become sticky. Substance B does not become sticky even in the open container. The fact that it remained without any change in the open container indicates that it is neither efflorescent nor deliquescent. It may be a hygroscopic salt or may not absorb moisture at all.

Level 3

1. (i) comparison of densities of water and ice
   (ii) variation of temperature at different layers in the sea
   (iii) change in density of water with change in temperature
2. (i) cohesive, adhesive forces
   (ii) composition of polythene
   (iii) composition of glass
   (iv) forces between water and polythene
   (v) forces acting between water and glass
   (vi) comparison of these forces
3. (i) relation between specific heat and intermolecular force of attractions
   (ii) relation between kinetic energy and temperature
   (iii) relation between kinetic energy and intermolecular forces of attraction in A and B
   (iv) relation between intermolecular forces of attraction and the heat required
4. (i) nature of water molecules
   (ii) relation between light absorbed/emitted/scattered and colour
   (iii) light absorbed/emitted by water
   (iv) comparison of amount of light absorbed/emitted in deep waters and shallow waters
5. (i) the mode of reaction between zinc and acid
   (ii) role of Zn
   (iii) change in property of Zn in granulated and pure forms.
   (iv) comparison of the reactivity of hydrogen in presence of granulated zinc and pure zinc
6. The curve indicates that the solubility of the solute at 100°C is 250 g. However, the given solution contains only 150 g of solute. The solution at point A is an unsaturated solution. Therefore, no precipitation takes place up to point B at 80°C, where the solution becomes saturated with just 150 g of the solute. Point B indicates a saturated solution. Point C at 40°C indicates that the solution still contained 150 g of solute which is a supersaturated solution. That means, it is possible to cool solution from 80°C to 40°C without any crystallisation by maintaining suitable conditions. At 40°C, when crystallisation starts, the solution ultimately becomes saturated represented by point D. At point D (40°C), the solubility is 75. That means, 75 g of solute would have been precipitated out. At E also the solution remains saturated by precipitating 25 g more of solute.
7. At 100°C, the solubilities of NaCl and KCl are 40 and 55, respectively. Therefore, the entire sample dissolves in 100 g of water. When 90 g of water is evaporated, 10 g of water remains and since the solution is to cooled to 0°C, it can contain 3.5 g NaCl and 2.8 g KCl. That means the entire KCl (1 g) remains in the solution which remains unsaturated wrt KCl. In 10 g of water only 3.5 g remains in dissolved state thereby making the solution saturated wrt NaCl. The rest of the NaCl, i.e., 35.5 g gets precipitated out. This is the maximum amount of NaCl that can be obtained in pure form.
8. In coastal regions, the amount of water is more and the specific heat of water is much higher than that of the land. Hence, a major part of heat coming from the sun is absorbed by water. The increase in temperature of water is less because of its high specific heat. Hence, the temperature of the land does not change much.
9. Desiccant materials have a high affinity for water vapour. The process involves exposing the desiccant material to humid air stream, allowing it to attract and retain some of the water vapour and then exposing the same desiccants to a dry air stream which has the effect of drawing the retained moisture from the desiccant. The first air stream is the air that is being dehumidified while the second air stream is used only to regenerate the desiccant material.
10. The vapour pressure of these hydrated crystals is greater than that of the water vapour present in the atmosphere at room temperature.

Chapter 6

Carbon and its Compounds

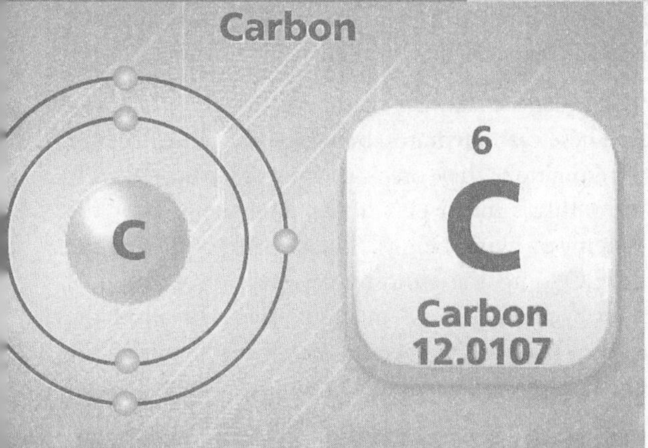

Remember

Before beginning this chapter, you should be able to:

- define metals and non-metals.
- classify substances as metal or non-metals and their properties.

Key Ideas

After completing this chapter, you should be able to:

- learn the carbon cycle.
- know the preparation, properties and uses of different allotropic forms of carbon and different commercially important compounds of carbon.
- study the oxides of carbon, their laboratory preparation, properties and uses.
- learn about fossil fuels, coal and petroleum.
- understand working principle of different types of fire extinguishers.
- know the occurrence, preparation and properties of methane.

INTRODUCTION

Carbon is one of the most important non-metallic elements. This is because all the biomolecules invariably possess carbon and hydrogen as the major constituents. The special significance of carbon lies in the fact that it forms two types of compounds—organic and inorganic compounds. The compounds which are analogous with the corresponding compounds of other non-metallic elements are studied under the branch of inorganic chemistry. The chemistry of the wide range of the allotropic forms of carbon also comes in the realm of inorganic chemistry.

CARBON CYCLE

The various compounds of carbon are responsible for the growth and the development of living organisms. Though the various life processes involve complex organic reactions, carbon dioxide, which is basically an inorganic compound, is invariably associated with them.

Atmosphere acts as a reservoir of carbon dioxide. Plants make use of this gas for the process of photosynthesis, thereby producing carbohydrates. These carbohydrates, being the sources of energy, are consumed by animals. During the process of respiration, they break down and carbon dioxide gas is released back into the atmosphere. Apart from this, a major part of the food taken up by the animals is also assimilated into the basic organ systems of living beings. The decomposition of the dead organic matter also results in the release of CO_2 into the atmosphere. Some proportion of CO_2 gets dissolved in sea water, which is used up by the aquatic plants. The degradation of the dead aquatic plants and animals over a long period of time under specific conditions results in the formation of fossil fuels, like, coal and petroleum. Further the burning of these fossil fuels releases CO_2 into the atmosphere.

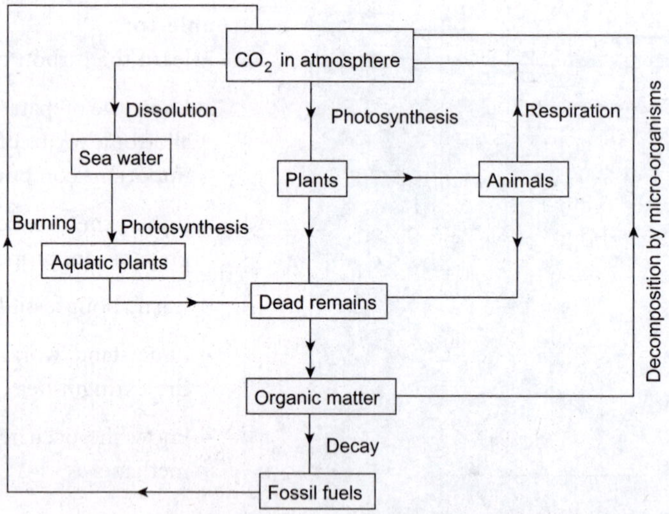

FIGURE 6.1 Carbon cycle

Carbon

Occurrence

Carbon occurs in both free and combined states.

Free State

Carbon exists as the native element in the form of coal in the earth's crust as the native element. It occurs in a very small amount in its allotropic forms, like, diamond and graphite. Diamond and graphite are pure forms of carbon. Coal is an impure form of carbon. Another allotropic form of carbon, fullerene, has been discovered by geologists in a crater made by a meteorite in Germany and in ancient rocks in New Zealand.

Combined State

Carbon exists in the combined state in all the three physical states, namely, solid, liquid and gas.

1. **Solid state:** Carbon occurs in the solid state in the form of mineral carbonates, like, calcium carbonate ($CaCO_3$), magnesite ($MgCO_3$), calamine ($ZnCO_3$), etc. In plants and animals carbon occurs in the form of fats, proteins, carbohydrates and various other complex chemical compounds.

2. **Liquid state:** Carbon commonly exists in liquid state in fuels and vegetable oils. The fuels mainly comprise petrol, diesel, kerosene, LPG, etc.

3. **Gaseous state:** In gaseous state, carbon exists either in the form of oxides, hydrocarbons or in water as dissolved carbon dioxide. Carbon dioxide and carbon monoxide are the oxides of carbon. About 0.03% by volume of atmosphere is of carbon dioxide while carbon monoxide is present in volcanic gases and furnace emissions of industries.

   A wide variety of hydrocarbons occur naturally. The naturally occurring hydrocarbons are natural gas, petroleum gas, marsh gas and others. Carbon dioxide dissolves in water to form carbonic acid, which is present in all kinds of natural waters.

ALLOTROPY

Allotropy is a phenomenon in which an element exhibits different physical forms with almost similar chemical properties. Some elements, like, carbon, phosphorous, sulphur, iron, etc., exhibit this phenomenon. The different physical forms exhibited by the element are called **allotropes**. Carbon is an element that can exhibit various allotropic forms which have a wide variety of applications. The allotropic forms exhibited by carbon are broadly of two types, namely, crystalline forms and non-crystalline forms or amorphous forms.

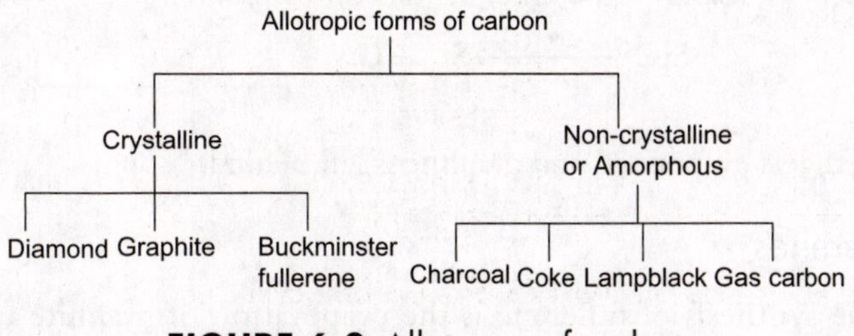

FIGURE 6.2 Allotropes of carbon

Crystalline Allotropic Forms of Carbon

They have well defined regular geometrical arrangements of carbon atoms. Diamond and graphite are the widely known crystalline allotropes of carbon. A third form of crystalline allotrope of carbon called **fullerene** was discovered in recent times. They have extensive technological applications in various fields.

Formation and Synthesis of Diamond

Diamonds are formed in nature by the crystallisation of carbon. The carbon present beneath the surface of the earth under specific conditions dissolves in the molten rock material present there. The liquid so formed is commonly called **magma**. When the magma containing carbon is pushed up to the surface of the earth due to the volcanic eruption, it gets solidified. The iron present in the magma expands on solidification, exerting a great pressure on carbon, which, in turn, crystallises to form diamonds.

Diamonds are also synthesised artificially for specific applications. In the synthesis of diamond, carbon is prepared from sugar and molten iron is obtained by melting iron in an electric furnace by raising its temperature to the range of 3000°C–3500°C. Carbon prepared from sugar is added to the molten iron to form a homogeneous solution. This solution is suddenly cooled by pouring it into molten lead at 327°C. On sudden cooling, the molten iron on outer surface suddenly cools, whereas the inner surface remains at high temperature. On further cooling, the expansion of iron takes place which exerts a great pressure on carbon producing diamonds.

Formation or Manufacture of Graphite By Acheson Process

The raw material taken for the manufacture of graphite is a mixture of powdered coke, sand and ferric oxide along with saw dust. This mixture is filled in an electric furnace lined inside with fire clay bricks. The carbon rods act as a cathode and an anode in the furnace. These rods are inserted in such a way that they are held in contact with each other through the particles of coke, which is commonly called **coke bed**. The mixture is covered with a layer of sand and coke on the top so as to cut off the entry of air into it.

When an electric current is passed through the electrodes, the temperature of the furnace increases to 3500°C. The coke bed connecting the two electrodes offers large resistance to the flow of the electricity.

When the current is allowed to pass through the reaction mixture for a period of 30 hours, the following reactions take place with the formation of graphite:

$$\underset{\text{(Sand)}}{SiO_2} + \underset{\text{(Coke)}}{3C} \xrightarrow{3500°C} \underset{\text{(Silicon carbide)}}{SiC} + 2CO$$

$$SiC \xrightarrow{3500°C} Si_{(s)} + C_{(s)}$$

The silicon formed gets evaporated and graphite is left behind.

Synthesis of Fullerenes

The first step in the synthesis of fullerene is the evaporation of graphite using laser radiation and subsequent condensation of carbon vapour. When these vapours are cooled in the atmosphere of noble gases, fullerene molecules consists of mainly C_{60}, with smaller amount of C_{70} and traces of other fullerene molecules consisting of even number of carbon atoms up to 350 are formed. From these, C_{60} and C_{70} are separated through chromatographic separation.

Comparative Study of Various Crystalline Allotropes

Structure

Diamond	Graphite	Fullerenes
Diamond has a regular tetrahedral arrangement. This is due to the bonding of each atom of carbon with four other carbon atoms, forming a single unit of crystal. These crystal units lie in different planes accounting for a rigid three-dimensional structure. Carbon has a valency of four and each carbon is bonded to four other carbon atoms forming a tetrahedral unit. These tetrahedral units lie in different planes, thus, forming a rigid three-dimensional structure.	In graphite each carbon atom is bonded covalently to three other carbon atoms resulting in the arrangement of hexagonal rings in a single plane. The bonds between the atoms of two single crystals, in the parallel planes are weak. Each carbon is bonded to three carbon atoms only leaving behind one free valency. A three-dimensional arrangement of hexagonal rings is resulted. These rings lie on a single plane. The entire structure is such that the layers of hexagonal rings are arranged parallel to each other.	Fullerenes are large spherical carbon cage molecules and were named Buckminster fullerenes in honour of American architect Robert Buckminster Fuller. The name fullerene originated from the structure that resembled the geodesic dome structures designed by the architect.

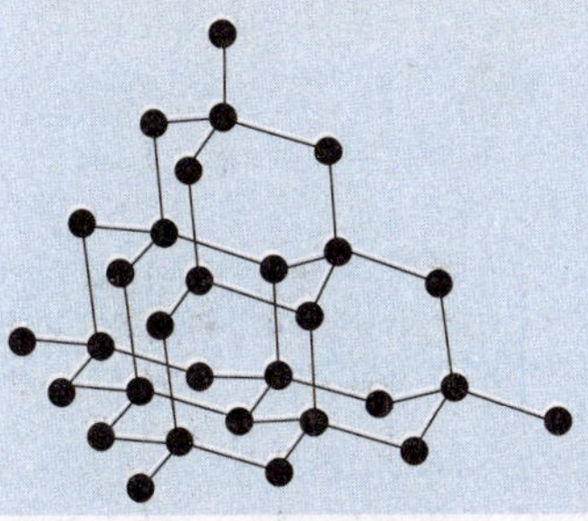

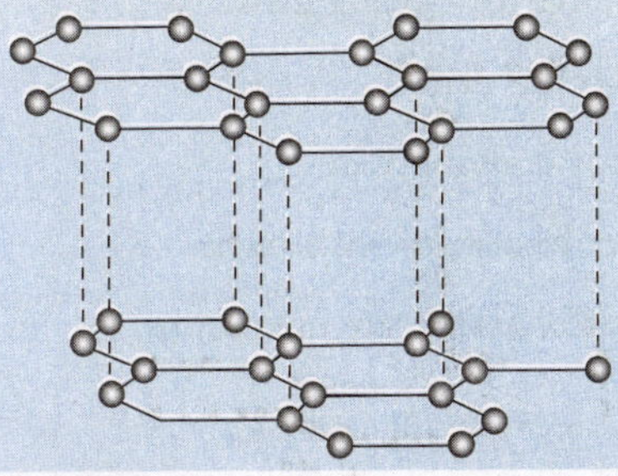

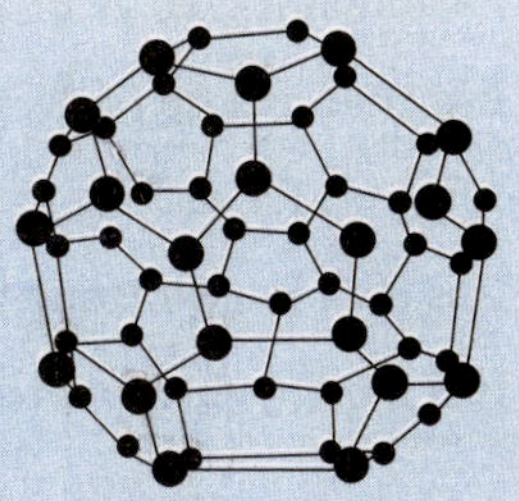

Physical Properties

Diamond	Graphite	Fullerenes
A pure diamond is a colourless and transparent crystal. It is the hardest among naturally occurring solids.	Graphite is a dark grey and very soft solid with metallic lustre.	Brown or black powder.
Diamond is a good conductor of heat and a bad conductor of electricity.	It is a good conductor of heat and electricity.	It becomes a super conductor when it forms compounds with noble gases.
It has a high-refractive index of 2.5.	It is opaque.	Refractive index of fullerene is 2.2.
It is insoluble in common solvents.	It is insoluble in common solvents.	Soluble in common solvents, such as, benzene, toluene or chloroform.
Diamond is the densest form of carbon with a density of 3.5 g/cm^3.	Density is 2.25 g/cm^3.	Density is 1.65 g/cm^3.
The melting point of diamond is about 3700°C.	It has a melting point of about 3600°C.	It undergoes sublimation at about 527°C.
Presence of impurities impart colour to diamonds.	–	–

Chemical Properties

Diamond	Graphite
Action with oxygen: diamond catches fire at 900°C; when heated in oxygen, it catches fire at 800°C to form CO_2 (carbon dioxide). $C_{(s)} + O_{2(g)} \xrightarrow{800°C} CO_{2(g)}$	Graphite on heating in the presence of pure oxygen catches fire at 700°C and burns brightly forming a mixture of carbon dioxide and carbon monoxide. $3C_{(s)} + 2O_{2(g)} \xrightarrow{700°C} CO_{2(g)} + 2CO_{(g)} + \Delta Q$
Reaction with sodium carbonate: on heating diamond very strongly with solid sodium carbonate, sodium oxide and carbon monoxide are formed. $Na_2CO_{3(s)} + C_{(s)} \longrightarrow Na_2O_{(s)} + 2CO_{(g)}$	Graphite does not burn in air. On heating the fused mixture of sodium carbonate and graphite, sodium oxide and carbon monoxide gas are formed. $Na_2CO_{3(s)} + C_{(s)} \xrightarrow{Fuse} Na_2O_{(s)} + 2CO_{(g)}$

Uses of Diamond

1. Diamonds are used for making various kinds of jewellery as they sparkle brilliantly.
2. Diamond is used as an abrasive for cutting glass.
3. It is used as a tip of deep boring drills.
4. It is used for making dies for drawing wires.
5. It is used in generating laser beams in electronics.
6. It is used by surgeons to perform delicate operations.

Graphite

1. Graphite is used in making leads of pencils.
2. It is used as a dry lubricant as ordinary lubricating oil gets charred at high temperature.
3. It is used in making refractory crucibles which can withstand very high temperatures.
4. Graphite is used to make suitable black paint and printer's ink.
5. Graphite fibres can be used to reinforce plastic as they are strong.
6. A strong, light weight composite material of graphite and plastic is used to make fishing rods, bicycle frames, spacecraft parts, dish antennae and tennis rackets.
7. It is used in nuclear reactors as a moderator.

Conversion of Graphite into Diamond

Graphite can be transformed into diamond by applying a pressure greater than 1,00,000 times the atmospheric pressure at the sea level and by burning at a temperature of about 3700°C. These conditions of temperature and pressure help in rearranging the atoms of carbon in graphite into a diamond structure.

Amorphous Allotropes of Carbon

Charcoal, coke, lamp black and gas carbon are amorphous forms of carbon. In these forms of carbon, the carbon atoms are not arranged in an orderly manner. Recent X-ray study reveals that these allotropic forms are tiny graphite crystals cemented together by impurities.

Charcoal

Charcoal is one of the manmade amorphous forms of carbon. It is used as a fuel. Depending on the source from which charcoal is obtained, it is of three types.

Wood Charcoal Laboratory Preparation

A dry hard glass test tube is taken, and it is filled half with wood shavings. These wood shavings are subjected to heating in the absence of air by using a Bunsen burner. Wood shavings get charred, and fumes are evolved. These fumes get condensed in the conical flask placed in cold water and form two separate layers. A matchstick is brought near the jet tube, and the gas coming out of it catches fire. This gas is wood gas. The products of destructive distillation of wood are wood charcoal, wood tar, pyroligneous acid and wood gas.

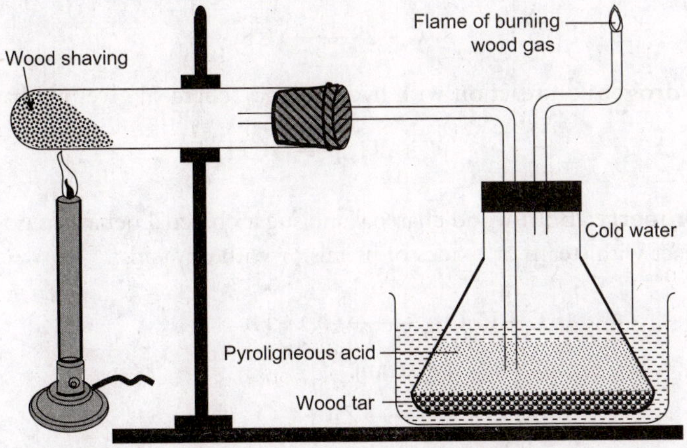

FIGURE 6.3 Laboratory preparation of wood charcoal

Bone Charcoal

Bone charcoal is also known as animal charcoal or bone ash or ivory black. Animal bones contain organic matter and calcium phosphate. The crushed fine powder of the animal bones if subjected to destructive distillation produces residue. This residue is called **bone charcoal**.

Sugar Charcoal

One of the purest forms of amorphous allotropes of carbon is sugar charcoal and it is prepared by destructive distillation of sugar. Sugar crystals lose water and get converted to pure carbon. This pure carbon obtained from sugar is known as sugar charcoal. The chemical reaction of sugar with concentrated sulphuric acid produces sugar charcoal.

$$C_{12}H_{22}O_{11} \xrightarrow{H_2SO_4} 12C + 11H_2O$$

Physical Properties of Charcoal

Charcoal is a porous black solid. It has a huge surface area due to its porosity. It has the ability to adsorb specific substances, like, coloured impurities, poisonous substances, etc.

Chemical Properties

1. **Reaction with non-metals:** Charcoal reacts with non-metals, like, oxygen, sulphur and hydrogen.

   (a) **With oxygen**: oxides of carbon are formed:

$$C + O \longrightarrow CO_2$$
$$\text{(Excess)}$$
$$C + O_2 \longrightarrow 2CO$$

   (b) **With sulphur**: on passing sulphur vapour through red hot charcoal, a vapour of carbon disulphide is formed:

$$C + 2S \longrightarrow CS_2$$

   (c) **With hydrogen**: on reaction with hydrogen gas, charcoal gives methane:

$$C + 2H_2 \longrightarrow CH_4$$

2. **Reducing property:** Both wood charcoal and sugar charcoal behave as good reducing agents when they react with steam or oxides of metals or with oxyacids:

$$\underset{\text{steam}}{C + H_2O_{(g)}} \longrightarrow CO + H_2$$
$$ZnO + C \longrightarrow Zn + CO$$
$$C + 2H_2SO_4 \xrightarrow{\text{boiling}} CO_2 + 2H_2O + 2SO_2$$

Since bone charcoal contains maximum percentage of calcium phosphate, it cannot act as a good reducing agent.

Uses of Charcoal

Wood charcoal	Bone charcoal	Sugar charcoal
It is used as an excellent household fuel for keeping rooms warm in winter.	Bone charcoal is used to remove colour from sugar cane juice due to the adsorbing impurities.	It is used for extracting metals from their oxides.
It is used extensively for small-scale production of metals. When wood charcoal is heated with oxides of less active metals, they get reduced to free metals.	It is used in the extraction of yellow phosphorous.	It is used as an adsorbent material in place of activated charcoal.
It is used as a deodorant and disinfectant.		
Charcoal is used as one of the constituents of the gunpowder.		
It is used in gas masks.		

Other Amorphous Forms of Carbon

	Lamp black	Coke	Gas carbon
Preparation	Lamp black is prepared by burning mustard oil, turpentine oil and petroleum in the absence of oxygen. The preparation of lamp black can be done at home by placing a clean dry glass slide over the flame of mustard oil lamp. After some time a deep black powdery substance is coated on the slide, which is known as lamp black.	Coke is prepared by heating coal in the absence of air up to a temperature of 1300°C in huge iron retorts. The products obtained by the decomposition of coal are coal gas, carbon, coal tar, liquor ammonia and coal gas.	Gas carbon can be prepared by destructive distillation of coal. The thermal vaporisation of small amounts of carbon from coal on condensation produces a grey solid. This grey solid obtained is called **gas carbon**.
Properties	Lamp black is a light, powdery black substance, having a velvet touch. It has an oily feel due to the presence of the vapours of some amount of oil.	It is greyish black porous solid.	It is a dull grey solid. It is a good conductor of electricity.
Uses	(i) Lamp black is used as a stabilizing filler for rubber in making tyres and plastics. (ii) It is used as a black pigment in inks and paints. (iii) It is used for making black shoe polishes. (iv) It is used in the manufacture of black carbon papers and carbon ribbons for type writers.	(i) It is used as a household fuel. (ii) It is used extensively in the extraction of metals, like, iron copper, lead, etc., from their oxide and sulphide ores as it is an excellent reducing agent. (iii) It is used in the manufacture of graphite and calcium carbide. (iv) It is used in the manufacture of water gas and producer gas.	It is used for making electrodes for dry cells.

COMPOUNDS OF CARBON

The compounds of carbon are basically classified into two categories, namely, inorganic carbon compounds and organic compounds. In contrast to the vast number of organic compounds, the number of inorganic carbon compounds is very limited. Among them, oxides, carbides, carbonate and bicarbonate salts and cyanides are important.

Oxides of Carbon: Carbon monoxide and carbon dioxide are the two stable oxides formed by carbon.

Carbon Monoxide

Occurrence

Carbon monoxide is not a natural component of atmospheric air. It is mainly added to the atmosphere due to the incomplete combustion of fossil fuels, like, wood, coal, petrol, etc., Degradation of organic matter in swamps also gives out minor proportions of carbon monoxide along with carbon dioxide. Since carbon monoxide is found to be one of the components of volcanic eruptions, the atmosphere in the volcanic regions contains slightly greater proportions of carbon monoxide.

Laboratory Method of Preparation

Principle: When CO_2 gas is passed over red hot charcoal, charcoal gets oxidised and forms carbon monoxide. This is a highly endothermic reaction.

$$C_{(s)} + CO_{2(g)} \xrightarrow[\text{(red hot)}]{} 2CO_{(g)} - Q$$

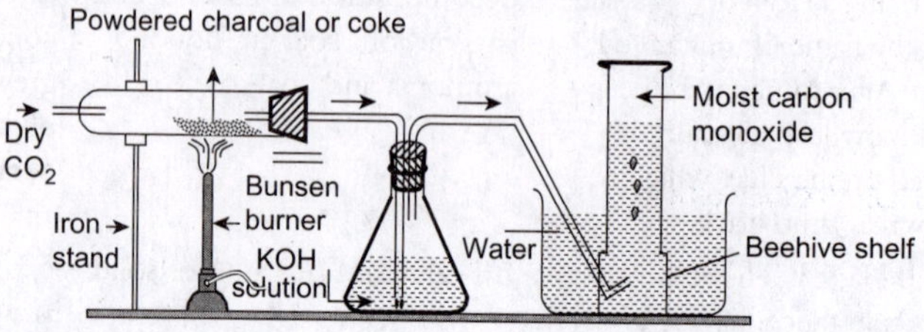

FIGURE 6.4 Laboratory preparation of carbon monoxide

Process: Powdered charcoal is taken in a hard glass test tube and is heated. Then, carbon dioxide gas is passed over this. CO_2 gas oxidises carbon and turns it into carbon monoxide.

Purification: Carbon monoxide prepared by the above process may contain CO_2 gas as an impurity. This can be removed by passing the products through caustic potash solution.

Precautions

1. The powdered charcoal is kept red hot throughout the reaction.
2. The initial bubbles of the gas are left out and only then the collection of the gas is started.
3. Carbon monoxide being a poisonous gas, the entire process of preparation is carried out in a fume chamber.

In the laboratory, CO can also be prepared from oxalic acid and formic acid.

(a) From oxalic acid: Sulphuric acid absorbs water from oxalic acid, producing carbon monoxide and carbon dioxide.

$$\begin{matrix} COOH \\ | \\ COOH \end{matrix} + H_2SO_4 \xrightarrow{\Delta} H_2SO_4.H_2O + CO + CO_2$$

(b) From formic acid: Sulphuric acid absorbs water from formic acid, forming carbon monoxide.

$$HCOOH + H_2SO_4 \xrightarrow{100°C} H_2SO_4.H_2O + CO$$

Carbon Dioxide

Occurrence

Carbon dioxide occurs in nature both in free and in combined states.

Free State

1. Atmospheric air contains 0.03% of CO_2.
2. Dry wells, mines and caves near lime kilns contain larger proportions of CO_2.
3. Dissolved CO_2 in water in oceans, lakes, etc.

Combined State

Minerals, like, limestone, magnesite, etc., contain large amount of CO_2 in the form of carbonate salts.

General Methods of Preparation

1. **Burning of charcoal or carbon or coke**: When charcoal or coke is burnt in adequate supply of air, it enhances the level of carbon dioxide. The reaction is highly exothermic.

$$C + O_2 \longrightarrow CO_2 + Q$$

2. **Thermal decomposition of metal carbonates**: All carbonate except those of sodium or potassium on heating evolve carbon dioxide along with the formation of metal oxide.

$$CaCO_3 \longrightarrow CaO + CO_2$$
$$ZnCO_3 \longrightarrow ZnO + CO_2$$

3. **Thermal decomposition of bicarbonates**: Bicarbonates on strong heating evolve carbon dioxide along with the formation of the corresponding carbonate and water

$$NaHCO_3 \longrightarrow Na_2CO_3 + H_2O$$

4. **Action of dilute mineral acids on carbonates and bicarbonates**: Dilute HCl or H_2SO_4 when added to the carbonate or bicarbonate salt, neutralisation reaction takes place with the liberation of carbon dioxide gas:

$$Na_2CO_3 + H_2SO_4 \longrightarrow Na_2SO_4 + CO_2 + H_2O$$
$$NaHCO_3 + HCl \longrightarrow NaCl + H_2O + CO_2$$

Laboratory Method of Preparation

Principle: Marble chips contain calcium carbonate which, on the addition of dilute hydrochloric acid, releases CO_2 gas:

$$CaCO_3 + 2HCl \longrightarrow CaCl_2 + H_2O + CO_2$$

Process: Marble chips are taken in a conical flask. A two holed rubber cork is introduced into this. Through one hole, a thistle funnel is inserted and through another hole, a delivery tube is inserted. Dilute hydrochloric acid is added dropwise through the thistle funnel. CO_2 gas generated during the reaction comes out through the delivery tube.

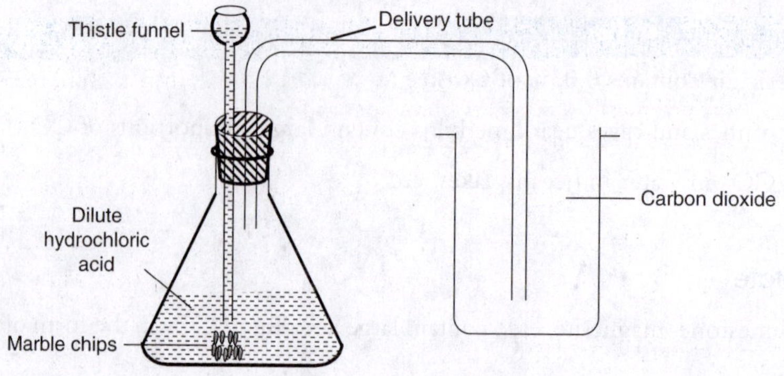

FIGURE 6.5 Laboratory preparation of carbon dioxide

Collection of Gas

It can be collected by the upward displacement of air since it is heavier than air.

Comparative Study of Carbon Monoxide and Carbon Dioxide

Physical Properties

Properties	Carbon monoxide	Carbon dioxide
Colour	Colourless	Colourless
Odour	No characteristic smell	No characteristic smell
Vapour density (VD)	Slightly lighter than air, VD = 14	Heavier than air, VD = 22
Solubility	Insoluble in water	Highly soluble in water
Nature	Neutral and does not respond to litmus test	Acidic. Changes blue litmus to red.
Boiling point	−192°C	−78.5°C

Chemical Properties

Properties	Carbon monoxide	Carbon dioxide
Combustibility	(a) Combustible, burns in air with a pale blue flame. A mixture of CO and air burns spontaneously resulting in an explosive reaction. (b) Not a supporter of combustion	Non-combustible Not a supporter of combustion
Reaction with alkalis	No reaction	Neutralisation takes place with the formation of salt and water: $CO_2 + 2NaOH \longrightarrow Na_2CO_3 + H_2O$
Reaction with lime water	No reaction	Turns milky due to the formation of insoluble $CaCO_3$: $CO_2 + Ca(OH)_2 \longrightarrow CaCO_3 + H_2O$

Properties	Carbon monoxide	Carbon dioxide
Reaction with metals	When CO gas is passed over the finely-divided metals, like, nickel, chromium and iron metal carbonyls are formed: $Ni + 4CO \xrightarrow{\Delta} Ni(CO)_4$ $Cr + 6CO \longrightarrow Cr(CO)_6$ $Fe + 5CO \longrightarrow Fe(CO)_5$	Na, K and Ca combine with CO_2 to form their respective carbonates along with carbon, whereas Mg and Al give their respective oxides and carbon: $4Na + 3CO_2 \longrightarrow 2Na_2CO_3 + C$ $2Mg + CO_2 \longrightarrow 2MgO + C$
Reaction with non-metals	Reaction with oxygen gives CO_2 gas and reaction with Cl_2 gas gives phosgene: $2CO + O_2 \longrightarrow 2CO_2$ $CO + Cl_2 \longrightarrow COCl_2$	No reaction with O_2 and Cl_2
As reducing agent/oxidising agent	CO reduces oxides of less active metals: $Fe_2O_3 + 3CO \longrightarrow 2Fe + 3CO_2$	Oxidises carbon to carbon monoxide: $CO_2 + C \longrightarrow 2CO - Q$
Biochemical process	Combines with haemoglobin of blood to form carboxyhaemoglobin. This makes CO gas poisonous	Green plants synthesise carbohydrates by the combination of CO_2 and water in the presence of sunlight. The process is called **photosynthesis** $6CO_2 + 6H_2O \longrightarrow C_6H_{12}O_6 + 6O_2$

Action of CO_2 When It is Passed Through Lime Water

Limited amount of CO_2	Excess amount of CO_2
When limited amount of CO_2 is passed through lime water, it turns milky due to the formation of insoluble $CaCO_3$: $Ca(OH)_{2(aq)} + CO_{2(g)} \longrightarrow CaCO_3 + H_2O$	When an excess amount of CO_2 is passed through lime water, it first turns milky, and then the milkiness disappears due to the formation of soluble $Ca(HCO_3)_2$: $Ca(OH)_2 + CO_2 \longrightarrow CaCO_3 + H_2O$ $CaCO_3 + CO_2 + H_2O \longrightarrow Ca(HCO_3)_2$

Uses of Carbon Monoxide (CO)

1. Carbon monoxide can be used as a fuel as it produces a large amount of heat on combustion. The fuels, like, coal gas, water gas and producer gas contain carbon monoxide as an important constituent.
2. Carbon monoxide is used in the extraction of metals like nickel from the mixture of other metals. This is done by passing carbon monoxide through the mixture of other metals.
3. In the manufacture of chemicals.
4. It behaves as a reducing agent in the extraction of metals.
5. In the preparation of war gas like phosgene.

Uses of CO_2

Apart from being the natural and indispensable raw material for photosynthesis, CO_2 finds many important applications in various fields.

1. Carbon dioxide is used for the hardening of mortars (mixture of $Ca(OH)_2$, sand and water). Thus, the mortar applied to join bricks slowly hardens due to the absorption of carbon dioxide from the atmosphere forming calcium carbonate.
2. Carbogen, a mixture of 95% of oxygen and 5% of carbon dioxide, is used to stimulate respiratory system.
3. It is used in soft drinks or aerated drinks to give them a tangy taste.
4. Solid carbon dioxide called **dry ice** is used as a refrigerant.
5. Carbon dioxide is extensively used in the production of industrial compounds, such as, washing soda, baking soda, white lead, etc.
6. Atmosphere of carbon dioxide can be used in the preservation of food grains, fruits, etc.
7. Carbon dioxide is used in fire extinguishers to put off fires since it is a non-combustible gas and does not support combustion.
8. Baking powder which contains sodium bicarbonate produces carbon dioxide gas on heating. This gas helps in the aeration of dough.

EXAMPLE

Give the reactions involved between carbon dioxide and metals.

SOLUTION

Na, K, Ca, combine with CO_2 to form their respective carbonates along with carbon, whereas Mg and Al give their respective oxides and carbon

$$4Na + 3CO_2 \rightarrow 2Na_2CO_3 + C;\ 2Mg + CO_2 \rightarrow 2MgO + C$$

EXAMPLE

How is dry ice manufactured?

SOLUTION

Dry ice can be prepared by liquifying CO_2 below 31°C by compression and then the liquid is allowed to evaporate rapidly, a portion of it solidifies to dry ice.

Fire Extinguishers

A fire extinguisher is a device used for putting off fires. Though many kinds of fire extinguishers are available, carbon dioxide is the basic source for extinguishing fires in most of the extinguishers.

Principle

Carbon dioxide gas is not a supporter of combustion. Being heavier than air, it forms a layer below air. Thus, CO_2 layer formed between the flames and air cuts off the contact between air and fire. As a result of this, the fire is prevented from spreading and is finally put off due to the shortage of the supply of oxygen to the fire.

Types

The most important types of fire extinguishers in use are the following:

1. soda acid fire extinguisher and
2. foam type fire extinguisher.

Soda Acid Fire Extinguisher

A fire extinguisher consists of a metallic cylinder filled with a solution of sodium bicarbonate. At the bottom of the cylinder, a thin sealed glass tube containing concentrated sulphuric acid is placed. This tube is surrounded by a fixed wire gauze cage. A plunger with a sharp end is placed at the bottom of the cylinder in such a way that the sharp end is placed at the sealed thin glass tube, as shown in the above figure. On the top of the cylinder, a nozzle which is sealed with wax is provided.

When the plunger is hit against the floor, the sharp tip of the plunger breaks the glass test tube. The acid in the test tube reacts with sodium bicarbonate solution to produce carbon dioxide gas. Carbon dioxide gas is forced out through the nozzle. The wax seal is broken off, thus, forcing CO_2 gas out through the nozzle. The fire is put off when the gas is directed against the fire.

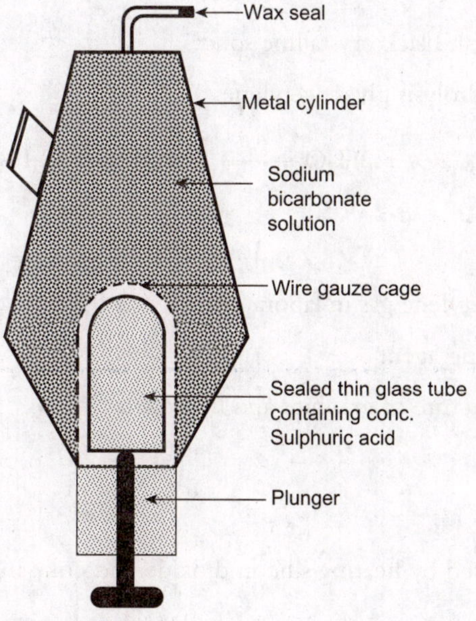

FIGURE 6.6 Soda acid fire extinguisher

Limitations

This fire extinguisher is used to extinguish fire caused by solid inflammable materials only. In the case of extinguishing fires caused by inflammable liquids, such as, petrol; it is rendered useless because the solution coming out of the cylinder, being denser than oil sinks in the oil and disables it to cut off the supply of air to the fire. It should not be used to extinguish the flames caused by electricity as the solution is a good conductor of electricity.

Foam Type Extinguisher

Foam type extinguisher is used to extinguish fire caused by inflammable liquids, such as, petrol, alcohol, diesel, etc. The construction and working of the extinguisher is similar to that of soda acid fire extinguisher. However, the solution of sodium bicarbonate contains saponin (a material which produces lot of foam). Sulphuric acid is replaced by aluminium sulphate solution. As a result, the following reaction takes place, which helps in extinguishing fire:

$$Al_2(SO_4)_3 + 6NaHCO_3 \longrightarrow 3Na_2SO_4 + 2Al(OH)_3 + 6CO_2$$

Limitation

This fire extinguisher cannot be used to extinguish fire caused by electricity.

Other Inorganic Compounds of Carbon

Calcium Carbide (CaC_2)

Preparation: Calcium carbide is prepared by heating pulverised calcium oxide and coke:

$$2CaO + 6C \longrightarrow 2CaC_2 + 2CO$$

Physical Properties: Greyish black crystalline solid.

Chemical Properties: Hydrolysis gives acetylene:

$$CaC_2 + 2H_2O \longrightarrow Ca(OH)_2 + C_2H_2$$

Uses

1. It is used to prepare acetylene gas in laboratory
2. It is used as a dehydrating agent
3. It is used in the manufacture of graphite and hydrogen

Silicon Carbide (SiC)

Preparation: SiC is produced by heating silicon dioxide and coke in an electric furnace. It is also known as carborundum.

$$SiO_2 + 3C \longrightarrow SiC + 2CO\uparrow$$

Physical Properties

1. It is a very hard substance with high melting point nearly 2700°C.
2. It is insoluble in water.
3. Its density is 3.22 g/cm^3.

Chemical Properties: Silicon carbide is oxidised by fused sodium hydroxide in the presence of air:

$$SiC + O_2 + 4NaOH \longrightarrow Na_2CO_3 + Na_2SiO_3 + 2H_2O$$

Uses

1. It is used as an abrasive.
2. It is also used as a grinding stone to cut and sharpen tools.

Calcium Carbonate ($CaCO_3$)

Preparation

1. Carbonic acid reacts with calcium hydroxide to produce $CaCo_3$.
2. It is prepared by passing CO_2 into a solution of calcium hydroxide, calcium carbonate precipitates out:

$$Ca(OH)_2 + CO_2 \longrightarrow CaCO_3 + H_2O$$

Physical Properties

1. It is a white crystalline solid with melting point of 825°C.
2. It is insoluble in water.

Chemical Properties

1. It reacts with strong acids releasing CO_2:

$$CaCO_3 + 2HCl \longrightarrow CaCl_2 + CO_2 + H_2O$$

2. It reacts with water that is saturated with CO_2 to form the soluble calcium bicarbonate:

$$CaCO_3 + CO_2 + H_2O \longrightarrow Ca(HCO_3)_2$$

Uses: It is used as an antacid.

Sodium Carbonate (Na_2CO_3)

Preparation: It is prepared by heating carbonic acid with NaOH:

$$H_2CO_3 + 3NaOH \longrightarrow Na_2CO_3 + 2H_2O$$

Physical Properties

1. It is a white crystalline solid with melting point of 851°C.
2. It is soluble in water.

Chemical Properties

1. It reacts with water to form carbonic acid and sodium hydroxide:

$$Na_2CO_3 + 2H_2O \longrightarrow H_2CO_3 + 2NaOH$$

2. It reacts with metal salts to form insoluble basic carbonates.

Uses

1. It removes greasy dirt from clothes and vessels.
2. It is used in the manufacture of glass.
3. It is used to soften hard water.

Sodium Bicarbonate ($NaHCO_3$)

Preparation: It forms when sodium hydroxide reacts with carbonic acid:

$$H_2CO_3 + NaOH \longrightarrow NaHCO_3 + H_2O$$

Physical Properties

1. It is a white crystalline substance.
2. It is sparingly soluble in water.

Chemical Properties

1. It reacts with water to form carbonic acid and sodium hydroxide:

$$NaHCO_3 + H_2O \longrightarrow H_2CO_3 + NaOH$$

2. It reacts with acids to evolve CO_2:

$$NaHCO_3 + HCl \longrightarrow NaCl + H_2O + CO_2$$

Uses

1. It is used in the preparation of sodium carbonate.
2. It is used as an antacid.
3. It is used in the preparation baking powder.

Compounds of Carbon and Hydrogen

Carbon has the unique capability of forming long chains by means of self-linkage among the atoms. This ability of an element to form either straight chains or branched chains is called **catenation.**

Due to this unique feature of catenation, carbon can form an innumerable number of compounds. These compounds containing only carbon and hydrogen are called **hydrocarbons.**

Depending on the relative proportions of carbon and hydrogen, hydrocarbons are further classified into saturated and unsaturated hydrocarbons. Saturated hydrocarbons have larger proportions of hydrogen and have a general formula, C_nH_{2n+2}. The saturated hydrocarbons containing 1, 2, 3 and 4 carbon atoms are called **methane**, **ethane**, **propane** and **butane**, respectively. All these compounds exist in a gaseous state at room temperature.

Methane

It is the simplest member of saturated hydrocarbons with the molecular formula CH_4.

Occurrence

Natural gas contains mainly methane. Natural gas is formed by the anaerobic decomposition of organic matter by bacteria present inside the earth's crust.

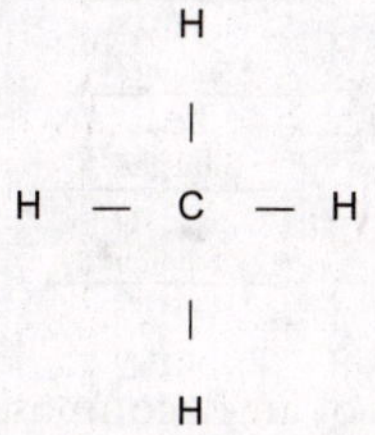

FIGURE 6.7 A molecule of methane

Methane is also found in marshy places. Hence, it is commonly known as marsh gas. (In coal mines, methane which causes explosions and fire, accumulates). For the safety of miners, Davy's safety lamp is used for illumination inside the mines. This lamp was designed by Sir Humphrey Davy.

Preparation of Methane

On heating anhydrous sodium acetate (sodium salt of acetic acid) with soda lime (a mixture of sodium hydroxide and calcium oxide), methane is formed along with sodium carbonate.

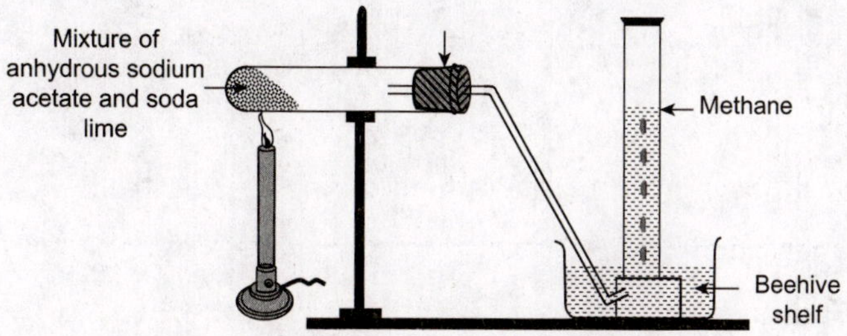

FIGURE 6.8 Preparation of methane

$$\underset{\text{(Sodium acetate)}}{CH_3COONa} + NaOH \xrightarrow{\Delta} \underset{\text{(Methane)}}{CH_4Na_2CO_3}$$

Methane gas produced during the reaction is collected over water by the downward displacement of water since it is lighter than air and insoluble in water.

Physical Properties

1. Methane is a colourless and odourless gas.
2. It is insoluble in water.
3. It is lighter than air.
4. It causes global warming as it is a greenhouse gas.
5. CNG which contains mainly methane can be stored in cylinders.

Chemical Properties

1. Methane on combustion burns with a blue flame giving out carbon dioxide and water:

$$CH_4 + 2O_2 \longrightarrow CO_2 + 2H_2O + \text{Energy}$$

2. Methane reacts with chlorine gas in the presence of sunlight, by displacing one, two, three or all of its hydrogen atoms:

$$CH_4 + Cl_2 \xrightarrow{\text{Sunlight}} CH_3Cl + HCl$$

$$CH_3Cl + Cl_2 \xrightarrow{\text{Sunlight}} CH_2Cl_2 + HCl$$

$$CH_2Cl_2 + Cl_2 \xrightarrow{\text{Sunlight}} CHCl_3 + HCl$$

$$CHCl_3 + Cl_2 \xrightarrow{\text{Sunlight}} CCl_4 + HCl$$

3. Methane on heating in the absence of air decomposes into carbon and hydrogen. The carbon so obtained is called **carbon black**. This reaction is called **pyrolysis** or **cracking**.

$$CH_4 \longrightarrow C + 2H_2.$$

TEST YOUR CONCEPTS

Very Short Answer Type Ques.tions

1. What is meant by allotropy?
2. Mention any three physical properties of graphite.
3. ______________ is used in the manufacture of black carbon papers.
4. Bone charcoal contains maximum percentage of ______________.
5. What is meant by carbonisation?
6. Describe a method of preparing carbon dioxide.
7. Give any two uses of calcium carbonate.
8. The major component of CNG is______________.
9. Discuss any two chemical properties of methane.
10. Give three uses of diamond.
11. ______________ acid on reaction with H_2SO_4 gives only carbon monoxide gas.
12. Explain how sugar charcoal is prepared.
13. What is a fire extinguisher? Mention its types.
14. Mention two physical properties of methane.
15. Give the chemical properties of calcium carbide.
16. How is bone charcoal prepared?
17. Melting point of diamond is ______.
18. Explain the structure of graphite.
19. What are fullerenes?
20. Name the purest form of charcoal.
21. Explain the reducing property of wood charcoal.
22. Mention the chemical properties of sodium carbonate.
23. Name the different allotropes of carbon.
24. Colour is imparted to diamond due to the presence of ______.
25. How is coke formed? Give two uses of coke.
26. Write the reaction involved in the preparation of silicon carbide.
27. The composition of lime mortar is ______.
28. The poisonous gas, phosgene is prepared from ______________ and ______________ gases.
29. Mention any two physical properties of carbon dioxide.
30. Give two properties and two uses of lamp black.

Short Answer Type Questions

31. Describe a laboratory method of the preparation of wood charcoal.
32. Describe the structure of diamond.
33. Why is soda acid fire extinguisher used to extinguish fire caused by solid inflammable materials?
34. Explain the reactivity of graphite with oxygen and sodium carbonate with chemical equations.
35. What are the different products formed when methane and chlorine are made to react in the presence of sunlight?
36. Mention the chemical properties of diamond.
37. How is methane prepared in the laboratory?
38. Write short notes on gas carbon.
39. Discuss the reactivity of carbon monoxide with metals and non-metals.
40. Explain the reactivity of carbon dioxide with metals.
41. What are the physical properties of carbon monoxide?
42. State the physical properties of diamond.
43. Give the preparation method of the following compounds:

    (i) CaC_2 (ii) SiC

    (iii) $CaCO_3$ (iv) Na_2CO_3

    (v) $NaHCO_3$

PRACTICE QUESTIONS

44. Discuss three important uses of
(i) graphite (ii) wood charcoal
(iii) carbon monoxide (iv) sugar charcoal
(v) bone charcoal (vi) carbon dioxide
(vii) methane

45. Discuss the physical properties of
(i) CaC_2 (ii) SiC
(iii) $CaCO_3$ (iv) Na_2CO_3
(iv) $NaHCO_3$

Essay Type Questions

46. Write a note on
(i) calcium carbide (ii) silicon carbide

47. Explain the manufacture of graphite by Acheson process.

48. Discuss the laboratory preparation of carbon monoxide.

49. Discuss carbon cycle in nature.

50. Explain the working of the two types of fire extinguishers.

For Answer key, Hints and Explanations, please visit:
www.pearsoned.co.in/IITFoundationSeries

CONCEPT APPLICATION

Level 1

Directions for questions from 1 to 7
State whether the following statements are true or false.

1. Graphite is used in the manufacture of crucibles as it possesses high-electrical resistance.
2. Fullerene is the amorphous allotrope of carbon.
3. Lamp black is used as filler in making rubber tyres.
4. Carbon monoxide is neither combustible nor a supporter of combustion.
5. In methane, all the hydrogen atoms can be replaced by chlorine atoms when the reaction takes place in presence of sunlight.
6. Sugar charcoal is a good reducing agent.
7. Foam type extinguisher is used to extinguish any kind of fire.

Directions for questions from 8 to 14
Fill in the blanks.

8. Crystallisation of carbon to form diamonds takes place when ______________ metal expands during solidification.
9. Carbon monoxide is slightly ______ than air.
10. The compound of carbon used to soften hard water is _______.
11. ______________ acid on reaction with H_2SO_4 gives only carbon monoxide gas.
12. Methane is prepared in a laboratory by heating anhydrous sodium acetate with ______.
13. Sugar on reaction with ______________ gives sugar charcoal.
14. Gas carbon is used as ______ in dry cells.

Directions for question 15
Match the entries in column A with the appropriate ones in Column B.

15.

Column A	Column B
A. Carbon dioxide	( ) a. Glass industry
B. Carbon monoxide	( ) b. Abrasive
C. Calcium carbide	( ) c. Fire extinguisher
D. Silicon carbide	( ) d. Antacid
E. Calcium carbonate	( ) e. Reducing agent
F. Sodium carbonate	( ) f. Baking powder
G. Sodium bicarbonate	( ) g. Used to make acetylene

Directions for questions from 16 to 45
For each of the questions, four choices have been provided. Select the correct alternative.

16. The existence of an element in different allotropic forms is due to the
(a) different arrangement of atoms
(b) different amounts of energy associated in the formation of each allotrope
(c) different methods of formation
(d) all of the above

17. Which among the following properties of coke is exploited in the preparation of graphite by Acheson process?
(a) bad conductor of electricity
(b) good conductor of heat
(c) highly porous nature
(d) low-melting point

18. Which of the following substances is used in place of H_2SO_4 in foam type fire extinguishers?
(a) saponin
(b) aluminium sulphate
(c) sodium carbonate
(d) alcohol

19. Generally $CaCO_3$ is insoluble in water but in the presence of carbon dioxide it is soluble. This is because
(a) of the formation of carbonic acid
(b) of the formation of soluble $Ca(HCO_3)_2$
(c) CO_2 makes $CaCO_3$ porous, thus, dissolving it in water
(d) of the formation of highly concentrated acids

20. Identify endothermic reaction among the following:
(a) passage of CO_2 through red hot carbon
(b) passage of O_2 through red hot carbon
(c) burning of methane
(d) burning of water gas

21. Nature of the products obtained by complete combustion of methane is
(a) acidic, basic (b) acidic, neutral
(c) basic, neutral (d) both are neutral

22. Which of the following carbonates does not decompose to give CO_2?
(a) $NaHCO_3$ (b) $CaCO_3$
(c) K_2CO_3 (d) $ZnCO_3$

23. A compound X made of two non-metals in a reaction with another non-metal Y gives the hardest substance and carbon monoxide. Identify the compound X and the non-metal Y.
(a) CO_2, Si (b) SiO_2, C
(c) SiC, O_2 (d) CO, Si

24. Which of the following allotropes of carbon is used for the manufacture of fullerenes?
(a) graphite (b) diamond
(c) coke (d) charcoal

25. Graphite cannot be used as a lubricant in space because
(a) absence of external pressure transforms crystalline graphite to amorphous form
(b) there is no atmosphere in space, and hence, graphite sublimes in space
(c) there is no atmosphere in space, and hence, there is no adsorbed air and water between layers of graphite
(d) none of the above

26. Coke can be used as
(a) an oxidising agent (b) a household fuel
(c) printer ink (d) electrodes

27. In the reaction:

$$2CaO + C \longrightarrow CaC_2 + 2CO$$

$$2CaC_2 + 2H_2O \longrightarrow A + B$$

if A is involved in the neutralisation reaction with acid, then B may be
(a) CH_4 (b) C_2H_2
(c) $Ca(OH)_2$ (d) CaH_2

28. Carbon occurs as the native element in the earth's crust in the form of
(a) diamond (b) methane
(c) carbon dioxide (d) gas carbon

29. Why shouldn't we light a candle in a closed room with people?
(a) The CO_2 formed causes breathlessness.
(b) Carbon particles are formed which are dangerous for respiratory tract.
(c) Methane gas, which is poisonous, is formed.
(d) Carbon monoxide gas which reduces the ability of blood to carry oxygen is formed.

30. Why do black shoe polishes have an oily feel?
(a) Shoe polish is a mixture of oil and powdered graphite.
(b) On exposure to air, these undergo chemical changes and produce oily substances.
(c) Vapour of some amount of oil is left over after its preparation.
(d) These are formed by dissolving charcoal in oil.

31. Arrange the steps in the process of carbon cycle, starting from the abundant state of existence of carbon in the combined state in their correct sequence.

(1) dead remains (2) CO_2 in atmosphere
(3) organic matter (4) plants
(5) fossil fuels

(a) 2 1 3 4 5 (b) 2 4 1 3 5
(c) 4 2 3 1 5 (d) 4 5 2 3 1

32. Arrange the steps in the process of carbon cycle starting from the substances which possess a mixture of hydrocarbons in a proper sequence.

(1) sea water (2) dead remains
(3) aquatic plants (4) CO_2 in the atmosphere
(5) organic matter (6) fossil fuels

(a) 3 1 4 5 6 2 (b) 6 3 4 1 2 5
(c) 4 1 3 2 5 6 (d) 6 4 1 3 2 5

33. Graphite fibres are used to reinforce plastic as they

(a) have weak carbon bonds
(b) have high-tensile strength
(c) are brittle
(d) have weak forces of attraction between layers

34. In the manufacture of graphite by Acheson process, the charge filled between the cathode and anode consists of

(a) powdered coke, sand and ferric oxide
(b) powdered coke
(c) sand
(d) ferric oxide

35. The compound which builds up the greenhouse effect is

(a) carbon monoxide (b) gas carbon
(c) carbon dioxide (d) none of these

36. The use of diamond as a gem is due to its

(a) extreme hardness (b) poor conductance
(c) low density (d) high-refractive index

37. To a small quantity of X, few drops of HCl are added. Consequently, a colourless, odourless gas is produced. This gas on passing through lime water turns it milky proving the presence of _______ in X.

(a) carbonate (b) bicarbonate
(c) carbide (d) either (1) or (2)

38. _______ is used extensively in the manufacture of washing soda

(a) carbon dioxide (b) carbon monoxide
(c) methane (d) lamp black

39. Which of the following can be considered as spontaneous combustion?

(a) burning of LPG
(b) burning of magnesium ribbon
(c) burning of camphor
(d) burning of potassium in moist air

40. Water gas is mixture of

(a) CO_2 and H_2 (b) H_2 and CH_4
(c) CO and H_2 (d) CO and N_2

41. Heating of methane in the absence of air is called

(a) combustion (b) decarboxylation
(c) pyrolysis (d) photolysis

42. Arrange the different types of coal in sequence in the increasing order of the quality coal.

(1) lignite (2) peat
(3) anthracite (4) bituminous

(a) 1 3 4 2 (b) 4 2 3 1
(c) 2 1 4 3 (d) 2 3 4 1

43. Graphite is a greasy, soft lubricant because it

(a) has low density
(b) has weak forces of attraction between layers
(c) is greyish-black in colour
(d) has a three-dimensional structure

44. Arrange the given combustible substances in decreasing order of calorific value:

(1) hydrogen (2) charcoal
(3) petrol (4) LPG
(5) wood

(a) 2 3 1 4 5 (b) 1 4 3 2 5
(c) 2 1 4 5 3 (d) 2 1 3 5 4

45. Graphite is used in a nuclear reactor as

(a) a moderator (b) a fuel
(c) an electrode (d) a lubricant

PRACTICE QUESTIONS

Level 2

1. Why is graphite used as a pencil lead?
2. Can molten copper be used in place of molten iron for the manufacture of artificial diamonds? Give a reason in support of your answer.
3. Diamond is a good thermal conductor like metals. However, it is a poor electrical conductor unlike metals. How do you account for this?
4. Why is activated charcoal widely used in water purifiers?
5. Burning more and more fossil fuels creates an imbalance in the natural carbon cycle as well as in the natural water cycle. Give reasons.
6. Carbon monoxide gas can be detected by passing it through a blood sample. Explain.
7. A building constructed from mortar becomes stronger on long standing. Give a reason.
8. Why is CNG replacing petrol as an automobile fuel?
9. Dry ice should not be stored in a sealed bottle. Explain with an appropriate reason.
10. Two non-metal atoms contain the same number of electrons in their valence shells. One of the non-metals in its most abundant form reacts with the other non-metal forming a very stable compound A. Compound A on reaction with oxygen and fused sodium hydroxide gives two products B and C. B is used as a raw material for the manufacture of glass and C is the major constituent of glass. Identify A, B and C. Write balanced chemical equations for the above reactions.
11. Burning more and more fossil fuels creates an imbalance in the natural carbon cycle as well as in the natural water cycle. Give reasons.
12. Tiny diamonds find applications in coating the tips and edges of cutting tools. Which properties of diamonds are made use of for this purpose?
13. Explain the role of baking soda as a leavening agent and as an antacid?
14. An oxide of a bivalent metal on heating with coke gives a compound X and a gas Y. The gas Y reacts with chlorine gas to give a poisonous gaseous compound. X undergoes hydrolysis to give a hydrocarbon Z with two carbon atoms. Identify the compounds X, Y and Z. Also, give the reactions involved.
15. Graphite is used as a solid lubricant. Give reasons.
16. How does a dry powder type fire extinguisher work?
17. A naturally occurring mineral of sedimentary rocks on heating to high temperatures decomposes giving a solid A and a gas. The solid on dissolution in water undergoes chemical reaction which is associated with hissing sound and the solution appears to be boiling. Compound B formed during this reaction on long standing forms a layer of white powder. When excess CO_2 is passed through this milky white solution, a clear solution is formed again. Identify the substances and justify the above observations. Give reasons wherever required.
18. In the manufacture of silicon carbide by Acheson process, sawdust is used along with sand and coke in the electric furnace. What is the main purpose of using sawdust as one of the constituents of the mixture?
19. The genuineness of a pearl can be verified by dipping it in lemon juice. Why?
20. Why does fogging occur while using a soda acid fire extinguisher?
21. Why is wood charcoal considered to be an excellent household fuel?
22. Two compounds X and Y, when dissolved in water, produced sodium bicarbonate. If hydrochloric acid is added to compound X, compound Y is liberated. Identify X and Y.
23. A student of VIII class broke a dry cell to examine its parts and correlate them with his teacher's explanations about dry cells. In the chemistry class, the student asked his teacher that though

graphite is a non-metal, why is it used as electrodes in the electrolytic process, especially where a high temperature is maintained. Write down the explanation the teacher gave to the student.

24. Sam and his family went to watch a Hollywood movie in which the hero along with his friends rescues 76 people trapped in mines where poisonous gas was being released. During the process, gas masks containing wood charcoal were given to the people. In the movie the hero and his friends were research students in the nearby university. Sam asked his scientist father regarding the role of wood charcoal in gas masks. Write the scientist's explanation in this regard.

25. An eleven-year old naughty boy Krish took keys of his father's car without his father's permission. He went inside the garage, closed it and started the ignition. After a few minutes, he started coughing. His father fortunately went into the garage, opened it, immediately brought him out and rescued him. Krish's mother asked her husband the reason for Krish's condition. What explanation did the father give?

Level 3

1. Explain the role of dry ice in the occurrence of artificial rain.
2. Wood charcoal floats on water, but if it is boiled in water it sinks. Explain with appropriate reasons.
3. Compare and contrast the principle involved in the usage of $NaHCO_3$ and dry ice for cleaning industrial equipment by blasting the given substances with compressed air.
4. Why is molten iron used in the preparation of artificial diamond?
5. What is the advantage of liquid CO_2 fire extinguisher over soda–acid fire extinguisher? Explain.
6. Though coke is made from coal, it is used for metallurgical processes instead of coal. Give reasons.
7. Draw a comparison among petrol, LPG and CNG as automobile fuels.
8. Compare and contrast the principle involved in the usage of $NaHCO_3$ and dry ice for cleaning industrial equipment by blasting the given substances with compressed air.
9. Pinku and Rinku are TIME IIT-F students. They went to a jewellery shop with their mother. They were delighted to see the lustrous gold ornaments. Pinku peeped through the showcase to see a diamond necklace and told Rinku—Really, the glitterance of diamonds is incomparable to the lustre of gold! Rinku complained that their chemistry teacher explained the lustre of metals in detail but didn't mention about diamonds at all. They both decided to ask their chemistry teacher the next day. What explanation will the teacher give?
10. Ocean acidification due to the disposal of industrial waste has a negative effect on oceanic calcifying organisms. Why?

CONCEPT APPLICATION

Level 1

True or false

1. false
2. false
3. true
4. false
5. true
6. true
7. false

Fill in the blanks

8. iron
9. lighter
10. Na_2CO_3
11. formic
12. soda lime
13. conc. H_2SO_4
14. electrodes

Match the following

15. A →c
B →e
C →g
D →b
E →d
F →a
G →f

Multiple choice questions

16. d
17. a
18. b
19. b
20. a
21. b
22. c
23. b
24. a
25. c
26. b
27. b
28. a
29. d
30. c

31. (i) CO_2 in the atmosphere
(ii) plants
(iii) dead remains
(iv) organic matter
(v) fossil fuels

32. (i) fossil fuels
(ii) CO_2 in the atmosphere
(iii) sea water
(iv) aquatic plants
(v) dead remains
(vi) organic matter

33. Graphite fibres are used to reinforce plastic as they have high-tensile strength.

34. In the manufacture of graphite by Acheson process, the charge filled between the cathode and anode consists of powdered coke, sand and ferric oxide.

35. CO_2 builds up the greenhouse effect.

36. The use of diamond as a gem is due to its high-refractive index.

37. To a small quantity of X a few drops of HCl are added; then, a colourless, odourless gas is produced. This gas on passing through lime water turns it milky proving the presence of carbonate and bicarbonate in X.

38. Carbon dioxide is used extensively in the manufacture of washing soda:

$$CO_2 + 2NaOH \rightarrow Na_2CO_3 + H_2O$$

39. Burning of potassium can be considered as spontaneous combustion.

40. Water gas is a mixture of CO and H_2.

41. Heating of methane in the absence of air is called pyrolysis.

42. (i) peat
(ii) lignite
(iii) bituminous
(iv) anthracite

43. Graphite is a greasy and soft lubricant because it has weak forces of attraction between layers.

44. (i) hydrogen
(ii) LPG
(iii) petrol
(iv) charcoal
(v) wood

45. Graphite is used in a nuclear reactor as a moderator

Level 2

1. (i) structure of graphite
(ii) type of bonding in graphite
(iii) colour of graphite

2. (i) condition required for the manufacture of diamond
(ii) comparison of change in volume of fixed mass of iron and copper during solidification
(iii) effect of this change on the rearrangement of atoms of carbon
(iv) relation between the arrangement of atoms and the allotropic form

3. (i) requisite for a substance to be a good thermal and electrical conductor
(ii) comparison of arrangement of atoms in metal and diamond, respectively
(iii) effect of the above arrangement on the thermal conductivity
(iv) reason behind the electrical conductivity in metals
(v) number of electrons involved in bond formation of carbon in diamond

4. (i) properties of activated charcoal
(ii) surface area of activated charcoal
(iii) effect of surface area on process of removal of impurities

5. (i) products of combustion of fuels
(ii) effect of products formed on environment
(iii) reactivity of products with rain water
(iv) effect on carbon and water cycle

6. (i) interaction between carbon monoxide and haemoglobin
(ii) reaction of CO with O_2 carrier in blood
(iii) product formed
(iv) colour of the product formed

7. (i) constituents of mortar
(ii) purpose of mortar in construction
(iii) reaction between one of the components present in mortar with the component present in air
(iv) the percentage abundance of the above component present in air
(v) relation between the availability of the reactant and the time taken for the reaction

8. (i) chemical composition of CNG
(ii) energy released per unit mass due to the burning of the major component of CNG
(iii) the products formed during burning of CNG
(iv) effect of these products on the atmosphere

9. (i) properties of dry ice
(ii) change in dry ice at normal temperature and pressure conditions
(iii) comparison of volume before and after the change

10. (i) raw material used in the manufacture of glass and the major constituent of glass
(ii) identification of B and C
(iii) identification of A based on the composition of B and C

11. (i) products of combustion of fuels
(ii) effect of products formed on environment
(iii) reactivity of products with rain water
(iv) effect on carbon and water cycles

12. (i) properties of cutting tools
(ii) characteristics of tools used for cutting
(iii) arrangement of atoms in diamond

13. (i) chemical property of baking soda
(ii) reaction of baking soda with other components present in baking powder

(iii) physical state of the products formed

(iv) effect of the physical state of the product on bakery products

(v) reaction of baking soda with the excess acid produced in the stomach

(vi) nature of the reaction

14. (i) identification of hydrocarbons

(ii) identification of metal which gives hydrocarbon with two carbon atoms on hydrolysis

(iii) products formed on reaction of metal oxide with coke

(iv) reaction of gaseous product with chlorine

15. (i) properties of lubricants

(ii) structure of graphite

(iii) bonding in graphite

(iv) melting point of graphite

16. A mixture of sand and sodium bicarbonate can be used to put off the burning material. The heat released from the burning material decomposes sodium bicarbonate and the carbon dioxide produced being heavier than air puts off the flame.

$$2NaHCO_3 \rightarrow Na_2CO_3 + H_2O + CO_2$$

17. Limestone is the naturally occurring mineral in sedimentary rocks. This contains calcium carbonate which on decomposition at high temperature gives solid CaO and CO_2.

CaO on reaction with water forms $Ca(OH)_2$. This is a highly exothermic reaction and CO_2 gas is evolved during this reaction. Therefore, the solution appears to be boiling and is associated with a hissing sound. On long exposure to air, this reacts with atmospheric CO_2 to form $CaCO_3$ as a white-powdered layer. On passing excess CO_2, $CaCO_3$ reacts with this forming soluble calcium bicarbonate. Therefore, a clear solution is formed again.

18. Sawdust used in the charge increases its porosity. The increase in porosity allows a continuous escape of carbon monoxide that burns at the top of the charge. It also prevents heat loss.

19. Real pearl is nothing but calcium carbonate which gives effervescence of carbon dioxide when dipped in citric acid present in lemon juice. But imitation pearl is made up of plastic which does not give out carbon dioxide with lemon juice.

20. Carbon dioxide comes out with great force through a small nozzle from soda acid fire extinguisher. This reduces the temperature of the carbon dioxide to a great extent and moisture present in air condenses on the carbon dioxide molecules and appears like fog.

21. When wood burns, most of the gases and tars present in wood vaporise and charcoal remains. Charcoal is almost 100% carbon and burns with a red glow and leaves very little flame or smoke. Charcoal is a good fuel that burns easily and cleanly in the presence of adequate supply of air.

22. $X + Y + H_2O \rightarrow NaHCO_3$

$$X + HCl \rightarrow Y$$

X should be the carbonate of sodium which produces bicarbonate; secondly, X on reaction with acids like HCl produces CO_2, hence, Y is CO_2. The reaction is

$$\underset{(X)}{Na_2CO_3} + CO_2 + H_2O \rightarrow \underset{(Y)}{2NaHCO_3}$$

23. Graphite is a good conductor of electricity and it is inert to most of the electrolytes. It has a very high-thermal resistivity. Due to these properties, graphite is used in making electrodes in the process of electrolysis.

24. Wood charcoal has a good adsorbing capacity. In areas where the inhaled air contains harmful gases, gas masks containing wood charcoal are used to adsorb these gases. The charcoal in the gas masks adsorbs these gases and the pure air enters the respiratory track.

25. The burning of a fuel takes place while starting a car. If the fuel is burnt in a closed system, incomplete combustion takes place resulting in the formation of CO due to an inadequate supply of air. CO is very harmful for health because of the formation of carboxyhaemoglobin.

Level 3

1. (i) reason behind the occurrence of natural rain
 (ii) composition of dry ice
 (iii) condition required for the formation of clouds
 (iv) type of phase transition that takes place in dry ice
 (v) effect of the above phase transition on the temperature of the surroundings

2. (i) physical properties of wood charcoal
 (ii) principle of floating
 (iii) factors affecting density
 (iv) relation between temperature and kinetic energy of gases

3. (i) effect on the unwanted coating due to the blasting of soda or dry ice
 (ii) nature of sodium bicarbonate
 (iii) mechanical impact on the industrial equipment due to blasting of $NaHCO_3$ and dry ice
 (iv) changes that takes place in dry ice after blasting
 (v) change in temperature due to the above phenomenon
 (vi) effect of change in temperature on the coating of impurities on the surface of industrial equipment

4. (i) change in volume during solidification of iron
 (ii) conditions required for preparation of diamond
 (iii) comparison of volume of iron before and after solidification
 (iv) effect of change in volume on pressure
 (v) effect of pressure in preparation of diamond

5. (i) comparison of the working principle of the given fire extinguishers
 (ii) comparison of composition of the materials used in soda fire extinguisher with that used in liquid CO_2 fire extinguisher
 (iii) transformations that takes place during the usage of both the fire extinguishers
 (iv) comparison of physical properties of the products formed
 (v) types of fire where soda–acid fire extinguisher cannot be used

6. Coal is fed into the coke oven and heated in an oxygen free atmosphere and devolatised. The heating is done in various steps which subject the coal to different temperatures for varying time periods. During each step different volatile compounds are driven off. At the end of the heating process coke remains. It is porous with good strength. Since coke is a purer form of carbon than coal and is porous, it is a better reducing agent than coal.

7. Petrol is a fraction containing hydrocarbons with more than five carbon atoms (C_5–C_{10}). LPG contains butane as a major component with four carbon atoms. CNG contains methane with one carbon atom as a major component. With decrease in number of carbon atoms in the hydrocarbon, the calorific value increases and also the extent of incomplete combustion decreases. Therefore, the fuel efficiency increases. Apart from this, petrol contains sulphur and nitrogen which release harmful pollutants into the atmosphere, whereas LPG and CNG do not contain sulphur and nitrogen. Petrol being a liquid leaves residue in the engine. Among LPG and CNG, burning of CNG produces less amount of CO_2 than LPG. Hence, CNG is considered as the best fuel.

8. Soda blasting is a technique employed to strip off the paints and unwanted materials from all surfaces. This technique involves blasting of $NaHCO_3$ on the required surface with the help of compressed air. Dry ice blasting is also used for the same purpose. But it is more advantageous than soda blasting because dry ice pellets sublime as soon as they are blasted on any surface leaving no residual matter on the surface. Since huge amount of heat is absorbed for sublimation process, thermal shock (due to sudden contraction) in generated in the coating which is an added advantage for the removal of unwanted coating.

9. Metals possess free electrons and on absorption of light, these electrons undergo excitation and deexcitation. This gives metals their lustre. Diamond does not possess any free electrons. However, when light falls on it, the edges of the diamond reflect light at a certain angle and this phenomenon is called **total internal reflection**. This leads to the sparkling of diamond which is responsible for its unique position among all gemstones.

10. The disposal of the industrial wastes in the ocean increases the acidity of ocean water which damages the shells of the oceanic calcifying organisms. Therefore, their self-protection system becomes weaker.

Chapter

7

Some Important Elements and their Compounds

Remember

Before beginning this chapter, you should be able to:

- expalin the properties of metals and non-metals, and their applications in various fields.
- know the commonly know elements such as Nitrogen, Sulphur, Chlorine—their preparation, properties of different compounds that find wide applications in our daily life.

Key Ideas

After completing this chapter, you should be able to:

- study about the preparation, properties and uses of nitrogen, phosphorus and their compounds, like, Ammonia (NH_3), Nitric Acid (HNO_3), Phosphoric acid (H_3PO_4) etc.
- know the preparation, properties and uses of Sulphur and its compounds, like, SO_2, H_2SO_4, H_2S.
- expalin the preparation, properties and uses of chlorine and its compounds, like, HCl, $CaOCl_2$.
- study the industrial applications of chlorine and its derivatives.

INTRODUCTION

The 111 authorised elements can be broadly categorised as metals and non-metals. Metals gained significance not only due to their large number but also due to their widespread use in various fields of industry. Nevertheless, the role of non-metals is not insignificant in day-to-day life. The importance of oxygen and carbon in the biosphere is incredible. Apart from this, some non-metals in the form of their compounds occupy the most pivotal position in the industrial sector and they are rightly called **industrial chemicals**.

Nitrogen, the element which is well known for its abundance in the atmospheric air, is the most important nutrient for plants. Therefore, the various compounds of nitrogen are manufactured for the use as fertilisers. Sulphur and phosphorous also form a part of the fertiliser industry. In addition to this common use, certain compounds are useful for specific purposes such as phosphorous in the match industry. Similarly common salt, a compound of chlorine, forms an important part of our diet.

However, there are some compounds, such as, nitric acid, sulphuric acid, hydrochloric acid, etc., which form an inevitable part of almost every chemical industry. In fact, the yearly consumption of sulphuric acid in a country is taken as an indication which reflects the status of chemical industry in that country. In this context, it should be recalled that sulphuric acid is popularly known as the king of chemicals.

NON-METALS AND THEIR COMPOUNDS

Owing to the significant industrial importance attached to non-metals and their compounds, the study of these forms an important area in chemistry.

Occurrence

Elements	Free state	Combined state
Nitrogen	Nitrogen exists in a free state in the atmospheric air. It is the major constituent of air comprising 78% by volume and 75% by weight.	Nitrogen occurs in a combined state in various forms. It is present in the form of minerals, like, nitre (KNO_3) and Chile salt petre ($NaNO_3$). Nitrogen is present in major amounts in organic matter, such as, proteins, nucleic acids, enzymes and various compounds of biological importance.
Phosphorus	Phosphorous, being highly reactive, does not exist in the free state.	In the combined state, it exists in the form of phosphates, in inorganic as well as organic matter. Examples: chlorapatite $3Ca_3(PO_4)_2.CaCl_2$, fluorapatite $3Ca_3(PO_4)_2.CaF_2$, phosphorprotein of yolk, bone marrow, etc.
Sulphur	Sulphur, in the free state is found in the earth's crust (0.03% of the earth's crust is elemental sulphur). In the volcanic regions, such as, Sicily and Japan; it is present near the earth's crust and in the non-volcanic regions of the United States, such as, Texas and Louisiana; it is found much below the earth's crust (300 to 400 m below the earth crust).	Sulphur in the combined state is found in the form of sulphides (in ores), sulphates (in salts) and in organic matter. Examples: cinnabar (HgS), iron pyrites (FeS.CuS), gypsum $CaSO_4.2H_2O$, insulin, glucosionates, etc.
Chlorine	Chlorine does not occur in the free state in nature due to its high reactivity.	Chlorine exists in the combined state in the form of chlorides, like, common salt (NaCl), potassium chloride (KCl), carnalite ($KCl\ MgCl_2\ 6H_2O$) and mineral horn silver (AgCl).

Nitrogen

Manufacture of Nitrogen

Principle: Since nitrogen is abundantly available in the atmospheric air, it is manufactured mainly by the fractional distillation of liquid air.

Process: The process of manufacturing of nitrogen from air involves two stages:

Stage 1: liquefaction of air

Stage 2: isolation of nitrogen from liquid air

Liquefaction of air: Before subjecting air to liquefaction, air should be free from dust particles, moisture and carbon dioxide.

Components to be removed	Methods of removal
Dust particles	By passing through electric precipitators or filters
Moisture (water vapour)	By passing through conc. H_2SO_4 or anhydrous $CaCl_2$
Carbon dioxide gas	By passing through caustic soda (NaOH) or caustic potash (KOH)

Application of high pressure of 100 atm to 200 atm over dry air and subsequent expansion of this compressed air through a fine jet results in cooling. Repeating the above process a number of times results in the conversion of this air to liquid state.

Isolation of nitrogen from liquid air: Nitrogen and oxygen, the major constituents of air, have different boiling points of −195°C and −182.9°C, and can be separated by fractional distillation. Nitrogen has a lower-boiling point than oxygen, and hence, gets evaporated first leaving behind oxygen in the liquid form.

Detection of nitrogen gas: There is no direct test for the identification of nitrogen gas due to its chemical inertness. However, it is possible to identify nitrogen by an indirect method.

Test	Reactions involved
A burning magnesium ribbon when introduced into a jar of nitrogen, continues to burn giving a pale yellow powder.	$3Mg + N_2 \longrightarrow Mg_3N_2$
The powder on treating with water evolves a colourless pungent smelling gas, which produces white dense fumes on exposure to a glass rod dipped in HCl solution.	$Mg_3N_2 + 6H_2O \longrightarrow 3Mg(OH)_2 + 2NH_3$ $NH_3 + HCl \longrightarrow NH_4Cl$

Physical Properties of Nitrogen

Parameter	Characteristic
Solubility	Slightly soluble in water (2.3 vol in 100 vol)
Vapour density	14.0
Liquefaction	It can be liquefied to a colourless liquid which boils at −195.8°C
Solidification	It can be solidified under high pressure to a white snow like mass which melts at −209.8°C.
Nature	It is a chemically unreactive gas. Due to this unreactive nature, it is used in (i) filling of electric bulbs to prevent the oxidation of the filament present in it (ii) preservation of food stuffs

Chemical Properties of Nitrogen

Property	Reaction
Combustibility	(a) No reaction with oxygen under normal conditions (b) Not combustible (c) Not a supporter of combustion
Action with litmus	No response to litmus test (neutral gas)
Reaction with non-metals	
(i) Reaction with hydrogen	Nitrogen reacts with hydrogen at high temperature and pressure to give ammonia gas: $N_2 + 3H_2 \longrightarrow 2NH_3$
(ii) Reaction with oxygen	Nitrogen and oxygen react in equal volumes to form nitric oxide: $N_2 + O_2 \longrightarrow 2NO$
Reaction with metals	
(i) Reaction with magnesium	Magnesium reacts with nitrogen to form magnesium nitride: $3Mg + N_2 \longrightarrow Mg_3N_2$
(ii) Reaction with calcium	$3Ca + N_2 \longrightarrow Ca_3N_2$
(iii) Reaction with aluminium	$2Al + N_2 \longrightarrow 2AlN$
Reaction with compounds	
Reaction with calcium carbide	Heating calcium carbide with nitrogen at 800°C to 1000°C forms a mixture of calcium cyanamide and graphite: $CaC_2 + N_2 \xrightarrow{800°C} CaCN_2 + C$

Uses of Nitrogen

1. Dilutes the activity of oxygen in natural processes, like, combustion and respiration.
2. Manufacture of ammonia by Haber's process. Ammonia finds application in the manufacture of fertilisers.
3. Nitric oxide combines with oxygen to give various other oxides and these oxides of nitrogen react with water to give oxyacids of nitrogen.
4. The mixture of calcium cyanamide and graphite is known as nitrolim which is an important fertiliser.

Nitrogen is also needed in the soil for both plants and animals. The process of fixing nitrogen in the soil is called **nitrogen fixation**.

Nitrogen Fixation

Though atmosphere contains large proportion of free nitrogen, it is not assimilated by either plants or animals directly. The process of conversion of the atmospheric nitrogen into the usable form either by natural or artificial means is called **nitrogen fixation**.

(a) Natural Fixation

Natural fixation of nitrogen takes place by leguminous plants and also by lightening.

Fixation of Nitrogen by Leguminous Plants

Only leguminous plants, like, peas, beans, etc., are capable of taking in atmospheric nitrogen. These plants possess root nodules which absorb nitrogen from the atmospheric air. The symbiotic bacteria living in these root nodules convert nitrogen into various nitrogen compounds which plants can easily assimilate and the soil becomes rich in nitrogen compounds. These compounds become the source of nitrogen for the plants which are grown in that soil.

By Lightening

When discharges of lightening take place in the atmosphere, due to the high temperature the atmospheric nitrogen combines with oxygen forming nitrogen monoxide which gets oxidised further to nitrogen dioxide:

$$N_2 + O_2 \rightleftharpoons 2NO$$

$$2NO + O_2 \longrightarrow 2NO_2$$

This gas dissolves in the water droplets in clouds and forms nitric acid which comes down to soil in the form of rain water:

$$4NO_2 + 2H_2O + O_2 \longrightarrow 4HNO_3$$

Nitric acid further reacts with minerals, like, metal carbonates or basic oxides present in the deeper layers of soil to form respective metal nitrates which can be assimilated by plants:

$$2HNO_3 + MCO_3 \longrightarrow M(NO_3)_2 + CO_2\uparrow + H_2O$$

(b) Artificial Fixation by Haber's Process

Nitrogen which is isolated from the atmospheric air by the fractional distillation of liquid air is made to react with hydrogen in the ratio of 1: 3 under high pressure (200–900 atm) in the presence of a catalyst (finely divided iron with molybdenum as a promoter) at about 450°C to 500°C to produce ammonia gas:

$$N_2 + 3H_2 \rightleftharpoons 2NH_3$$

Ammonia so manufactured can be used for the manufacture of various ammonium fertilisers. The ammonia can also be converted to nitric acid which can further be converted to various nitrate fertilisers, like, calcium ammonium nitrate.

Recovery of nitrogen back to the atmosphere: Nitrate salts are assimilated by plants through their roots and are converted into proteins. These proteins are consumed by animals. Now the proteins present in the animals are decomposed into simpler substances like urea during metabolic process which are later converted to ammonium salts. Decay products of dead plants and animals are converted into ammonium salts by ammonifying bacteria which are further converted to nitrites and nitrates by nitrifying bacteria. *Nitrosomonas* bacteria help in the conversion of ammonium salts to nitrites and subsequent conversion of these nitrites to nitrates is carried out by *nitrobacter.* The nitrates so obtained are further converted to nitrogen gas by denitrifying bacteria. Thus, the nitrogen consumed during different processes is returned to the atmosphere again.

Nitrogen Cycle

The atmospheric nitrogen is converted to nitrogenous compounds by means of nitrogen fixation. However, the percentage of nitrogen in the atmospheric air remains unaltered. That means, the nitrogen which is converted into compounds is returned back into the atmosphere by the above processes. The entire process of nitrogen fixation and the reconversion of this fixed nitrogen into free nitrogen is called **nitrogen cycle.**

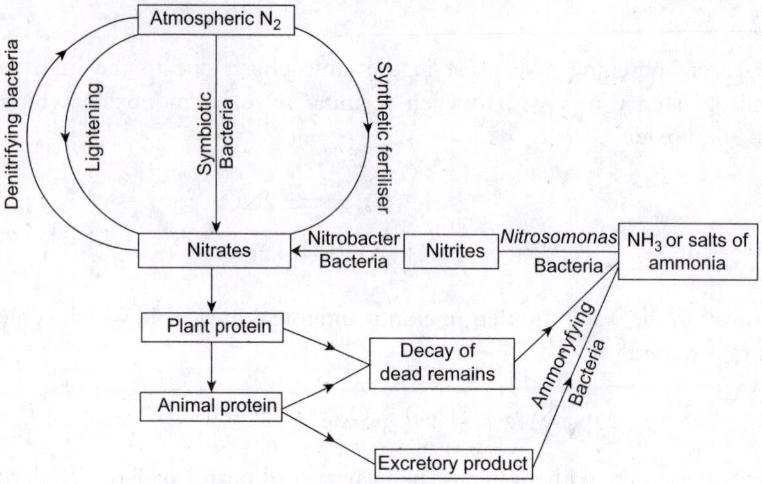

FIGURE 7.1 Nitrogen cycle

Phosphorus

Preparation

Phosphorous is prepared by the electrolytic reduction of mineral phosphate.

Procedure

The mineral phosphate (calcium phosphate) is mixed with sand and coke. This mixture is taken in an electric furnace with carbon electrodes. The mixture is electrically heated up to 1775 K.

The following reactions take place:

$$2Ca_3(PO_4)_2 + \underset{\text{(sand)}}{6SiO_2} \longrightarrow \underset{\text{(slag)}}{6\ CaSiO_3} + P_4O_{10}$$

$$P_4O_{10} + 10C \longrightarrow P_4 + 10CO$$

The slag formed settles at the bottom and is removed. Phosphorous vapours and carbon monoxide gas formed are let out of the furnace from the top. The subsequent cooling of these vapours under water results in the condensation of phosphorous into solid phosphorous.

Purification

The phosphorous obtained is purified using potassium dichromate in an acidic medium. The impurities are oxidised and removed as vapours or slag. Pure liquid phosphorous settles at the bottom where it is collected, filtered through chamois leather and sent through water cooled pipes for solidification.

Allotropy

The phenomenon of existence of an element in more than one form is called **allotropy**, and those different forms of an element are called **allotropes**. Allotropes have almost same chemical properties but different physical properties.

Phosphorous exists in two important allotropic forms:

1. white phosphorous and
2. red phosphorous

Comparative study of white phosphorous and red phosphorous:

Properties	White Phosphorous	Red Phosphorous
State	Soft solid	Brittle powder
Colour	White initially, gradually changes to yellow	Dark red
Odour	Garlic smell	Odourless
Density	1.82 g/cm^3	2.1 g/cm^3
Melting point	317 K	–
Boiling point	553.5 K	Sublimes at 565 K
Ignition temperature	308 K	533 K
Physiological nature	Poisonous	Non-poisonous
Atomicity	Four	Exists as chains
Structure	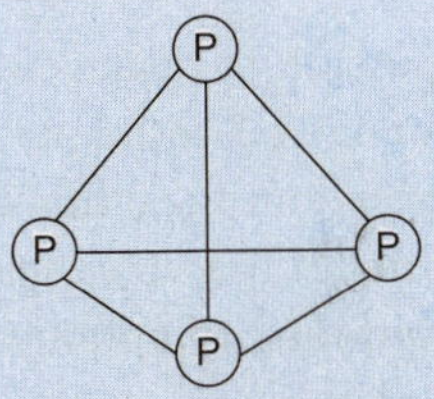 Isolated tetrahedral P_4 units	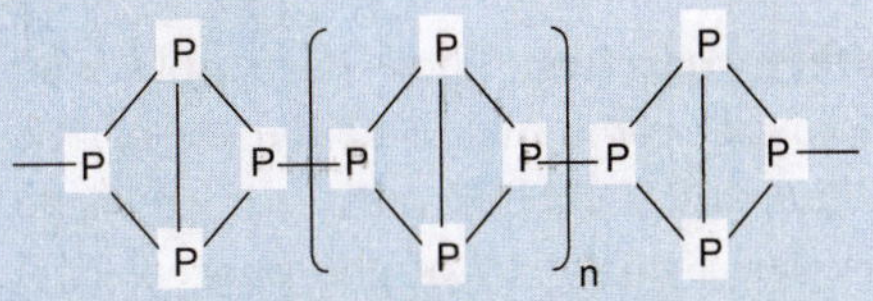 Chains of tetrahedral P4 units linked to each other by P–P bonds.

Chemical Properties

Property	Reaction
Reaction with oxygen	Phosphorus reacts with oxygen or air and forms white dense fumes of phosphorus pentoxide: $4P + 5O_2 \longrightarrow 2P_2O_5$
Reaction with chlorine	A piece of phosphorus introduced into a jar containing chlorine reacts initially to form phosphorus trichloride and on further reaction forms phosphorus pentachloride: $2P + Cl_2 \longrightarrow 2PCl_3$
Reaction with calcium	Phosphorus can directly combine with calcium to give calcium phosphide: $3Ca + 2P \longrightarrow Ca_3P_2$
Reaction with NaOH	Phosphorus when boiled with a solution of sodium hydroxide, phosphine gas and sodium hypophosphite are formed: $4P + 3NaOH + 3H_2O \longrightarrow PH_3 + 3NaH_2PO_2$

Reaction with HNO_3 — Phosphorus on reaction with concentrated nitric acid produces phosphoric acid and nitrogen dioxide:

$$P + 5HNO_3 \longrightarrow H_3PO_4 + 5NO_2 + H_2O$$

Phosphorus acts as a powerful reducing agent.

Uses of Phosphorus

1. Phosphor bronze, an alloy of phosphorus, copper and tin can be manufactured from phosphorus.
2. White phosphorus is used as a rat poison.
3. Phosphorus is used in the manufacture of compounds, like, hypophosphates, phosphoric acid and phosphorus chlorides.
4. Phosphorous is used in the manufacture of bombs, smoke screens and fireworks.
5. Phosphorous is very widely used in the match industry, as it has a low-ignition temperature. Depending upon the activity of the matches, they are categorised into two types:
   (a) Lucifer matches
   (b) Safety matches

Lucifer matches: These are 'strike anywhere matches.' They are called so because they catch fire when they are rubbed against any hard surface. In these matches, the tip of the match stick is composed of antimony trisulphide, red phosphorous and potassium chlorate in addition to a binding material like glue.

Safety matches: These burn only when they are made to strike on a particular surface. The chemical on the stick is composed of potassium chlorate and antimony sulphide mixed with glue. When this is rubbed on a surface made of red phosphorous, antimony sulphide and fine glass powder, a small part of phosphorous detaches and catches fire. This spark initiates the ignition of antimony sulphide which further helps in the decomposition of potassium chlorate which provides oxygen for combustion.

EXAMPLE

Farmers are advised to include bean plants in the crop rotation system. What purpose does it serve?

SOLUTION

Nitrogen is an essential nutrient required in large quantities for plants. Nitrogen in the soil is consumed fast when a particular type of crop is grown. The bean plant belongs to leguminous family and is capable of taking atmospheric nitrogen directly and converting it to nitrate salts. Thus, they help in the replenishment of soils with nitrogen. When the bean plants are removed from the soil, the next crop can get plenty of nitrogen from the soil.

Sulphur

Sulphur has a wide variety of uses in the industries. It is extracted from the earth's crust by the following processes:

1. Sicilian process
2. Frasch process

1. Sicilian Process

This process is used to extract sulphur which is near to the earth's crust (deposits in Sicily).This process is carried out in brick kilns built on sloping hill sides.

Process: Large amounts of clay and stone are mixed with crude sulphur and is stacked inside the brick kiln leaving small spaces in between. This is covered with a layer of powdered sulphur which is then subjected to burning. The heat evolved during the burning of this sulphur leads to melting of the remaining sulphur that lies in the bottom layers. The molten sulphur is allowed to flow down and is collected in wooden moulds.

Purification: The sulphur obtained in the above process contains about 5% of earthly impurities. Depending on the applications, it is used in the natural form or in the purified form. The purification is carried out by distillation process. The liquid sulphur obtained after distillation is collected in the form of solid rolls, and hence, called **roll sulphur**.

2. Frasch Process

This process is used to extract the sulphur which lies 150–400 m below the earth's crust. This process is also called **Louisiana process** as large deposits of this are found in Louisiana. A direct mining is not possible as the sulphur is present in layers of quick sand and gravel.

Process: In this process three concentric pipes of diameters 25 mm, 76 mm and 152 mm are drilled through the ground to the sulphur deposits. Superheated steam (170°C) under pressure is sent through the outer most pipe. This melts the sulphur present below (MP of sulphur = 112°C). Hot compressed air (up to 35 atm) is sent through the innermost pipe, which froths up the molten sulphur below. The sulphur foam formed rises up the middle pipe and is collected.

Advantages

The sulphur extracted in this process is 99·5% pure and does not need further purification.

Allotropes of sulphur: The phenomenon of existence of an element in more than one physical form is called allotropy; and the other forms of the same element are called allotropes. Sulphur exists in different allotropic forms. Allotropes have same chemical properties but different physical properties.

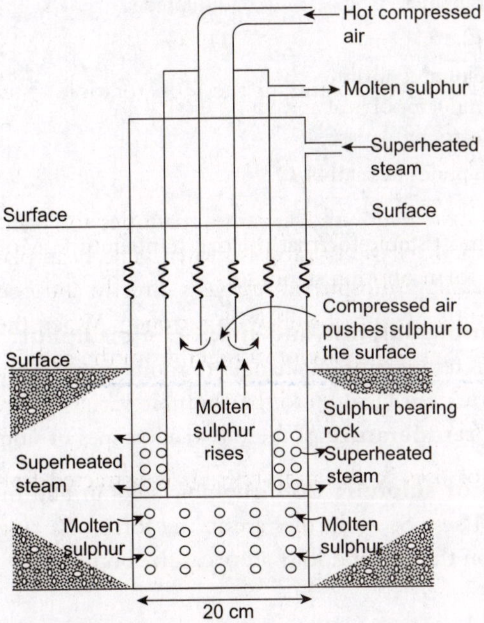

FIGURE 7.2 The Frasch process for extracting sulphur

The three main allotropic forms of sulphur are the following:

1. Rhombic sulphur
2. Monoclinic sulphur
3. Plastic sulphur

Rhombic sulphur and monoclinic sulphur are crystalline, whereas plastic sulphur is amorphous.

Comparative Study of the Allotropic Forms of Sulphur:

	Rhombic sulphur	Monoclinic sulphur	Plastic sulphur
Other names	Octahedral sulphur, alpha sulphur	Prismatic sulphur, beta sulphur	Gamma sulphur
Preparation	Roll sulphur is dissolved in carbon disulphide. This is allowed to evaporate slowly by slight heating. Rhombic sulphur crystals are left behind	Roll sulphur is heated on an evaporating dish till it melts to pale yellow liquid. This on cooling forms a crust on the surface. Holes are pierced on the crust and the molten sulphur is drained out. Needle-shaped sulphur (monoclinic sulphur) crystals are left behind	Roll sulphur is heated to above 300°C till it turns to dark brown, this is poured into cold water and the sulphur formed is plastic sulphur
Colour	Pale yellow	Amber	Dark brown
Shape/structure	Octahedral 	Needle shaped 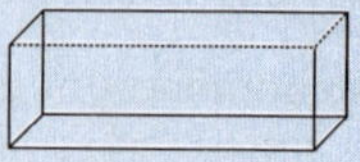	Amorphous
Density	2.08 g/cm^3	1.98 g/cm^3	1.92 g/cm^3
Solubility	Soluble in carbon disulphide	Soluble in carbon disulphide	Insoluble in carbon disulphide
Melting point	112.8°C	119°C	No sharp melting point
Conductivity	Sulphur is a bad conductor of heat and electricity		
Boiling point	Sulphur boils at 444°C		

Rhombic sulphur is the most stable form at normal temperature. Monoclinic sulphur and plastic sulphur change to rhombic form on long standing.

Transition between rhombic sulphur and monoclinic sulphur: Rhombic sulphur is stable below 95.6°C and above this temperature it changes to monoclinic sulphur. Conversely, monoclinic sulphur is stable above 95.6°C, but changes to the rhombic variety below this temperature. Hence, 95.6°C is called **transition temperature** of these two allotropes of sulphur.

Puckered-ring structure of sulphur: Both rhombic sulphur and monoclinic sulphur exists in the form of S_8 molecules. These S_8 molecules are in the form of a ring. It forms a crown-shaped molecule with four atoms on the top and four atoms at the bottom.

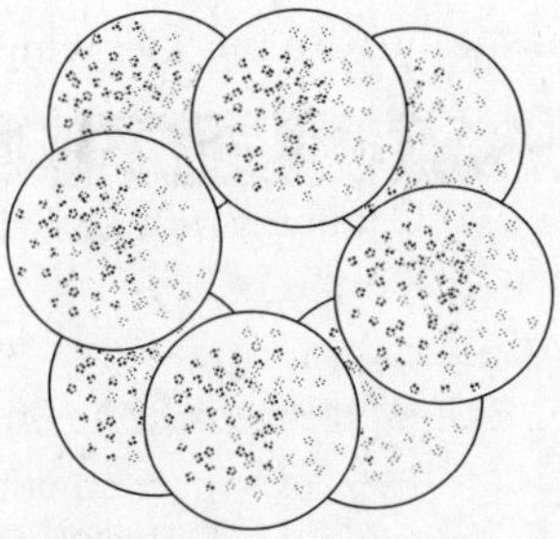

FIGURE 7.3 Puckered-ring structure of sulphur

The rhombic form and the monoclinic form differ in the arrangement of these S_8 puckered rings. In rhombic sulphur, these rings fit snugly into each other while in monoclinic sulphur the rings are stacked one on top of the other.

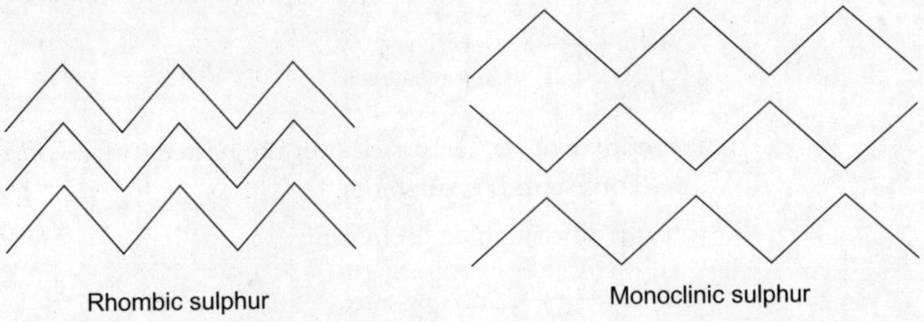

FIGURE 7.4 Structures Rhombic sulphur and Monoclinic sulphur

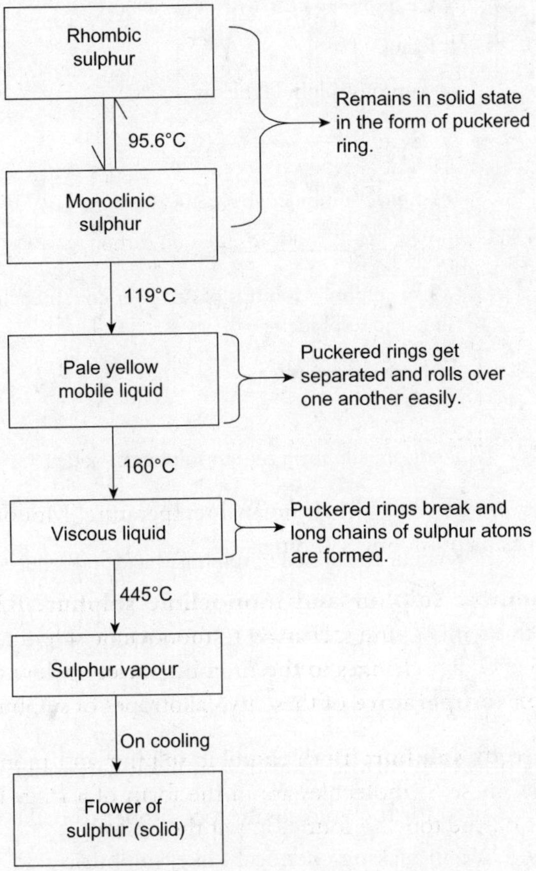

FIGURE 7.5 Action of heat on sulphur

Chemical Properties

Properties	Reaction
With non-metals	
Oxygen	Above 300°C it burns with a pale blue flame giving out two oxides of sulphur. $S + O_2 \longrightarrow \underset{\text{(Sulphur dioxide)}}{SO_2}$ $2S + 3O_2 \longrightarrow \underset{\text{(Sulphur trioxide)}}{2SO_3}$ (trace amounts)
Hydrogen	Boiling sulphur with hydrogen gas gives a gas with the smell of rotten eggs $S + H_2 \longrightarrow \underset{\text{(hydrogen sulphide)}}{H_2S}$
Carbon	Sulphur vapours when passed over red hot coke give carbon disulphide $\underset{\substack{\text{Coke}\\\text{(red hot)}}}{C} + S \longrightarrow \underset{\text{(Carbon disulphide)}}{CS_2(\ell)}$
With metals	Sulphur vapour when passed over the heated surface of certain metals gives corresponding sulphides.
Zinc	It forms zinc sulphide on heating: $Zn + S \longrightarrow ZnS$
Iron	It forms ferrous sulphide on heating: $Fe + S \longrightarrow FeS$
Copper	It forms (a) cuprous sulphide (below 400°C): $2Cu + S \xrightarrow{< 400°C} Cu_2S$ (b) cupric sulphide (above 400°C): $Cu + S \xrightarrow{< 400°C} CuS$
Mercury	When sulphur vapour is passed over cold metallic mercury, it gives mercuric sulphide: $Hg + S \longrightarrow HgS$
With acids	
Sulphuric acid	Reduces sulphuric acid to sulphur dioxide: $S + H_2SO_4 \longrightarrow 3SO_2 + H_2O$
Nitric acid	Sulphur is oxidised to sulphuric acid and reduces nitric acid to nitrogen dioxide: $S + 6HNO_3 \longrightarrow H_2SO_4 + 6NO_2 + 2H_2O$

Uses of Sulphur

Sulphur has a wide variety of uses in various industries as listed hereunder:

1. **Rubber industry**: It is used for the vulcanisation of rubber to make it hard and elastic.
2. **Chemical industry**: Used in making chemicals, like, sulphuric acid, carbon disulphide, etc.
3. **Explosive industry**: Sulphur along with charcoal and nitre is used in making gunpowder.

EXAMPLE

When molten sulphur (above 195°C) is poured in water, an amorphous variety of sulphur is formed. Give the reason.

SOLUTION

When sulphur is heated above 160°C, some of the eight member ring break and open-chain structures are formed. When this liquid sulphur is poured into water, suddenly it cools. Due to the sudden cooling, the rearrangement of rings is not possible. Hence, amorphous sulphur is formed.

EXAMPLE

The viscosity of sulphur increases from 160°C to 195°C and subsequently decreases above this range. Explain with appropriate reasons.

SOLUTION

The viscosity of liquids usually decreases as temperature increases. When liquid sulphur is heated from 160°C to 195°C, the viscosity increases. This is due to breaking of S_8 rings followed by polymerisation of the chains of sulphur atoms. Due to polymerisation interlocking of sulphur, chains takes place with each other. The longer the chains of S atoms, the more the chains interlock with each other and the more viscous the sulphur becomes. Above 195°C, the long chains begin to break up, and thus, viscosity gradually decreases.

Chlorine

Laboratory Method of Preparation

Oxidation of hydrochloric acid: Hydrochloric acid on oxidation with MnO_2 or $KMnO_4$ or $K_2Cr_2O_7$ gives chlorine gas. Oxidation of HCl by MnO_2 is the most common method employed for the preparation of chlorine gas in laboratory.

Principle

When manganese dioxide is heated with concentrated HCl, HCl gets oxidised to chlorine gas:

$$MnO_2 + 4HCl \longrightarrow MnCl_2 + 2H_2O + Cl_2$$

Process

A round-bottomed flask fitted with a two holed rubber cork is taken. MnO_2 is taken in this flask. A thistle funnel is introduced into the flask through one hole. Concentrated HCl can be added through this thistle funnel. Through the second hole, a delivery tube is inserted into the flask. The mixture of MnO_2 and HCl taken in the round-bottomed flask is heated gently. The liberated chlorine gas which comes out of the delivery tube is collected into a gas jar.

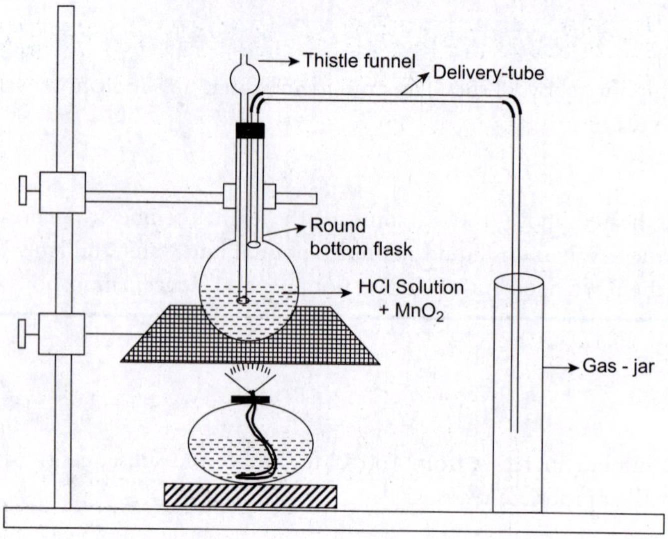

FIGURE 7.6 Preparation of chlorine

Collection of Gas

Chlorine gas being heavier than air is collected by the method of upward displacement of air.

Physical Properties of Chlorine

Parameters	Characteristics
Colour	Greenish Yellow
Odour	Pungent smell
Solubility	Sparingly soluble in water
Density	Heavier than air. Vapour density is 35.5
Atomicity	2

Chemical Properties

Properties	Reactions
Reaction with air	Under normal conditions chlorine does not react with oxygen. Chlorine is non-combustible and also not a supporter of combustion
Reaction with water	Chlorine dissolves in water. A mixture of hydrochloric acid and hypochlorous acid is formed. This reaction is responsible for the bleaching action of chlorine since HOCl dissociates giving nascent oxygen: $Cl_2 + H_2O \longrightarrow HCl + HOCl$ $HOCl \longrightarrow HCl + [O]$
Reaction with metals	Chlorine reacts with most of the metals: $2Na + Cl_2 \longrightarrow 2NaCl$ For example, when burning magnesium ribbon reacts with chlorine gas, the corresponding metallic chlorides are formed. MgCl2 is formed with the evolution of light energy: $Mg + Cl_2 \longrightarrow MgCl_2$

Properties	Reactions
Reaction with non-metals	At high temperature chlorine reacts with some non-metals E.g., $2P + 3Cl_2 \longrightarrow 2PCl_3$ $2P + 5Cl_2 \longrightarrow 2PCl_5$ Corresponding non-metallic chlorides are formed
(a) Reaction with alkalies (cold and dilute) (b) Reaction with alkalies (hot and concentrated)	(a) On reaction with cold dilute NaOH the products are sodium chloride and sodium hypochlorite: $Cl_2 + 2NaOH \longrightarrow 5NaCl + NaOCl + 3H_2O$ (b) On reaction with hot concentrated NaOH the products are sodium are sodium chloride and sodium chlorate: $3Cl_2 + 6NaOH \longrightarrow 5NaCl + NaOCl_3 + 3H_2O$
Reaction with other compounds	Reaction of chlorine with excess of ammonia products gives ammonium chloride and nitrogen: $8NH_3 + 3Cl_2 \longrightarrow 6NH_4Cl + N_2$ Reaction of chlorine with limited amount of ammonia. Products formed are nitrogen trichloride and HCl: $NH_3 + 3Cl_2 \longrightarrow NCl_3 + 3HCl$
	On reaction with H_2S, chlorine oxidises H_2S to sulphur And a yellow coloured sulphur powder is formed: $H_2S + Cl_2 \longrightarrow S + 2HCl$
Reaction with turpentine	Chlorine gas is passed over a filter paper dipped in hot turpentine. It burns with a black sooty flame with the formation of black soot of carbon: $C_{10}H_{16} + 8Cl_2 \longrightarrow 10C + 16HCl$

Uses of Chlorine

1. In the manufacture of bleaching power ($CaOCl_2$).
2. For bleaching wood pulp, cotton, paper, silk, rayon, etc.
3. For preparing poisonous gas, like, mustard gas (ClC_2H_4-S-C_2H_4Cl), phosgene ($COCl_2$) and tear gas (CCl_3NO_2).
4. In the preparation of hydrochloric acid.
5. In the extraction of metals, like, platinum, gold, titanium, etc.
6. In the manufacture of chloroform ($CHCl_3$), carbon tetrachloride (CCl_4), dichloro diphenyl trichloro ethane (DDT), etc., and also in rubber, plastic and paint industries.
7. In the purification of drinking water.

The elements are very useful in forming certain compounds which play a major role in industries.

Compounds of Nitrogen

Since nitrogen is the most essential element for the growth of plants and most of the plants are incapable of absorbing nitrogen directly from the atmosphere, the manufacture of useful compounds from nitrogen has lot of industrial significance. The most important compounds are ammonia and nitric acid which form the basic raw materials for the manufacture of a number of fertilisers.

AMMONIA

It is prepared by the action of quick lime on ammonium chloride:

$$NH_4Cl + CaO \longrightarrow CaCl_2 + H_2O + 2NH_3$$

Physical Properties of Ammonia

Parameters	Characteristics
Colour	Colourless
Odour	Pungent smell, causes burning sensation in the upper part of nasal track and brings tears to eyes
Taste	Bitter in taste
Physiological nature	Poisonous, damages respiratory system
Density	It is lighter than air (vapour density is 8.5)
Solubility	Highly soluble in water, so, it cannot be collected by downward displacement of water. Further, 1300 volumes of NH_3 can be dissolved in 1 volume of water at STP
Boiling point	–33.4°C
Freezing point	–78°C

Chemical Properties of Ammonia

Properties	Reaction and Observation
Combustibility	A burning match stick is introduced into ammonia gas chamber. The match stick is put off. Ammonia gas is neither combustible nor a supporter of combustion
Action with litmus	A moist red litmus paper is dipped into a jar of ammonia Red litmus is turned to blue colour. Ammonia is basic in nature
Action with acids	When ammonia gas is passed into the acids, like, HCl or H_2SO_4, ammonium salts are formed: $NH_3 + HCl \longrightarrow NH_4Cl$ $NH_3 + H_2SO_4 \longrightarrow (NH_4)_2SO_4$
Action with non-metals (i) Reaction with oxygen	A burning match stick when introduced into a jar containing ammonia and oxygen burns with a pale blue flame: $4NH_3 3O_2 \longrightarrow 2N_2 + 6H_2O$ When the above mixture of ammonia and oxygen is passed over heated platinum, nitric oxide and water vapour are formed with the evolution of heat $4NH_3 + 5O_2 \xrightarrow[900°C]{P} 4NO + 6H_2O$ $2\,NO + O_2 \longrightarrow 2NO_2$ $2NO_2 + H_2O \longrightarrow HNO_2 + HNO_3$

Properties	Reaction and Observation
(ii) Reaction with chlorine	(1) Limited amount of Cl_2 White dense fumes of ammonium chloride are formed along with nitrogen: $8NH_3 + 3Cl_2 \longrightarrow 6NH_4Cl + N_2$ (2) Excess amount of Cl_2 Nitrogen trichloride and HCl are formed: $NH_3 + 3Cl_2 \longrightarrow NCl_3 + 3HCl$
Reaction with metals	On reaction with active metals corresponding amides are formed: $2NH_3 + 2Na \longrightarrow 2NaNH_2 + H_2$ $2NH_3 + 2K \longrightarrow 2KNH_2 + H_2$
Reducing properties	Ammonia gas when passed over heated metal oxides, reduces them to respective metals: $3CuO + 2NH_3 \longrightarrow 3Cu + N_2 + 3H_2O$ $3PbO + 2NH_3 \longrightarrow 3Pb + N_2 + 3H_2O$

Uses of Ammonia

1. In the manufacture of fertilisers, like, urea, ammonium sulphate, etc.
2. As a solvent
3. As a refrigerant in ice plants
4. In the manufacture of nitric acid, sodium carbonate and sodium bicarbonate

Some Important Ammonium Salts

Preparation	Applications
Ammonium chloride $NH_4OH + HCl \longrightarrow NH_4Cl + H_2O$	(i) Soldering (ii) Electrolyte in dry cell and Leclanche cell (iii) Dyeing and calico printing (iv) Laboratory reagent
Ammonium sulphate $NH_3 + H_2SO_4 \longrightarrow (NH_4)_2SO_4$	(i) Fertiliser (ii) Preparation of other ammonium salts, like, ammonium carbonate and ammonium nitrate
Ammonium nitrate $(NH_4)SO_4 + 2NaNO_3 \longrightarrow Na_2SO_4 + 2NH_4NO_3$	(i) Fertiliser (ii) Explosives, like, amatol (NH_4NO_3 + 20% TNT) and ammonal (NH_4NO_3 + Al powder) (iii) Manufacture of nitrous oxide
Calcium ammonium nitrate—mixture of calcium carbonate and ammonium nitrate	Fertiliser
Ammonium phosphate $NH_3 + H_3PO_4 \longrightarrow NH_4H_2PO_4$ $2NH_3 + H_3PO_4 \longrightarrow (NH_4)_2HPO_4$ $3NH_3 + H_3PO_4 \longrightarrow (NH_4)_3PO_4$	Fertiliser

NITRIC ACID

Nitric acid is prepared by heating a mixture of potassium nitrate and concentrated sulphuric acid, when taken in a proportion in a retort. The vapours of nitric acid are passed into a receiver and cooled by water.

$$KNO_3 + H_2SO_4 \longrightarrow HNO_3 + KHSO_4$$

Physical Properties of Nitric Acid

Parameters	Characteristics
Colour	It is a colourless liquid but commercial nitric acid is yellowish brown in colour
Odour	Suffocating smell
Taste	Sour taste
Nature	Hygroscopic and fuming liquid
Density	Pure nitric acid has a density of 1.54 g/cm^3 and commercial nitric acid has lower density than the pure one, i.e., 1.42 g/cm^3
Solubility	Highly soluble in nature
Physiological action	Non-poisonous but stains skin yellow and causes very painful blisters
Boiling point	86°C
Melting point	–42°C

Chemical Properties of Nitric Acid

Properties	Reactions and observations
Action of heat	Nitric acid when subjected to simple heating decomposes to give reddish brown vapours of NO_2: $4HNO_3 \xrightarrow{\Delta} 2H_2O + 4NO_2 + O_2$
Dilution	When excess of water is added, self-ionisation takes place giving hydronium ion and nitrate ion: $HNO_3 + H_2O \longrightarrow H_3O^+ + NO_3^-$
Reaction with metal oxides	Treating dilute HNO_3 with metallic oxide leads to the formation of metal nitrates and water: $CuO + 2HNO_3 \longrightarrow Cu(NO_3)_2 + H_2O$
Reaction with bases	On addition of dil HNO_3 to bases, metal nitrates and water are formed: $NaOH + HNO_3 \longrightarrow NaNO_3 + H_2O$
Reaction with metal carbonates	On addition of dil. HNO_3 to metal carbonates, metal nitrates are formed with evolution of CO_2 gas: $CaCO_3 + 2HNO_3 \longrightarrow Ca(NO_3)_2 + CO_2 + H_2O$
Oxidising properties	It is a strong oxidising agent due to the liberation of nascent oxygen: $2HNO_3 \longrightarrow 2HNO_2 + 2[O]$

Properties	Reactions and observations
Oxidation of non-metals	Heating a non-metal with conc. HNO_3 leads to the formation of oxyacid of that non-metal: $S + 6HNO_3 \longrightarrow H_2SO_4 + 6NO_2 + 2H_2O$ $P + 5HNO_3 \longrightarrow H_3PO_4 + 5NO_2 + H_2O$
Oxidation of metals	Metals with dilute nitric acid form metal nitrates and liberate other gases:
(i) Metals with dilute nitric acid	$3Cu + 8\ HNO_3 \longrightarrow 3Cu(NO_3)_2 + 2NO + 4H_2O$ $4Zn + 10HNO_3 \longrightarrow 4Zn(NO_3)_2 + N_2O + 5H_2O$ $Mg + 2HNO_3 \longrightarrow Mg(NO_3)_2 + H_2$ $Mn + 2HNO_3 \longrightarrow Mn(NO_3)_2 + H_2$
(ii) Metals with conc. nitric acid	Metals with concentrated nitric acid also form metal nitrates and liberate nitrogen dioxide gas: $Cu + 4HNO_3 \longrightarrow Cu(NO_3)_2 + 2NO_2 + H_2O$ $Zn + 4HNO_3 \longrightarrow Zn(NO_3)_2 + 2NO_2 + 5H_2O$
(iii) With Fe, Co, Ni	Certain metals, like, iron, cobalt, nickel, however, become passive and do not react with nitric acid.
Reaction with other inorganic compounds	Some inorganic compounds, like, H_2S, KI, SO_2 get oxidised by reducing HNO_3 to NO_2. $3H_2S + 2HNO_3 \longrightarrow 4H_2O + 2NO_2 + 3S$ $2KI + 2HNO_3 \longrightarrow 2KNO_3 + 2H_2O + 2NO + I_2$ $SO_2 + 2HNO_3 \longrightarrow H_2SO_4 + 2NO_2$ $6FeSO_4 + 3H_2SO_4 + 2HNO_3 \longrightarrow 4H_2O + 3Fe_2(SO_4)_3 + 2NO$ $3HCl + HNO_3 \longrightarrow 2H_2O + NOCl + Cl_2$

Nitric acid due to its unique chemical properties and strong oxidising nature is useful in many ways. It is used in making fertilisers, explosives, artificial silk and as a laboratory reagent.

Phosphorus

Compounds of Phosphorous

Compounds	Preparation	Uses
Phosphorous pentoxide	$4P + 5O_2 \longrightarrow 2P_2O_5$	As a dehydrating agent In making phosphoric acid
Phosphoric acid	$P_2O_5 + 3H_2O \longrightarrow 2H_3PO_4$	In the preparation of pharmaceuticals. In the manufacture of phosphates and phosphatic manures

Compounds	Preparation	Uses
Salts of phosphoric acid	$NaOH + H_3PO_4 \longrightarrow NaH_2PO_4 + H_2O$ (Sodium dihydrogen. phosophate) $2NaOH + H_3PO_4 \longrightarrow NaH_2PO_4 + H_2O$ (Disodium hydrogen phosphate) $3NaOH + H_3PO_4 \longrightarrow 3H_2O + Na_3PO_4$ (Sodium phosphate)	As anti-microbials coagulants, food preservatives, etc. In electronics, aviation, petroleum field. Used along with sodium bicarbonate in making baking powder. To clean out the intestines before a medical examination
Sodium hypophosphite	$4P + 3NaOH + 3H_2O \longrightarrow PH_3 + 3NaH_2PO_2$	As a reducing agent in electroplating
Metal phosphides	$2P + 3Ca \longrightarrow Ca_3P_2$ $2P + 3Zn \longrightarrow Zn_3P_2$	Zinc phosphide is used in making rat poison
Chlorides of phosphorus	$2P + 3Cl_2 \longrightarrow 2PCl_3$ $PCl_3 + Cl_2 \longrightarrow PCl_5$	In making $POCl_3$ and $PSCl_3$ which are used in making herbicides, insecticides and plasticisers
Superphosphate of lime	$Ca_3(PO_4)_2 + 2H_2SO_4 + 5H_2O \downarrow \underbrace{Ca(H_2PO_4)_2H_2O + 2CaSO_4.2H_2O}_{\text{Super phosphate of lime}}$	As a fertiliser

Compounds of Sulphur

The most important compounds of sulphur are the following:

1. Sulphur dioxide
2. Sulphuric acid
3. Hydrogen sulphide

SULPHUR DIOXIDE

This is an oxide of sulphur where one atom of sulphur is associated with two atoms of oxygen. It is found in exhaust emissions of internal combustion engine, in the industrial areas where coal and petroleum are used as fuels. In nature, it is found in volcanic gases.

Laboratory preparation of SO_2: Sulphur dioxide is prepared in the laboratory by heating copper turning with concentrated sulphuric acid:

$$Cu + 2H_2SO_4 \longrightarrow CuSO_4 + 2H_2O + SO_2\uparrow$$

Physical Properties of Sulphur dioxide

Parameters	Characteristics
Colour	Colourless
Odour	Pungent and suffocating
Taste	Sour

Parameters	Characteristics
Vapour density	32 (2.2 times heavier than air)
Solubility in water	Fairly soluble
Boiling point	−10°C
Freezing point	−76°C
Physiological nature	Poisonous

Chemical Properties of Sulphur dioxide

Chemical Properties	Reactions involved
Acidic nature	
(i) With litmus	Sulphur dioxide is acidic in nature and can change blue litmus to red
(ii) Reaction with water	Sulphur dioxide with water forms an unstable sulphurous acid: $H_2O + SO_2 \longrightarrow H_2SO_3$
Reducing properties	
Bleaching action	Sulphur dioxide is a good reducing agent. This on reaction with moisture or water produces nascent hydrogen which helps in the reducing action: $SO_2\uparrow + H_2O \longrightarrow H_2SO_4 + 2[H]$ (reducing agent)
	The nascent hydrogen produced on being exposed to moisture acts as a bleach. It reduces the coloured matter to colourless. This reaction is reversible. The colourless product on exposure to atmospheric oxygen can get oxidised, and thus, regain its colour
	Colour vegetable + [H] $\longrightarrow$ Colourless product + Water
	Bleached product + Atmospheric oxygen $\longrightarrow$ Original colour
Addition reactions	The reducing property of sulphur dioxide is also seen in its adduct formation: $2SO_2 + O_2 \xrightarrow[400-500°C]{Platinum} 2SO_3$
Oxidising property	When sulphur dioxide is introduced to burning potassium or magnesium metal, it oxidises the metal to its oxide and sulphide: $2Mg + SO_2 \longrightarrow 2MgO + MgS$

Sulphur dioxide, due to the above mentioned properties, is useful in various fields.

Sulphur dioxide is used:

1. In chemical industries for the preparation of sulphuric acid
2. In sugar industry to decolourise sugar cane juice
3. As a disinfectant due to its germicidal and insecticidal activity
4. As a bleaching agent
5. In refrigeration industry
6. As an anti-chlor to remove excess chlorine from articles

SULPHURIC ACID

The level of industrialisation of a country can be measured by the amount of sulphuric acid made by that country. It is also called **the king of the chemicals**, and **oil of vitriol** in certain cases.

In the free state it is found in the hot water of sulphur springs and beds of mineral sulphides. In the combined state, it is found as mineral sulphates.

Manufacture of Sulphuric Acid

The large-scale manufacture of sulphuric acid is carried out by the contact process.

Contact Process

In this process, the basic raw material required is SO_2 which is produced by burning sulphur:

$$S + O_2 \longrightarrow SO_2$$

Manufacture of sulphuric acid from SO_2 takes place in two steps:

Step I: Sulphur dioxide and oxygen in a ratio of 2 : 1 by volume is passed over vanadium pentoxide, maintained at 450°C under high pressure conditions. Under these conditions, the sulphur dioxide and oxygen react to form sulphur trioxide. Platinised asbestos can also be used in place of V_2O_5.

$$2SO_2 + O_2 \longrightarrow 2SO_3$$

Step II: Sulphur trioxide thus obtained is dissolved in sulphuric acid to form pyrosulphuric acid or oleum.

$$SO_3 + H_2SO_4 \longrightarrow \underset{\text{(Oleum)}}{H_2S_2O_7}$$

The pyrosulphuric acid on treatment with water gives sulphuric acid:

$$H_2S_2O_7 + H_2O \longrightarrow 2H_2SO_4$$

The sulphuric acid prepared by this method is pure and highly concentrated.

Physical Properties of Sulphuric Acid

Parameters	Characteristics
Colour	Colourless
Odour	Odourless
Taste	Sour
State	Dense oily liquid
Boiling point	338°C
Freezing point	−10.4°C
Solubility	Soluble in water
Physiological nature	Corrosive in nature

Chemical Properties of Sulphuric Acid

Properties	Reactions involved
Acidic nature	
(i) With metals	Metals which are more reactive than hydrogen, form metal sulphates with sulphuric acid, liberating hydrogen gas: $Zn + H_2SO_4 \longrightarrow ZnSO_4 + H_2 \uparrow$ $2Na + H_2SO_4 \longrightarrow Na_2SO_4 + H_2 \uparrow$ Copper and lead, however, react with sulphuric acid forming the corresponding sulphates, by liberating sulphur dioxide gas but not hydrogen gas: $Cu + 2H_2SO_4 \longrightarrow CuSO_4 + SO_2 + 2H_2O$
(ii) With basic oxides	Neutralisation reaction takes place on reaction of sulphuric acid with basic oxides, giving metal sulphates and water: $K_2O + H_2SO_4 \longrightarrow K_2SO_4 + H_2O$ $CuO + H_2SO_4 \longrightarrow CuSO_4 + H_2O$
(iii) With alkalis	Sulphuric acid and alkalis undergo neutralisation giving metal sulphates and water: $2NaOH + H_2SO_4 \longrightarrow Na_2SO_4 + H_2O$ $2KOH + H_2SO_4 \longrightarrow K_2SO_4 + H_2O$
(iv) With chlorides and nitrates	Sulphuric acid is a non-volatile acid. This on reaction with chlorides and nitrates gives hydrochloric acid and nitric acid: $NaCl + H_2SO_4 \longrightarrow NaHSO_4 + HCl \uparrow$ $KNO_3 + H_2SO_4 \longrightarrow KHSO_4 + HNO_3$
(v) With carbonates and sulphites	Reaction with carbonates and sulphites evolves carbon dioxide and sulphur dioxide gases, respectively, forming metal sulphates: $Na_2CO_3 + H_2SO_4 \longrightarrow Na_2SO_4 + H_2O + CO_2 \uparrow$ $Na_2SO_3 + H_2SO_4 \longrightarrow Na_2SO_4 + H_2O + SO_2 \uparrow$
Oxidising property	Sulphuric acid on heating undergoes thermal decomposition giving nascent oxygen. Thus, sulphuric acid acts as an oxidising agent. It can oxidise certain non-metals to its respective oxides
	$H_2SO_4 \longrightarrow H_2O \uparrow SO_2 \uparrow + [O]$ $S + 2H_2SO_4 \longrightarrow 2H_2O + 3SO_2 \uparrow$ $C + 2H_2SO_4 \longrightarrow 2H_2O + 2SO_2 \uparrow + CO_2 \uparrow$
Dehydrating property	Sulphuric acid is a very good dehydrating agent, i.e., it can remove hydrogen and oxygen in the form of water from a number of chemical compounds. Its dehydrating properties are clearly evident in removal of water from copper sulphate crystals, sugar and starch

Properties	Reactions involved
(i) Dehydration of hydrated salts	Blue coloured copper sulphate crystals ($CuSO_4.5H_2O$) which on treating with sulphuric acid turns to a white powdery mass. This is because the water molecules associated with the crystal are being removed $\underset{\text{(Blue)}}{CuSO_4.5H_2O} + \xrightarrow{H_2SO_4\text{(conc.)}} CuSO_4 + \underset{\text{(white powdery mass)}}{5H_2O}$
(ii) Dehydration of sugars and starch	Sugars and starch on treating with sulphuric acid turn to a black-coloured mass, i.e., carbon. All the hydrogen and oxygen atoms are removed, as water, leaving behind carbon: $\underset{\text{(sugar)}}{C_{12}H_{22}O_{11}} + \xrightarrow{\text{conc. } H_2SO_4} \underset{\text{(black mass)}}{12C} + 11H_2O$ $\underset{\text{(starch)}}{(C_5H_{10}O_5)_n} + \xrightarrow{\text{conc. } H_2SO_4} 5_nC + 5_nH_2O$

Uses

Sulphuric acid being 'the king of the chemicals' has many uses in industry as well as regular life.

It is used

1. In the manufacture of fertilisers
2. In making explosives, like, trinitrotoluene (TNT), trinitroglycerine (TNG), etc.
3. In storage batteries as an electrolyte
4. As a laboratory reagent
5. In extraction of metals
6. In pickling metals as sulphuric acid can remove metallic impurities

Hydrogen Sulphide

Hydrogen sulphide gas is well known for its rotten egg smell. In the free state, it is present in volcanic gases, water of springs and in the air near and around industrial areas.

Though the gas has bad smell and pollutes atmosphere, it is still prepared in the laboratory due to its certain unique properties and uses.

Laboratory preparation of hydrogen sulphide

Principle: Ferrous sulphides react with hydrochloric acid to give ferrous chlorides, liberating hydrogen sulphide gas:

$$FeS + 2HCl \longrightarrow FeCl_2 + H_2S \uparrow$$

Physical Properties of Hydrogen Sulphide

Parameters	Characteristics
Colour	Colourless
Odour	Smell of rotten eggs
Taste	Sour taste
Solubility	Fairly soluble in water
Vapour density	17 (1.2 times heavier than air)

Chemical Properties of Hydrogen Sulphide

Properties	Reactions involved
Acidic nature	Hydrogen sulphide is acidic in nature and can change blue litmus to red
Reducing nature	Hydrogen sulphide shows reducing properties by adding hydrogen atoms in some cases
(i) With oxygen	Hydrogen sulphide undergoes combustion during which it reduces oxygen to water: $2H_2S + O_2 \longrightarrow 2S + 2H_2O$ It, however, does not support combustion
(ii) With chlorine	Chlorine on reaction with hydrogen sulphide is reduced to hydrogen chloride: $H_2S + Cl_2 \longrightarrow 2HCl\uparrow + S$
(iii) With potassium permanganate	Decolourisation of potassium permanganate is observed on its reaction with H_2S. This is because potassium permanganate is reduced to manganese sulphate by hydrogen sulphide, thus, decolourising it: $2KMnO_4 + 3H_2SO_4 + 5H_2S \longrightarrow K_2SO_4 + 2MnSO_4 + 8H_2O + 5S$

Uses or Applications

The most important application of hydrogen sulphide gas is in analytical chemistry.

Hydrogen sulphide on reaction with aqueous solutions of metal salts converts them to metal sulphides. These metal sulphides are in the form of precipitates. The colour of the precipitate depends upon the nature of metal ion. Therefore, hydrogen sulphide is mainly used for the detection of metal cations present in the metal salts.

$$Pb(NO_3)_2 + H_2S \longrightarrow \underset{\text{(Black precipitate)}}{PbS} + 2HNO_3$$

$$CuSO_4 + H_2S \longrightarrow \underset{\text{(Black precipitate)}}{CuS} + H_2SO_4$$

$$ZnSO_4 + H_2S \longrightarrow \underset{\text{(White precipitate)}}{ZnS} + H_2SO_4$$

$$MnSO_4 + H_2S \longrightarrow \underset{\text{(Flesh coloured precipitate)}}{MnS} + H_2SO_4$$

This is the major use of hydrogen sulphide gas.

Compounds of Chlorine

Chlorine is used in the manufacture of various industrially useful compounds. The compounds of chlorine find applications in various fields, such as, textiles, paper, dyestuffs, etc. Most of the applications of chlorine are basically due to its oxidising and bleaching action.

Bleaching powder is one of the most important compounds of chlorine which is widely used for the purification of drinking water owing to its germicidal and disinfectant action.

The chemical name of bleaching powder is calcium chlorohypochlorite or calcium oxychloride. The formula of bleaching powder is $CaOCl_2$.

Principle

Chlorine gas on passing through slaked lime at high temperature (400°C) gives bleaching powder:

$$Ca(OH)_2 + Cl_2 \longrightarrow CaOCl_2 + H_2O$$

MANUFACTURE

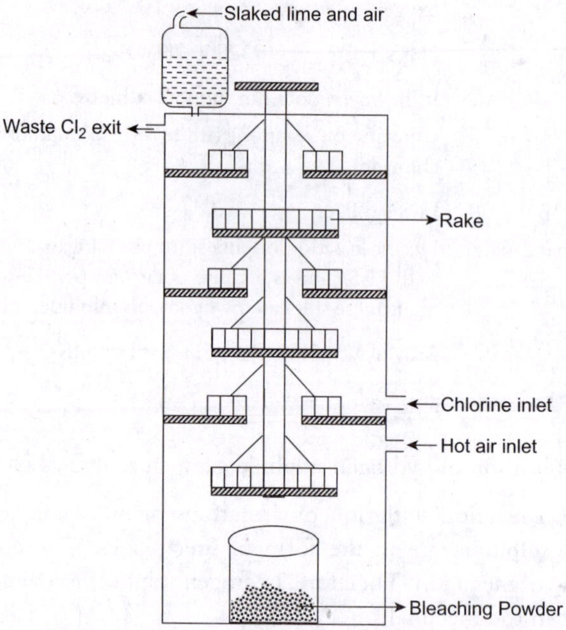

FIGURE 7.7 Preparation of bleaching powder

Process

Manufacture of bleaching powder can be done in two types of plants, namely, Hasen Clever plant and Bachmann plant.

Bachmann Plant

The plant consists of a vertical tower made of cast iron. This is called **chlorinating tower**. Two inlets are provided at the base of the tower for the entry of chlorine gas and hot air into the tower. A hopper is provided at the top of the tower for the introduction of slaked lime into the tower. The entire tower is made up of horizontal shelves provided with rotating rakes.

Dry slaked lime is introduced into the chlorinating tower through hopper. Hot air and chlorine gas are sent into the tower through the inlets provided at the bottom of the plant. Due to the movement of rotating rakes, slaked lime moves downwards, whereas chlorine gas along with hot air moves upwards. This counter-current mechanism helps the thorough mixing up of chlorine gas with slaked lime which leads to completion of the reaction.

Uses of Bleaching Powder

1. The most important use of chlorine is the bleaching of cotton, linen and wood pulp. Due to this bleaching property, bleaching powder finds its use in textile industry and manufacture of paper.

2. Bleaching powder being a mild bleaching agent is best suited for bleaching of delicate articles, such as, silk ivory, etc.
3. Another important application of bleaching powder is its use as a disinfectant and germicide.
4. Bleaching powder also finds its use in the manufacture of chloroform.

Industrial Application of Sodium Chloride

Common salt which is mainly used as a flavouring agent for foodstuffs had many industrial applications also. Sodium chloride is the most important raw material for the production of a number of compounds, such as, chlorine, hydrochloric acid, sodium hydroxide, etc.

Manufacture of Sodium Hydroxide

Principle

An aqueous solution of sodium chloride is called **brine**. This brine solution on electrolysis produces sodium hydroxide as the principal product. Hydrogen and chlorine are obtained as by-products.

$$NaCl \longrightarrow Na^+ + Cl^-$$

$$2Na^+ + 2H_2O \longrightarrow 2NaOH + 2H^+$$

$$2Cl^- \longrightarrow Cl_2 + 2e^-$$

$$2H^+ + 2e^- \longrightarrow H_2$$

The process of electrolysis can be carried out in two types of electrolytic cells. They are:

1. Nelson cell
2. Castner–Kellner cell

NELSON CELL METHOD

Construction of Nelson cell

Nelson cell consists of a perforated steel U tube insulated by asbestos lining. This U tube acts as a cathode. The U-shaped vessel is provided with an inlet and an outlet. Through the inlet, a brine solution is introduced into the U-tube. A graphite rod is suspended into the U-tube. This acts as an anode. This cell is suspended in a rectangular steel tank. This is also provided with an outlet and a side tube.

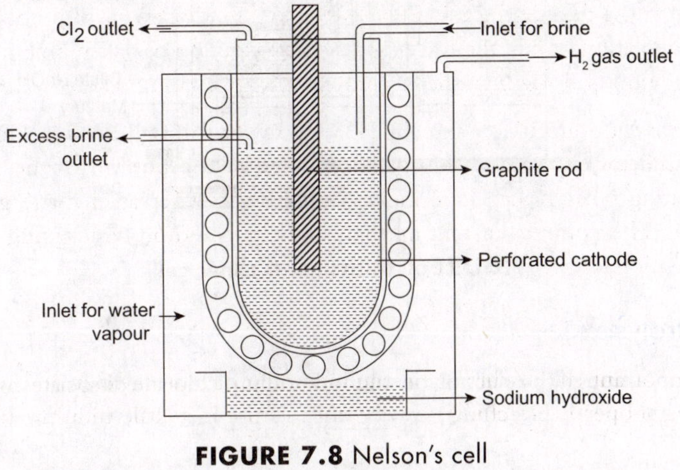

FIGURE 7.8 Nelson's cell

Process of Electrolysis

On passing electricity through the brine solution, sodium chloride dissociates to give

Na+ and Cl– ions:

$$NaCl \longrightarrow Na^+ + Cl^-$$

Chloride ions get discharged at anode liberating chlorine gas. This is collected through an outlet provided for the U-tube.

$$2Cl^- \longrightarrow Cl_2 + 2e^-$$

Steam is allowed to enter into the rectangular steel tank. Sodium ions penetrate through asbestos and react with steam thereby forming sodium hydroxide:

$$Na^+ + H_2O \longrightarrow NaOH + H^+$$

H+ ions get discharged at the cathode where they undergo reduction to liberate hydrogen gas which is collected through the outlet provided for in the rectangular steel tank:

$$2H^+ + 2e^- \longrightarrow H_2$$

CASTNER–KELLNER CELL

Construction of Electrolytic Cell

The cell consists of a rectangular iron tank which is made into three compartments by means of two non-porous slate partitions. These partitions should be suspended from the top in such a way that they do not touch the bottom of the cell. Mercury is taken at the bottom of the cell. This mercury can be made to circulate in the three compartments by means of the eccentric wheels arranged at the bottom of the cell. The mercury taken in the bottom part of the cell acts as an intermediate electrode. In the middle compartment it acts as an anode, whereas in the two outer compartments it acts as a cathode. The two outer compartments are filled with the brine solution and the central compartment is filled with dilute sodium hydroxide solution. Graphite rods are inserted in the outer compartments which act as the anode. A bunch of iron rods suspended in the middle compartment functions as the cathode.

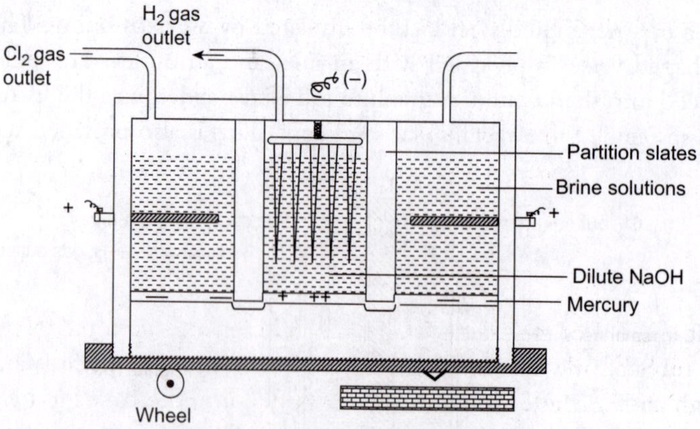

FIGURE 7.9 Castner–Kellner cell

Process of Electrolysis

On passing electricity through the electrolytic solution, sodium chloride dissociates as Na^+ and Cl^- ions:

$$2NaCl \longrightarrow 2Na^+ + Cl^-$$

Chloride ions get discharged at anode and chlorine gas is liberated at anode:

$$\text{Anode: } 2Cl^- \longrightarrow Cl_2 + 2e^-$$

Since mercury present in the outer compartments acts as a cathode, Na^+ ions get discharged there and lose their charge. Sodium metal which is formed combines with mercury to form sodium amalgam:

$$\text{Hg cathode: } Hg + 2Na^+ + 2e^- \longrightarrow Na_2Hg$$

Sodium amalgam thus formed in the outer compartments is brought into the central compartment by the rotatory movement of the eccentric wheels. Sodium amalgam reacts with water forming sodium hydroxide solution which is removed and concentrated.

On evaporation and subsequent cooling of concentrated NaOH solution, solid pellets of sodium hydroxide are obtained:

$$\text{Hg anode: } Na_2Hg - 2e^- \longrightarrow 2Na^+ + Hg$$

$$\text{Cathode: } 2H_2O + 2e^- \longrightarrow H_2 + 2OH^-$$

$$2\,Na^+ + 2OH^- \longrightarrow 2NaOH$$

Hydrogen Chloride

The electrolysis of a brine solution gives sodium hydroxide as the major product and hydrogen and chlorine as the minor products. These by-products are used in the manufacture of industrially useful compounds, such as, hydrogen chloride.

Preparation of Hydrogen Chloride

Laboratory Method

Principle: Metallic chlorides on heating with concentrated sulphuric acid liberate hydrogen chloride gas. This gas on dissolution in water produces hydrochloric acid. Example: sodium chloride on treatment with H_2SO_4 liberates hydrogen chloride gas:

$$NaCl + H_2SO_4 \xrightarrow{<200^\circ C} NaHSO_4 + HCl(g)$$

$$2NaCl + H_2SO_4 \xrightarrow{>200^\circ C} Na_2SO_4 + 2HCl(g)$$

$$NaHSO_4 + NaCl \xrightarrow{>200^\circ C} Na_2SO_4 + HCl(g)$$

Process: Specific amount of rock salt (NaCl) is taken in a round-bottomed flask. The flask is fitted with a two holed rubber cork. Thistle funnel is introduced through one hole and a delivery tube is introduced through another hole. Sulphuric acid is added into the flask through the thistle funnel. The flask is heated gently with the help of a Bunsen burner arranged on a tripod stand. HCl gas coming out through the delivery tube is collected into a gas jar.

Collection of gas: Since HCl is heavier than air, it is collected by upward displacement of air.

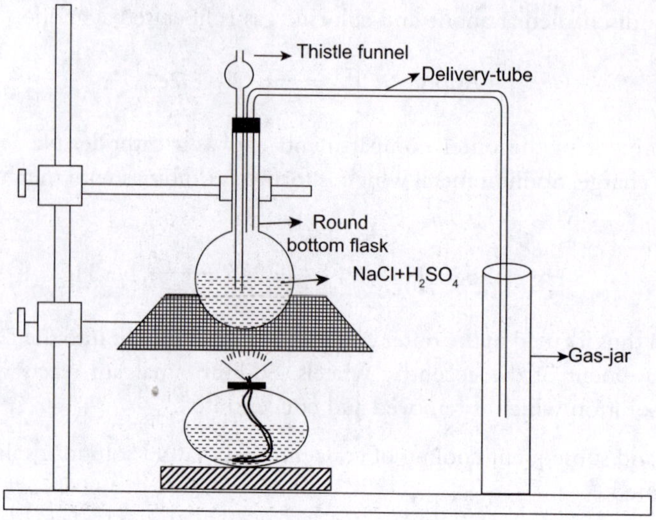

FIGURE 7.10 Preparation of hydrogen chloride

Industrial Method

Hydrogen and chlorine gas when taken in equal volumes and exposed to diffuse sunlight give hydrogen chloride. This is a photochemical reaction since it takes place in presence of light. Mild heating of hydrogen gas in the atmosphere of chlorine gas also gives hydrogen chloride:

$$H_2 + Cl_2 \xrightarrow{\text{Sunlight}} 2HCl$$

Physical Properties

Parameters	Characteristics
Colour	Colourless
Odour	Pungent smell
Density	Heavier than air (VD = 18)
Solubility	Highly soluble in water forming hydrochloric acid. Also soluble in moist air. Dense white fumes appear due to the formation of tiny droplets of hydrochloric acid

Chemical Properties

Properties	Reaction
Reaction with ammonia	When a glass rod dipped in ammonia is introduced into a gas jar containing hydrogen chloride gas, dense white fumes of ammonium chloride are formed: $NH_3 + HCl \longrightarrow NH_4Cl$
Reaction with sodium hydroxide	Hydrogen chloride gas on reaction with sodium hydroxide forms sodium chloride and water. This is called **neutralisation reaction**: $HCl + NaOH \longrightarrow NaCl + H_2O$
Reaction with silver nitrate	When a solution of HCl is added to silver nitrate solution, a white precipitate of silver chloride is formed: $HCl + AgNO_3 \longrightarrow AgCl\downarrow + HNO_3$

Uses

1. As a laboratory reagent
2. In the preparation of chlorine
3. In the manufacture of silver chloride needed for making photographic films

Human civilisation started with observation of nature. People observed nature and implemented their ideas to develop different articles, like, wheel, potteries, simple weapons by using some natural resources, like, clay, wood, sand, stone, etc., for minimizing their day-to-day struggle for existence. Then the discovery of certain metals and non-metals was a major breakthrough in the course of civilisation. Slowly people started exploring more and more natural resources and converting them into different forms to achieve a comfortable and easy lifestyle and this effort ultimately led to the industrial revolution. Invention of glass and ceramic was a big stride towards the modern civilisation. Invention of chemical fertilisers has brought major changes in the cultivation of crops and yield of food products which lead to the green revolution.

Other than this, invention of many other chemical substances, like, polymers, plastics, synthetic fibres; like, nylon, rayon and soaps and detergents brought a paradigm change in the comfort zone of human life. In view of their significant role in the socio-economic development of society, appreciable industrial importance has been attributed to these substances which make their study inevitable.

EXAMPLE

When not used for a long time, bleaching powder loses its bleaching quality. Justify.

SOLUTION

Bleaching powder reacts with excess of dilute acid liberating chlorine gas. The amount of chlorine gas liberated is called **available chlorine**. This determines the quality of a sample of bleaching powder. Generally a good sample of bleaching powder contains 35-38% of available chlorine.

$$CaOCl_2 + H_2SO_4 \rightarrow CaSO_4 + Cl_2 + H_2O$$

Bleaching powder that is not used for a long time undergoes auto oxidation forming calcium chloride and calcium chlorate. As a result, available chlorine decreases.

$$6CaOCl_2 \rightarrow 5CaCl_2 + Ca(ClO_3)_2$$

SOME INDUSTRIALLY IMPORTANT COMPOUNDS

Glass

Glass is a homogeneous supercooled liquid. Its very high viscosity gives it an appearance of a solid. Major constituents of glass are sodium silicate, calcium silicate and silica. The arrangement of the constituent particles in the glass does not follow any regular pattern.

Manufacture of Glass

Raw Material

The raw materials used in the manufacture of glass are soda ash (Na_2CO_3), limestone ($CaCO_3$) and silica (SiO_2).

Process

Finely powdered silica, sodium carbonate and calcium carbonate are mixed with broken glass pieces called **cullet** and heated at about 1600 K to 1700 K. Cullet increases the fusibility of the raw material. Sodium carbonate and calcium carbonate react with silica to form respective silicates with the evolution of CO_2. The most significant part of manufacture of glass is cooling of molten glass which should be carried out carefully at a moderate and uniform rate in order to achieve the required properties of glass.

Manufacture of Glassware

Different methods are adopted for the manufacture of different types of glass ware from molten glass.

Blowing

Hollow glass articles are manufactured by glass-blowing technology. There are two different methods of glass blowing:

1. Free-blowing
2. Mould-blowing

Free-blowing

The process of free-blowing involves the blowing of air to inflate the molten glass which is gathered at one end of the blowpipe to give the desired shape. Here the perfection depends on the skill of the glass worker.

Mould-blowing

Mould-blowing is an alternate glass-blowing method that was developed after the technique of free-blowing. In this process, molten glass is inflated into a wooden or metal-carved mould with the help of the blow pipe which gives the molten glass the shape and design of the interior of the mould.

Pressing

In this process, a motorised plunger is used to press the molten glass taken inside the blank mould to make the glass containers and utensils.

Float Glass Method

Besides the above processes, the flat or sheet glass which is widely used as window panes, glass walls, glass doors, etc., are manufactured by floating molten glass on a bed of molten tin. This sheet of glass made by this process possesses uniform thickness and very flat surface.

Types of Glass

Since glass has a wide variety of applications, the characteristics of glass are required to be changed to achieve the specific properties suitable for the end products. This can be done by doping different compounds in glass.

Silica Glass

The raw material of silica glass is almost 100% pure form of quartz, and hence, it is very expensive. It undergoes very less thermal expansion and has high chemical resistance. Due to these characteristics, it is used for the manufacture of laboratory apparatus.

Borosilicate Glass

Borosilicate glass is composed of about 80% silica, 13% boron trioxide, small amount of oxides of sodium and aluminium. Its coefficient of thermal expansion is low, softening point is very high and it is resistant to a wide variety of chemicals. These properties make it suitable for the manufacture of laboratory ware.

Alkali Silicate Glass

The raw materials of alkali silicate glass are sand and soda. It is also known as water glass because it is soluble in water and used only as a solution. It is generally used for making gums and adhesives.

Lead Glass

In lead glass, lead oxide is added which increases the density of the glass thereby increasing its refractive index. This type of glass is used for the manufacture of ornamental glassware, decorative articles, etc.

Optical Glass

Optical glass is required to be absolutely flawless because it is used for the manufacture of optical instruments, like, binoculars, spectacles, lenses, prisms, telescopes, microscopes, etc. This type of glass is completely transparent and can be ground into the required shape. Optical glass generally contains phosphorus and lead silicate with little cerium oxide which absorbs the UV radiation. However, it has the widest range of composition with slight variation in the ingredients which gives rise to slight variation in optical properties and makes the glass suitable for the specific end product.

Coloured Glass

The colour of the glass can be obtained by the homogeneous distribution of different ions throughout the glass during the manufacture of glass. Presence of different oxides of iron gives green or brown colour, whereas the presence of oxides of copper gives rise to light blue or red colour. This type of glass is used for decorative, technical and scientific purposes.

Compounds	Colours
Iron oxides	Green, brown
Manganese oxides	Deep amber, amethyst, decolouriser
Cobalt oxide	Deep blue

Processed Glass

Properties of glass are not only attributed to the slight alteration of the ingredients but also to the processing of the glass. Some of the examples of processed glass and their applications are given below:

Processed glass	Applications
Laminated glass	Doors and windows of automobiles because it provides good strength to the glass
Fibre glass	Used for reinforcing purpose due to its high-tensile strength
Foam glass	Light weight glass used for civil construction and insulation purposes
Opaque glass	Non-transparent glass filters the light entering into it and provides an aesthetic look

Ceramics

Ceramics are hard, brittle substances made up of oxides, nitrides, carbides, borides, etc., which have high resistance to heat, electricity and chemicals and can have high-mechanical strength and impact resistance. Ceramics find a wide variety of applications ranging from simple pottery, sanitary wave and floor tiles to nuclear fuel, superconductors and joint replacements in human body.

Pottery

Pottery is representation of the articles which are made up of clay. Clay is a mixture of fine particles of quartz, feldspar, mica, mineral carbonates, oxides and sulphides of iron in varying proportions. When mixed with the right proportion of water, it exhibits a unique property called **plasticity**. Due to this property, articles of different shapes can be made from the clay kneaded with definite proportion of water. After drying, the articles are strongly heated in a kiln. During heating at a suitably high temperature, different physical and chemical changes occur in those substances which convert clay to ceramic material.

Pottery can be classified into three categories depending on the raw materials used and the temperature at which the objects are fired:

1. earthenware,
2. stoneware and
3. porcelain.

Earthenware

In this type of potteries, clay is the major constituent and the objects are fired at a comparatively lower temperature. Colourful glazes can be used at this temperature to make the pottery impervious to liquid and give a glossy appearance. Earthenware includes utensils, crockery, decorative items, etc.

Stoneware

During the manufacture of this type of potteries, the clay articles are heated at a much higher temperature, and hence, it has a greater strength. Drain water pipes, sanitary ware, etc., are the examples of stoneware.

Porcelain

It is the purest and the most delicate type of pottery. The raw materials used are kaolin, a fine white clay, controlled amount of feldspar and flint. After firing at a higher temperature, these articles become impermeable. Porcelain ware are glazed and enamelled for further beautification. Different metallic oxides are used in the process of enamelling which imparts a variety of colours to the articles. Bone china is a kind of porcelain which is made translucent to light by adding calcium phosphate to clay. Porcelain finds applications ranging from crockery, statues, decorative items to plumbing fixtures, electrical insulators as well as in aerospace industries.

Fertiliser

Like other living beings, plants require food for their growth. A wide variety of elements are required for many different purposes for the nourishment of plants. Among these carbon, oxygen and hydrogen are the principal nutrients. Nitrogen, phosphorus, potassium, magnesium, sulphur, calcium and iron play significant role for the growth and development of plants. These elements are called **major plant nutrients**. Some other elements, like, manganese, molybdenum, copper, boron, zinc, iron, chlorine, etc., are used by the field crops in very small quantities. These are called **minor plant nutrients**.

The sources of carbon, hydrogen and oxygen are air and water, whereas the other elements are required to be absorbed by the plants from the soil. Assimilation of these nutrients in the required proportions leads to the growth of healthy plants. But the soil may become deficient of nutrients. Manures and fertilisers are added to replenish the nutrients in the soil. Some of the common manures are cow dung, compost, bone meal, remains of fish, etc. But the ever increasing demand for food crops which could not be met by the available natural manures necessitated the development and use of chemical fertilisers.

Chemical fertilisers can be broadly classified into three types:

1. **Nitrogenous fertilisers:** Ammonium sulphate and urea
2. **Phosphatic fertilisers:** Superphosphate and ammonium phosphate
3. **Potash fertilisers:** Potassium chloride and potassium sulphate

Micronutrients are also added to the soil in the form of fertiliser. These are called **secondary fertilisers**. Before applying the fertiliser, the soil is analysed chemically. The selection of the fertiliser depends upon the condition of the soil and the crops to be grown in that soil.

Fibre

Biologically fibres are the continuous filaments which hold tissues together, and hence, the natural sources of fibre are plants and animals. Application of fibre in our daily life is diverse. A simple thread which is used for stitching clothes, household decorative items, like, carpet, gunny bags for storage of food items and variety of fabrics are originated from fibres. Depending on the source and process of manufacture, fibres can be classified into the following two broad categories:

1. Natural fibres
2. Synthetic fibres

Natural Fibre

Fibre obtained from natural sources is known as a natural fibre. Cotton, silk, wool, etc., are the examples of the natural fibres. Basic constituent of cotton is cellulose which is obtained from plants, whereas wool and silk are obtained from animals the basic constituents of these fibres being the protein molecules.

Synthetic Fibre

Fibres which are manufactured artificially through chemical processes are called **synthetic fibres**. Rayon is a fibre which is manufactured from the natural resources like cellulose present in wood pulp and it is called **regenerated fibre**. Rayon can be considered as an intermediate between the natural and synthetic fibres. Nylon, dacron, terylene, etc., are obtained from petroleum (crude oil). The yarns, i.e., the long threads of synthetic fibre are manufactured by passing the solution of the polymers produced from the crude oil through a sieve with very fine holes.

Synthetic fibres have many advantages over natural fibres. These fibres can be manufactured in large scale and the cost of production is lesser. They are more durable and less wettable when compared to cotton. However, with respect to comfort, natural fibres are ahead of synthetic fibres.

Plastic

Plastics are made up of long chains of polymers obtained by the interlinkage of certain specific molecules each of same chemical composition. Examples of such polymers are polyethylene, polystyrene, polyamide, etc. Like fibre, plastic also has diversified fields of application from domestic articles to a wide range of industrial equipment, namely, body of automobiles, furniture, construction materials of buildings, telecommunication equipment, etc., owing to its unique properties, like, light weight, mechanical strength and aesthetic appearance. Based on the thermal behaviour, plastics can be divided into two categories—thermoplastics and thermosets.

Thermoplastics

This type of plastics can be processed repeatedly by melting and subsequent solidification without undergoing any chemical change. Hence, they can be reused. Examples of thermoplastics are polyethylene, polyvinyl chloride, etc.

Thermosets

Plastics of this variety cannot be softened by heating, and thus, they cannot be reused. Examples of thermosets are urea–formaldehyde resin, epoxy resin, etc.

Soaps and Detergents

Soaps and detergents are the two artificially synthesised substances which are indispensable in our daily activity. Based on chemical composition soaps are the sodium or potassium salts of fatty acids, whereas detergents are sodium or potassium salts of alkyl sulphonic acids. Both soaps and detergents are soluble in water and act as surfactants which reduce the surfaces tension of water to a great extent. This increases the water–fabric interaction as a consequence of which dirt particles, grease spots, etc., are washed away effectively. In other words, soaps and detergents enhance the cleansing action of water.

Detergents can be used with hard water containing soluble chloride and sulphate salts of calcium and magnesium effectively, while soaps being ineffective with hard water due to the formation of curdy precipitates with the above salts with poor lather formation.

EXAMPLE

Why is common salt sprinkled over pots during the heating process while making pots?

SOLUTION

At high temperature, common salt ionises to Na^+ and Cl^-. These ions fill up the pores of the pot giving it a smooth and glassy finish.

EXAMPLE

(a) Why are plastic containers preferred for storing chemicals?

(b) Why are the materials made of plastic more in use rather than other substances?

(c) Why are handles of screw drivers used for electrical works made of plastics?

(d) Mention two examples of plastics in the medical field.

(e) Name the special plastic used for non-stick coating pans.

SOLUTION

(a) Plastics are chemically resistant. Hence, plastic containers are preferred for storing chemicals

(b) Plastics are cheap, durable and available in attractive shapes and colours. Hence, the materials made of plastic more in use rather than other substances

(c) As plastics are poor conductors of electricity handles of screw drivers used for electrical works made of plastics

(d) Plastics are used in packing tablets, doctor gloves, syringes, etc.

(e) Teflon is the special plastic used for non-stick coating pans.

TEST YOUR CONCEPTS

Very Short Answer Type Questions

1. How are CO_2 and dust particles removed from air before subjecting air to liquefaction?
2. In rat poison, phosphorous is used in the form of ________.
3. Give the existence of chlorine in the combined state in nature.
4. Name the most commonly found phosphates in nature.
5. Explain the reaction of chlorine with magnesium.
6. In what forms does sulphur occur in the combined state in nature?
7. List the physical properties of plastic sulphur.
8. How can mercuric sulphide be prepared?
9. The bacterial conversion of nitrogen into nitrogen compounds is called ________.
10. What happens when chlorine reacts with phosphorus?
11. Explain the acidic nature of sulphur dioxide based on its reactivity with water.
12. Give a brief description of the structure of white phosphorous.
13. Explain the chemical reaction of chlorine with hydrogen sulphide.
14. Why soap is ineffective with hard water?
15. What is the valency of nitrogen in ammonia? What is CAN? How is it useful?
16. The transition temperature of rhombic and monoclinic sulphur is ________.
17. Define glass blowing. What are the different methods employed for glass blowing?
18. What are the advantages of synthetic fibres over natural fibres?
19. Formula of fluorapatite is ________.
20. How does nitrogen occur in the combined state?
21. Mention the chemical formulae of
    (i) phosgene, (ii) tear gas and
    (iii) chloroform
22. What is the composition of ceramics?
23. What are the major and minor plant nutrients? Give three examples for each.
24. Write the balanced chemical reaction of the burning of ammonia in oxygen
25. What is nitrolim? How is it obtained?
26. ________ process is used to extract sulphur from deposits near the earth's crust.
27. Discuss the physical properties of chlorine.
28. How is principle of countercurrents is useful in Bachmann plant?
29. Why are dense white fumes formed when hydrogen chloride is dissolved in moist air?
30. Equal volumes of nitrogen and oxygen react to give ________.

Short Answer Type Questions

31. Write the equation for the following:
    (i) addition of concentrated HNO_3 to copper
    (ii) addition of dilute HNO_3 to zinc
32. Write a note on safety matches.
33. Describe how sulphur is extracted using the Sicilian process.
34. Differentiate between rhombic and monoclinic sulphur.
35. How is H_2S used as an analytical reagent?
36. Mention the uses of chlorine.
37. Explain the reaction of chlorine gas with turpentine.
38. Name the products formed in the following reactions:
    (i) reaction of sodium nitrate with ammonium sulphate
    (ii) reaction of potassium iodide with nitric acid
    (iii) addition of HNO_3 to sulphur

39. Explain the cleansing action of a soap.

40. Write two uses of ammonia.

41. Discuss briefly the chemical properties of H_2S.

42. Explain various types of chemical fertilisers with examples.

43. Why does sulphur dioxide act as a bleaching agent?

44. What is plastic? Write a short note on different categories of plastic.

45. Explain with equations the electrical process for the extraction of phosphorous.

Essay Type Questions

46. Write in detail about the compounds formed by phosphorous and their uses.

47. Explain in detail how sulphuric acid is prepared by the contact process.

48. Explain the construction and working of a Nelson cell.

49. Discuss the method of preparation of bleaching powder.

50. Explain the basic working of the Castner–Kellner cell, used for producing NaOH (sodium hydroxide).

For Answer key, Hints and Explanations, please visit:
www.pearsoned.co.in/IITFoundationSeries

CONCEPT APPLICATION

Level 1

Directions for questions from 1 to 7
State whether the following statements are true or false.

1. The ignition temperature of red phosphorous is less than that of white phosphorous.

2. The chemical formula of nitre is $NaNO_3$.

3. Ammonia on reaction with excess chlorine gives white dense fumes.

4. Sodium is deposited at the cathode during the electrolysis of brine solution.

5. Zinc sulphate solution on passage of H_2S gives a flesh-coloured precipitate.

6. Generally laboratory apparatus are made with borosilicate glass.

7. Urea is a nitrogenous fertiliser.

Directions for questions from 8 to 14
Fill in the blanks.

8. Liquid ________ is used for preserving biological specimen.

9. Density of white phosphorus is ________ than red phosphorus.

10. In Castner–Kellner cell, sodium ions react with mercury to form ________.

11. In Nelson cell, H_2 is liberated at ________.

12. Oxygen required for the combustion of safety matches can be produced from ________.

13. ________ bacteria convert atmospheric nitrogen into nitrogenous compounds.

14. Ammonia on reaction with potassium gives ________.

Directions for question 15
Match the entries in column A with the appropriate ones in Column B.

15.

Column A		Column B
A. Phosgene	( )	a. Heating metallic chlorides with conc. H_2SO_4
B. $CaOCl_2$	( )	b. Reaction of HCl with NaOH
C. NaOCl	( )	c. $COCl_2$
D. HOCl	( )	d. Reaction of phosphorus with chlorine
E. Cl_2	( )	e. $CCl_3.NO_2$
F. Tear gas	( )	f. Reaction of Cl_2 on slaked lime
G. PCl_5	( )	g. Nascent oxygen
H. HCl	( )	h. Oxidation of HCl by $K_2Cr_2O_7$

Directions for questions from 16 to 45

For each of the questions, four choices have been provided. Select the correct alternative.

16. Which of following statements regarding glass is false?

(a) Glass has high viscosity, and hence, exists in a solid state.

(b) Glass has no definite melting point.

(c) Arrangement of silicate units in glass is similar to that in liquid state.

(d) Glass has regular crystalline arrangement, and hence, exists as a solid.

17. Phosphor bronze is an alloy of

(a) P, Cu and Sn (b) P, Cu and Sb

(c) P, Zn and Sn (d) P, Cu and As

18. Which of the following loses its activity on storing for a long time?

(a) chlorine (b) hydrogen chloride

(c) bleaching powder (d) sodium hydroxide

19. Gypsum is

(a) hydrated magnesium sulphate

(b) anhydrous magnesium sulphate

(c) hydrated calcium sulphate

(d) anhydrous calcium sulphate

20. Clay shows plasticity when

(a) right proportion of water is added to it

(b) it is fired (strongly heated)

(c) it is dried at room temperature after kneading

(d) it is glazed

21. Which of the following is false regarding epoxy resin?

(a) It is a thermosetting polymer.

(b) It is less brittle in nature.

(c) It has relatively weak bonds.

(d) It has cross-linking among polymeric chains.

22. When Mg is burnt in the atmosphere of an element X, a white powder is obtained. When this is dissolved in water, it gives a compound Y with a pungent smell. What are X and Y?

(a) C, CH_4 (b) N_2, NH_3

(c) P, PH_3 (d) S, H_2S

23. The reducing property of SO_2 is shown in which of the following reactions?

(a) $SO_2 + H_2O + Cl_2 \longrightarrow 2HCl + H_2SO_4$

(b) $2H_2S + SO_2 \longrightarrow 2H_2O + 3S$

(c) $KOH + SO_2 \longrightarrow K_2SO_3 + H_2O$

(d) none of the above

24. The transparency of glass is attributed to which of the following properties of glass?

(a) high viscosity

(b) regular pattern of arrangement of silicate units

(c) irregular pattern of arrangement of silicate units

(d) high coefficient of thermal expansion

25. A soil is supplied with ammonium phosphate fertiliser. Which of the following types of bacteria is not involved in the process of the absorption of this fertiliser by plants?

(a) ammonifying bacteria (b) nitrosifying bacteria

(c) nitrifying bacteria (d) none of these

26. The gas liberated when concentrated sulphuric acid is treated with copper is

(a) H_2 (b) SO_3

(c) H_2S (d) SO_2

27. A soil is highly deficient in nitrogen. The crop requires nitrogen for immediate requirement as well as long-term requirement. Which among the following is the most suitable fertiliser for the soil?

(a) urea

(b) ammonium sulphate

(c) ammonium nitrate

(d) calcium ammonium nitrate

28. The process of glazing of ceramic article does not

(a) make it impervious

(b) impart glossy appearance

(c) make it impact resistant

(d) all of these

29. Sulphur, on heating, follows which of the following sequence?

(a) solid $\longrightarrow$ thick viscous liquid $\longrightarrow$ thin liquid $\longrightarrow$ gas

(b) solid $\longrightarrow$ semisolid $\longrightarrow$ liquid $\longrightarrow$ gas

(c) solid $\longrightarrow$ thin liquid $\longrightarrow$ thick viscous $\longrightarrow$ thin liquid $\longrightarrow$ gas

(d) solid $\longrightarrow$ powdery solid $\longrightarrow$ thick viscous liquid $\longrightarrow$ gas

30. Which among the following is true with regard to thermoplastics and thermosetting?

(a) Thermosettings are permanent setting resins but thermoplastics are not since they can be softened on cooling.

(b) Thermoplastics are less brittle when compared to thermosettings due to the absence of long chain polymers.

(c) Thermosettings are more brittle when compared to thermoplastics due to the presence of strong bonds.

(d) The chemical nature of thermoplastics can be altered by repeated heating and cooling.

31. Steps involved in the Frasch process are given below. Arrange them in the correct sequence.

(1) This melts the sulphur below melting point.

(2) The sulphur foam formed rises in the middle pipe and is collected.

(3) Superheated steam under pressure is sent through the outermost pipe.

(4) Hot compressed air is sent through the innermost pipe, which froths up the molten sulphur below.

(5) Three concentric pipes are drilled through the ground to the sulphur deposits.

(a) 5 3 1 4 2 (b) 5 1 4 3 2
(c) 5 1 4 2 3 (d) 5 4 1 3 2

32. Different steps involved in the manufacture of sulphuric acid in the contact process are given below. Arrange them in the correct sequence.

(1) formation of oleum

(2) oxidation of SO_2

(3) hydrolysis of oleum

(4) combustion of sulphur

(a) 4 1 3 2 (b) 1 4 2 3
(c) 4 2 1 3 (d) 1 4 3 2

33. Arrange the different forms of sulphur formed during heating followed by cooling:

(1) μ sulphur (2) flower of sulphur
(3) rhombic sulphur (4) sulphur vapour
(5) lambda sulphur (6) monoclinic sulphur

(a) 5 3 6 1 4 2 (b) 3 6 5 1 4 2
(c) 3 6 1 5 4 2 (d) 3 6 5 1 2 4

34. Slaked lime on reaction with ammonium chloride gives

(a) calcium hydroxide and ammonia

(b) calcium hydroxide and nitrogen

(c) calcium chloride and nitrogen dioxide

(d) calcium chloride and ammonia

35. Different steps involved in the mechanism of preparation of sodium hydroxide by Castner process are given below. Arrange them in correct sequence.

(1) $2Cl^- \rightarrow Cl_2 + 2e^-$

(2) $Na_2Hg - 2e^- \rightarrow 2Na^+ + Hg$

(3) $2H_2O + 2e^- \rightarrow H_2 + 2OH$

(4) $Hg + 2Na^+ + 2e^- \rightarrow Na_2Hg$

(5) $2NaCl \rightarrow 2Na^+ + 2Cl^-$

(6) $2Na^+ + 2OH^- \rightarrow 2NaOH$

(a) 5 4 3 2 1 6 (b) 5 2 3 1 4 6
(c) 4 2 1 5 3 6 (d) 5 1 4 2 3 6

36. The steps involved in the manufacture of glass are given below. Arrange them in the correct sequence.

(1) moderate cooling

(2) addition of cullet

(3) formation of respective silicates

(4) preparation of fine powder of raw materials

(5) heating of cullet at about 1600 K to 1700 K

(a) 4 2 5 3 1 (b) 4 5 2 1 3
(c) 4 5 3 2 1 (d) 4 2 3 5 1

37. Different processes involved in the manufacture of pottery or ceramic materials are given below. Arrange them in a proper sequence.

(1) change in the physical and chemical properties of the substances

(2) heating to a suitable high temperature

(3) drying of the mixture

(4) preparation of mixture by adding water to raw materials

(a) 2 1 4 3 (b) 4 3 2 1
(c) 4 3 1 2 (d) 3 4 2 1

38. The compounds formed when ammonia reacts with excess of chlorine are

(a) NH_4Cl, HCl (b) NCl_3, HCl
(c) N_2, HCl (d) NH_4Cl, NCl_3

39. In electrothermic reduction, calcium phosphate is mixed with
(a) sand, sulphur
(b) coke, sand
(c) sulphur, coke
(d) sulphur, phosphorus

40. HNO_3 on reaction with phosphorus gives
(a) phosphorus acid
(b) phosphoric acid
(c) metaphosphoric acid
(d) hypophosphoric acid

41. Sulphur on reaction with HNO_3 gives _____, _____
(a) H_2SO_4, NO_2, H_2O (b) H_2SO_3, NO_2, H_2O
(c) H_2SO_4, NO, H_2O (d) H_2SO_3, NO, H_2O

42. Which of the following metals liberates hydrogen when it is treated with very dilute HNO_3?
(a) Cu (b) Zn
(c) Mg (d) Fe

43. The bleaching action of bleaching powder is due to the formation of
(a) chlorate ion (b) chloride ion
(c) chlorite ion (d) hypochlorite ion

44. Which among the following types of glass is used in the manufacture of doors and windows of automobiles?
(a) laminated glass (b) fibre glass
(c) foam glass (d) opaque glass

45. Which of the following plastics can be recycled?
(a) melamine (b) polyethylene
(c) bakelite (d) both (1) and (2)

Level 2

1. Two moist red roses are taken in two containers A and B into which anhydride of sulphurous acid and a greenish yellow coloured gas are passed, respectively. What changes are observed with respect to two roses in A and B? How do you account for these changes?

2. Among white phosphorous and red phosphorous which is more preferable for use in match sticks? Give a reason in support of your answer.

3. When a burning paraffin candle is introduced into two jars containing oxygen and chlorine gases separately, what observations can be made? Explain with appropriate reasons.

4. When chlorine reacts with hot and concentrated caustic alkali XOH, one of the products, Y is formed by this reaction is used as an oxidiser in the match industry. Identify the compound Y and the element X.

5. Two samples of sulphur are heated separately starting at 60°C. One sample is found to melt at 114°C and the other one melts at 119°C. How do you account for this?

6. Bone ash contains both micro- and macronutrients in it. However, it is not used as a fertiliser. It is converted to superphosphate of lime which is an important fertiliser. Justify.

7. An iron rod is dipped in conc. HNO_3. Then it is made to react with copper sulphate solution. What observations are made in this process? Give reasons in support of your answer.

8. 'Noble metals, like, gold and platinum are insoluble both in HCl and in HNO_3. But they are soluble in aquaregia.' Justify.

9. Farmers are advised to grow beans or pea plants in crop rotation. Give reasons in support of your answer.

10. When copper metal is subjected to treatment with nitric acid, different oxides of nitrogen are liberated with different concentrations of nitric acid. Explain the reason.

11. Ammonium chloride on reaction with quick lime gives a gas X which turns red litmus blue. Excess of X and greenish yellow gas are taken in container A and excess of greenish yellow gas and X are taken in container B which on reaction gives different sets of products. When moist litmus paper is introduced into the jars, it turned to red in jar B. Identify the reactions involved and give equations.

12. Hydrogen chloride gas can be subjected to drying only with conc. H_2SO_4 but not with quick lime or phosphorus pentoxide. Explain.

13. Why are soaps ineffective during usage with hard water which contains soluble salts of calcium and magnesium?

14. When a binary salt of iron reacts with hydrochloric acid, it gives out a gas which can be used for identification of many metal ions. Identify the salt, the gas and explain how it is useful in detecting metal ions.

15. Nitric acid is colourless when freshly prepared. But, on long standing, it turns to yellow. How do you account for this?

16. Two research scholars Rony and Jony, needed red phosphorus and white phosphorus, respectively, for a research programme. Both of them went to a chemical store to purchase red phosphorus and white phosphorus. The storekeeper gave a normal glass bottle containing red phosphorus and a glass bottle containing white phosphorus which was kept in water. Justify the above observations.

17. A solid non-metal A on exposure to air forms a compound B which on dissolution in water forms the highest oxyacid C. Identify different type of salts which can be formed when C reacts with caustic potash.

18. Though P_2O_5 is a very good desiccant, its utility for drying is limited. Give reasons.

19. In an industry, H_2S gas is mixed with chlorine gas before releasing it into the atmosphere. Give the appropriate reason.

20. A solid non-metal X on burning gives a compound Y which under high temperature and pressure conditions in presence of catalyst gets oxidised to Z. Z can give the 'ic' acid of the non-metal on dissolution in water. However, it is not a preferred reaction for the preparation of the acid. Give reason and explain the method employed for the preparation of the ic-acid from Z and mention the precautions required during dilution of the acid.

21. Concentrated HNO_3 and concentrated H_2SO_4 can't be used for the preparation of H_2S. Give a reason.

22. Rekha and Lekha took two fresh red roses and kept them in two containers A and B into which anhydride of sulphurous acid and a greenish yellow-coloured gas are passed, respectively. After a few minutes these two roses lose their colour but on being exposed to the atmosphere, it was observed that Rekha's rose regained its colour but Lekha's rose did not. How do you account for the above changes?

23. During the summer vacation, a chemistry laboratory assistant stored the chemicals in their respective bottles. After a few months it was observed that the lids of the bottles in which sodium hydroxide was stored was struck tight. He went to a lecturer for finding the solution for this problem. What solution could be suggested by the lecturer?

24. Ranchu's father is working in a fertiliser industry. One day at home he heard his father making a suggestion to his colleague that 'between nitrate salts and ammonium salts, nitrate salts are preferable for use as a fertiliser.' The next day Ranchu asked his brother the reason for their father's suggestion. What answer did his brother give?

25. Thermoplastics can be moulded again and again, whereas thermosettings cannot be moulded. Give a reason.

Level 3

1. Two non-metallic gaseous elements react in 1 : 3 ratio to give another gas X. A mixture of X and oxygen is taken in a jar and a burning match stick is introduced into it. Another sample of the same mixture containing large excess of O_2 is passed over heated platinum. The mixture of gaseous products is dissolved in water to give Y and Z which are colourless. Z on long standing turns to yellow. Identify X, Y and Z by giving reasons wherever necessary. Also identify the exothermic reaction in the above sequence.

2. Both slow cooling and rapid cooling of glass are avoided. How do you account for this?

3. Phosphorite rock when treated with phosphoric acid gives a fertiliser which is preferred to a fertiliser

PRACTICE QUESTIONS

obtained from the same mineral on treatment with conc. sulphuric acid. Justify

4. Why is the compound AgCl used in photogrey lenses?

5. Bleaching powder in cold water is an excellent bleaching agent. But it cannot act as a good bleaching agent when dissolved in hot water. Why?

6. Hydrofluoric acid cannot be stored in glass bottles like all other acids. Give a reason.

7. Certain phosphates are helpful in making hard water soft. Which phosphates are used and how do they help in making water soft?

8. Both H_2SO_4 and HNO_3 cause damage to skin when the skin comes in contact with them. Compare and contrast the reasons.

9. Nitric acid attacks all the metals except noble metals but the nature of products of same metal along with corresponding nitrates depends upon the concentration of HNO_3. Explain.

CONCEPT APPLICATION

Level 1

True or false

1. False 2. False 3. False 4. False 5. False
6. True 7. True

Fill in the blanks

8. nitrogen
9. less
10. sodium amalgam
11. cathode
12. $KClO_3$
13. nitrogen-fixing bacteria (or) symbiotic
14. KNH_2

Match the following

15. A. →c
B. →f
C. →b
D. →g
E. →h
F. →e
G. →d
H. →a

Multiple choice questions

16. d 17. a 18. c 19. c 20. a
21. d 22. b 23. a 24. c 25. a
26. d 27. d 28. c 29. c 30. c

31. (i) three concentric pipes are drilled through the ground to the sulphur deposits
(ii) superheated steam under pressure is sent through the outermost pipe
(iii) this melts the sulphur below its melting point
(iv) hot compressed air is sent through the innermost pipe, which froths up the molten sulphur below
(v) the sulphur foam formed rises in the middle pipe and is collected

32. (i) combustion of sulphur
(ii) oxidation of SO_2
(iii) formation of oleum
(iv) hydrolysis of oleum

33. (i) rhombic sulphur
(ii) monoclinic sulphur
(iii) lambda sulphur
(iv) μ sulphur
(v) sulphur vapour
(vi) flower of sulphur

34. $Ca(OH)_2 + 2NH_4Cl \rightarrow CaCl_2 + 2NH_3 + 2H_2O$

35. (i) $2NaCl \rightarrow 2Na^+ + 2Cl^-$
(ii) $2Cl \rightarrow Cl_2 + 2e^-$
(iii) $Hg + 2Na^+ + 2e \rightarrow Na_2Hg$
(iv) $Na_2Hg - 2e^- \rightarrow 2Na^+ + Hg$
(v) $2H_2O + 2e^- \rightarrow H_2 + 2OH^-$
(vi) $2Na^+ + 2OH^- \rightarrow 2NaOH$

36. (i) preparation of fine powder of raw materials
(ii) preparation of cullet

(iii) heating of cullet at about 1600 K to 1700 K

(iv) formation of respective silicates

(v) moderate cooling

37. (i) preparation of mixture by adding water to raw materials

(ii) drying of the mixture

(iii) heating to a suitable high temperature

(iv) change in the physical and chemical properties of the substances

38. $2NH_3 + 6Cl_2 \rightarrow 2NCl_3 + 6HCl$

39. In an electrothermic reduction calcium phosphate is mixed with sand and coke.

40. $P + 5HNO_3 \rightarrow \underset{\text{phosphoric acid}}{H_3PO_4} + 5NO_2 + H_2O$

41. $S + 6HNO_3 \rightarrow H_2SO_4 + 6NO_2 + 2H_2O$

42. $Mg + 2HNO_3 \rightarrow Mg(NO_3)_2 + H_2\uparrow$

43. $CaOCl_2 + H_2O \rightarrow CaCl_2 + HOCl + HCl$

$HOCl \rightarrow H^+ + \underset{\text{hypochlorite ion}}{OCl^-}$

44. Laminated glass is used in the manufacture of doors and windows of automobiles because it provides good strength to the glass.

45. Since polyethylene is thermoplastic, it can be recycled.

Level 2

1. (i) identification of reason for decolourisation of moist roses

(ii) identification of the two gases

(iii) characteristic property of the above gases

(iv) the effect of characteristic property of the above gases on the colour of roses

(v) effect of atmospheric oxygen on revival of the colour of one of the roses

2. (i) comparison of property of red and white phosphorous

(ii) comparison of reactivity of white phosphorus and red phosphorus

(iii) comparison of ignition temperatures of white phosphorus and red phosphorus

3. (i) composition of paraffin candle and comparison of reactivity of the constituents present in candle with O_2 and Cl_2

(ii) affinity of the constituents of paraffin candle towards chlorine

(iii) products obtained when these constituents react with chlorine

(iv) physical states of the products

(v) products obtained due to the reaction between constituents of paraffin candle and oxygen

4. (i) oxidiser in match industry

(ii) identification of a substance used in match stick which supplies O_2

(iii) balanced chemical equation

(iv) identification of X from the balanced chemical equation

5. (i) allotropes of sulphur

(ii) stability of allotropes at different temperatures

(iii) comparison of melting points of different allotropes

(iv) pattern of heating to be employed

(v) effect of pattern of heating on the allotropic transformation

6. (i) requisite of a good fertiliser

(ii) constituent of bone ash which contains macronutrients required for plants

(iii) soluble nature of the above constituent

(iv) manufacture of superphosphate of lime from this constituent

(v) solubility of superphosphate of lime

7. (i) reactivity of iron with HNO_3

(ii) reactivity of iron with HNO_3

(iii) product obtained

(iv) reactivity of the product obtained

8. (i) product obtained from the mixture HCl and HNO_3
(ii) composition of aquaregia
(iii) reactivity of gold with aquaregia
(iv) product formed

9. (i) microorganism present in roots of bean or pea plants
(ii) the role of the microorganisms present in beans and pea plants in trapping the aerial nitrogen
(iii) role of nitrogen in the growth of plants

10. (i) property of HNO_3
(ii) nature of HNO_3
(iii) effect of concentration on oxidising capacity of HNO_3

11. (i) identification of product formed in the reaction of NH_4Cl and CaO
(ii) reaction between X and the greenish yellow gas in container A
(iii) reaction between X and the greenish yellow gas in container B
(iv) comparison of nature of the products formed in the two containers, A and B
(v) effect of nature of products on litmus paper

12. (i) reaction of P_2O_5 and CaO with HCl
(ii) reactivity of HCl with H_2SO_4, CaO, P_2O_5
(iii) reactions which are feasible
(iv) products obtained
(v) requisite for a drying agent

13. (i) composition of soap
(ii) reason for hardness of water
(iii) reaction between components of soap and salts imparting hardness to water
(iv) the nature of the products formed
(v) effect of the products on lather formation

14. (i) gas used for detection of ions
(ii) identification of the gas
(iii) balanced chemical equation
(iv) identification of binary salt from the balanced chemical equation
(v) reactivity of metal ions with the gas
(vi) products obtained
(vii) colour of the products formed

15. (i) decomposition of nitric acid
(ii) effect of light on HNO_3
(iii) effect of product formed on cold HNO_3

16. The ignition temperature of white phosphorus is very low as compared to red phosphorus. Hence, it catches fire in the presence of air. So, white phosphorous is preserved under water as its density is high. Therefore, the phosphorus settles down. As a result, it is not exposed to air. In contrats, red phosphorus has a high ignition temperature and does not catch fire on exposure to air. So, it is stored in normal glass bottles.

17. $$\underset{A}{4P} + 5O_2 \rightarrow \underset{B}{2P_2O_5}$$

$$\underset{B}{P_2O_5} + 3H_2O \rightarrow \underset{C}{2H_3PO_4}$$

$$H_3PO_4 + KOH \rightarrow KH_2PO_4 + H_2O$$

$$H_3PO_4 + 2KOH \rightarrow K_2HPO_4 + 2H_2O$$

$$H_3PO_4 + 3KOH \rightarrow K_3PO_4 + 3H_2O$$

18. P_2O_5 is a very good dehydrating agent, but is not used popularly as a dehydrating agent, because the water absorbed by this forms a protective viscous coating that inhibits further dehydration. However, granular form of P_4O_{10} can be used as a good dehydrating agent.

19. H_2S gas is poisonous and the antidote for this gas is chlorine. Chlorine has the property to destroy the effect of H_2S by oxidising it to sulphur:

$$H_2S + Cl_2 \rightarrow HCl + S$$

20. $$\underset{X}{S} + O_2 \rightarrow \underset{Y}{SO_2}$$

$$\underset{Y}{2SO_2} + O_2 \xrightarrow[V_2O_5]{\text{High pressure and temp}} \underset{Z}{2SO_3}$$

$$SO_3 + H_2O \rightarrow H_2SO_4$$

However, in the preparation of H_2SO_4, the above reaction is not preferred since it is highly exothermic and leads to explosion. Instead, SO_3 is dissolved in

HINTS AND EXPLNATION

H_2SO_4 to give oleum which on dilution with water gives H_2SO_4:

$$SO_3 + H_2SO_4 \rightarrow H_2S_2O_7$$

oleum

$$H_2S_2O_7 + H_2O \rightarrow 2H_2SO_4$$

Dilution of H_2SO_4 is also a highly exothermic reaction. Therefore, H_2SO_4 should not be diluted by adding water to the acid. Instead, water is taken and H_2SO_4 is added slowly by stirring. This leads to dissipation of released heat during dilution process.

21. Both concentrated HNO_3 and concentrated H_2SO_4 are strong oxidising agents. As a result, they react with H_2S formed and oxidises it to sulphur. Here the acids are reduced to SO_2 and NO_2, respectively:

$$H_2S + H_2SO_4 \rightarrow S + SO_2 + H_2O$$

$$H_2S + 2HNO_3 \rightarrow S + 2NO_2 + 2H_2O$$

22. Anhydride of sulphurous acid is SO_2.

Greenish yellow coloured gas is Cl_2.

When the two fresh red roses are exposed to SO_2 and Cl_2, the roses fade away as both SO_2 and Cl_2 act as bleaching agents. Once these two roses are exposed again to air, one of the roses which is bleached by SO_2 in jar A regains its colour. This is due to the reason that SO_2 bleaches by reduction and once the rose is exposed to air oxidation takes place. However, Cl_2 bleaches by oxidation.

23. Sodium hydroxide on being exposed to air reacts with the CO_2 present in the air to form sodium carbonate. This solidifies and the lid gets stuck due to this. The lids can be removed by using dilute acid with the help of cotton.

24. Both nitrate salts and ammonium salts are highly soluble in water and provide nitrogen to the soils. However, plants can take in and use nitrogen only in the form of nitrates. Nitrate salts when added to soils can be immediately made available for the plants. Ammonium salts cannot be directly taken in by the plants. Ammonium ions have to be first converted to nitrate ions and only then they are made available to the plants. Therefore, ammonium salts supply nitrogen after a long time, whereas nitrate salts serve the immediate requirement of the plants.

25. Thermoplastic plastics consist of long chains which can be moulded again and again, whereas in case of thermosetting plastics consist of long chain and are cross-linked with each other. Linkage prevents the displacement of individual chains on being heated, and thus, thermosetting polymers do not change once they have set.

Level 3

1. (i) identification of the acid which turns to yellow on long standing

(ii) identification of X

(iii) products obtained in the two jars

(iv) comparison of reactivity of products in the respective jars with water

(v) products obtained

(vi) identification of Y and Z

2. (i) thermal conductivity of glass

(ii) importance of process of cooling of softened glass to obtain good quality of glass

(iii) changes that takes place in the quality of glass on rapid cooling

(iv) changes that takes place in the quality of glass on slow cooling

(v) relation between the process of cooling of glass and its physical properties

3. (i) composition of superphosphate of lime and triple phosphate

(ii) composition of phosphorite rock

(iii) products formed when phosphorite rock is treated with H_3PO_4 and H_2SO_4 separately

(iv) comparison of percentage of phosphorus in the products

(v) comparison of soluble nature of the products

4. (i) change in AgCl in the presence of sunlight

(ii) effect of UV light on AgCl

(iii) products obtained

(iv) changes observed

(v) effect of the product on the colour of lenses

5. Bleaching powder reacts with cold water to produce chloride and hypochlorite ions. Hypochlorite ions dissociate producing nascent oxygen which is responsible for bleaching:

$$CaOCl_2 + H_2O \rightleftharpoons Ca^{+2} + Cl^- + ClO^- + H^+ + OH^-$$

Bleaching powder reacts with hot water and produces chloride and chlorate ions:

$$3ClO^- \rightarrow 2Cl^- + ClO_3^-$$

6. As glass is a silicate and HF reacts with the silicates to form SiF_4 and fluoride of metal:

$$Na_2SiO_3 + 6\ HF \rightarrow 2\ NaF + SiF_4 + 3H_2O$$

$$3SiF_4 + 3H_2O \rightarrow H_2SiO_3 + 2H_2SiF_6$$

7. Soluble phosphates when added to hard water form calcium and magnesium phosphates, which are insoluble precipitates. Thus, as the calcium and magnesium ions are precipitated, the water becomes soft and can give lather with soap.

8. H_2SO_4 being a dehydrating agent removes hydrogen and oxygen from the skin in the form of water thereby damaging the skin. HNO_3 reacts with skin proteins forming xanthoproteins, and hence, imparts yellow colour to skin and forms painful blisters.

9. In conc. HNO_3, more number of NO_3^- ions is present per unit volume, and these NO_3^- ions acts as an oxidising agent. It gets reduced to NO_2 due to more production of oxygen. In case of dilute HNO_3, less number of NO_3^- ions is present. So, it gets reduced to nitric oxide.

$$\underset{\text{(conc.)}}{Cu + 4\ HNO_3} \rightarrow Cu\ (NO_3)_2 + 2NO_2 + 2H_2O$$

$$\underset{\text{(dil.)}}{3Cu + 8\ HNO_3} \rightarrow 3Cu\ (NO_3)_2 + 2NO + 4H_2O$$

HINTS AND EXPLNATION